Bill Ratliff

To Taylor Chien
best wishes
Bill Ratliff

Bill Ratliff

A Profile of Courage and Leadership in American Politics

Robert Edward Sterken Jr.

LEXINGTON BOOKS
Lanham • Boulder • New York • London

Published by Lexington Books
An imprint of The Rowman & Littlefield Publishing Group, Inc.
4501 Forbes Boulevard, Suite 200, Lanham, Maryland 20706
www.rowman.com

Unit A, Whitacre Mews, 26-34 Stannary Street, London SE11 4AB

British Library Cataloguing in Publication Information Available

Library of Congress Cataloging-in-Publication Data

Names: Sterken, Robert Edward, Jr., author.
Title: Bill Ratliff : a profile of courage and leadership in American politics / Robert Edward Sterken Jr.
Description: Lanham, Maryland : Lexington Books, an imprint of The Rowman & Littlefield Publishing Group, Inc., 2016. | Includes bibliographical references and index.
Identifiers: LCCN2016042302| ISBN 9781498546935 (cloth : alk. paper) | ISBN 9781498546959 (pbk. : alk. paper) | ISBN 9781498546942 (electronic)
Subjects: LCSH: Ratliff, Bill, 1936- | Lieutenant governors--Texas--Biography. | Legislators--Texas--Biography. | Texas. Legislature. Senate--Biography. | Texas--Politics and government--1951-
Classification: LCC F391.4.R38 S74 2016 | DDC 328.73/092 [B] --dc23 LC record available at https://lccn.loc.gov/2016042302

Printed in the United States of America

For Alison, I am ever grateful, my love.
For my Bill, who set me on the road to academia.
And for Alexandra Grace, Bobby, and Taylor.

"Bill Ratliff is an inspiration to all who serve in government, and to all Americans, for his principled and bipartisan leadership, and his willingness to make the difficult and unpopular decisions necessary for good governance. Bill Ratliff showed great courage when he put his long and distinguished career of service at risk for the principle of fair and democratic elections which are the heart and soul of a successful democracy. [He] has demonstrated political courage worthy of our gratitude."

—Caroline Kennedy, announcing Governor Ratliff as winner of the 2005 John F. Kennedy Profile in Courage Award

Contents

Preface and Acknowledgments

Never Shade the Truth

I first met the Honorable William R. "Bill" Ratliff at "Herschel's Family Restaurant" in his hometown of Mt. Pleasant, Texas, in the spring of 2007. It was raining hard as he ducked his silver head inside the door of the restaurant. Dressed in a windbreaker, jeans, and a golf shirt, he shook the water from his windbreaker, smiled, waved, and motioned for me to join him at the counter. Over burgers and Diet Coke we visited for more than three hours. That afternoon I met an altruistic and generous man who spent almost two decades in the service of others at the peak of political power in Texas. By the time of my visit, Ratliff was a Texas legend—a giant who had stood against raw and self-serving political power, and faced long odds to do the right thing for the people of his district and the people of Texas. I had been asked to serve in the university's government relations post, after teaching and writing about government for many years, and I sought to learn from a man that many in the Texas Legislature affectionately called "Obi-Wan Kenobi."

In that first meeting, Lt. Governor Ratliff gave me stern advice. I asked, "tell me how can I best help my president, university, and our students?" Bill looked me in the eye and said, "First, you have to understand that you have no power. It is not that you have only a little power—but rather that you have no power. You only have information to share, and the true meaningful friendships that you forge." He went on, "Your information is only worth as much as your integrity—never, I repeat, never, shade the truth." I took those words to heart and they would eventually prove prophetic. I decided on the rainy drive back to my office that Lt. Governor Ratliff's story needed to be shared. It is a story of an inspiring and courageous man who did the right thing, even knowing well the likely and dire personal consequences. His is a story of a devoted and loving spouse and father, a man who worked very hard to build a professional life and after his career was well established decided to spend the rest of his life serving others, making a real and profound difference in the lives of his fellow Texans. This is a "hero's journey," a true story of how the work and dedication of one man of principle changed the lives of many. I hope that freshman college students will be inspired and that freshman legislators will vow to follow in his footsteps. I hope that my fellow citizens will be inspired to serve.

I am deeply grateful and honored to share this story. It is important to understand my purpose. I have written a profile in courage about Bill Ratliff's life. It was not my intention to write a comprehensive book of Ratliff's entire life, or to detail all of his work in politics, nor to index every policy area in which he worked. I did not write a book about all of the inner workings of the Texas Legislature or even the Senate, although much is covered. Rather, I aspired to share the story of a great Texan with the goal of inspiring others to act with courage. It is also important to note that in several places other scholars have written erroneous and incomplete information about Ratliff. In those places, I have worked to set the record straight.

GRATEFUL I AM

No work is completed alone. This book was made possible by the support and work of many people and to each I am ever grateful.

Bill's wife, Sally Ratliff, amassed marvelous, comprehensive, and extremely detailed scrapbooks of each and every year of Governor Ratliff's political life. Sally provided letters, invitations, golf scorecards, countless newspaper clippings, and even personal hand written notes written by the senator. Her work, now in the archives of the University of Texas at Tyler, was invaluable.

Of course, the greatest debt owed is to Governor Ratliff. I spent many hours and many full days in interviews with Governor Ratliff (and Sally). He is a modest man who was reluctant to talk about his own accomplishments, but he shared insights, wisdom, and historical details that greatly improved this book. It was an honor to work with such an open and honest man. Not once did he shy away from the truth, regrets, or the painful. Bill also patiently worked with me via email, clarifying, and answering many questions over the span of several years. Ever modest, Ratliff was reluctant to share personal successes. He did not see the final work until it was finished. Any and all errors are mine alone.

University of Texas School of Law Professor Jack Ratliff and Mr. Shannon Ratliff, Bill's brothers, also spent many hours answering questions and working to fill in the story of Bill's life. Professor Ratliff has published an excellent record of his parent's lives and that work greatly helped with the re-creation of Ratliff's formative years. I am grateful to both Jack and Shannon for their time and help.

I owe a debt of gratitude to the University of Texas at Austin's president Bill Powers for providing insights, recollections, and specific accounts of his meetings and specific work (torts) with all three Ratliff brothers. Texas Tech University Chancellor and Senator Robert Duncan was gracious in sharing stories, detailing meetings, and legislation, and offering his support.

Governor Ratliff's staff members also provided important information. Specifically, I wish to thank Mr. Don Edmonds and Ms. Vatra Solomon, both who were with Ratliff during his entire political life and spent many hours sharing his stories and details with me. Mr. Edmonds graciously shared extensive notes from his own book. I would also like to thank Mr. Eric Wright for his valuable time and contributions. I want to thank Mr. Carlos E. Martinez, Associate Vice President for Government Relations at the University of Texas at Austin. Mr. Martinez mentored and guided my work in the sometimes treacherous waters of the Texas Legislature, he is a friend, and a man of great integrity who provided guidance and help with my understanding of the inside game of legislative politics.

I am grateful to Dr. Marcus Stadelmann, Chair of the University of Texas at Tyler Department of Political Science, for many years of support and friendship. Dr. Stadelmann made this research possible by funding travel to Austin and many other places for interviews and by supporting the work in the many ways a good academic boss does. I am also indebted to Dr. Martin Slann, dean of the UT Tyler College of Arts and Sciences for his gracious and continued support of this research and writing. I am also thankful for the support and always available assistance of Ms. Terra Gullings, head of UT Tyler Archives and Special Collections, and to Mr. Aaron Ramirez, UT Tyler Archives assistant for help with the many boxes of Ratliff papers, photos, and special collections. This work would not have been possible without the work of the staff of the UT Tyler Archives and Special Collections. The labor intensive work of pulling up all of the photos was done by Texas Senate. I am grateful for the support of the Texas Senate Media Services.

I will ever be indebted for the encouragement, assistance, and editing skill of Stephen F. Austin State University President Emeritus William R. Johnson. Dr. Johnson edited this work with the careful and keen eye of a historian and greatly improved the book. Again, errors remain mine alone. My son, Robert Edward Sterken III, an outstanding lawyer, assisted in note taking, tort law, reviewing publishing contracts, and meeting with President Bill Powers when I was unable to make it to Austin for meetings. For his help I am ever grateful.

Finally, from the very beginning, this book would not have been possible without the love, support, encouragement, and many hours of discussion, planning, and editing by my life partner, Alison Johnson Sterken. Alison graciously supported me during the many days of doubt and patiently listened to too many long hours of detail. It is just not possible to adequately ever thank her for all she has done, but I will try.

—Robert Edward Sterken Jr.

ONE

Drawing Aces

Unalterable Opposition

The letter stating an "unalterable opposition," typed in a mere few sentences, was framed. Seated behind his desk, the gentleman with neatly trimmed silver hair, scholarly glasses, and an open-collar white-buttoned down shirt reached over to his left and took the letter from its place on the wall. The paper under the glass appeared heavy—suggesting the gravity of its contents. The seal at the top of the page was raised. The letter was signed in heavy black scrawling signatures by Texas senators—ten Democrats and one lone Republican. The eleventh and Republican signature had mattered in many ways and to many people. The southern gentleman holding the framed letter was the right and only Republican to sign it, to make a stand.

It is often said that good people do not run for public office. While this is most certainly not true, it is true that many good men and women choose not to serve and do not wish to engage in the ugliness of politics and governing. We undoubtedly need more good men and women in leadership. This book is—quite simply—a story of one good and decent man doing the right thing in a leadership role for his country; it tells the inspiring story of how one Texas public servant stood bravely and firmly on principle to fight for his constituents and for a fair, democratic, and good society. This is a story of courage, integrity, and of a leader who stood for the people—not his own personal interests. It is a story of a man whose personal courage and service has been honored on the national American political stage and whose name is now listed along with many other great and courageous Americans.[1] This is also a story of a man who stood firm on his principles. Many of those principles, ideas, and values are widely supported and others less so. A person of principle is one who

1

is guided by a set of values or principles—such as integrity. Ratliff was and is such a man and because of this he encountered his fair share of controversy and certainly has enemies—as evident in his need to take a principled stand in the face of enormous pressure to do otherwise. His story would be incomplete without an understanding of his position on some very difficult problems and policy.

This is also a story of personal and social responsibility, power, politics, and a change in the Republican Party. It is the story of being the "right Republican." The Republican Party has experienced significant and important factional differences over the years.[2] At both the state level and on the national stage a bloc of extremely conservative Christians—who are both fundamentalist and evangelical—have come to dominate the Republican Party and play an important role in the Ratliff story.[3] This group of evangelicals has changed the focus and split the party by placing specific emphasis on religion, salvation, and traditional Protestant Christian values. On the other hand, as Republican and former governor of New Jersey Whitman said, "there are a still lot of Republican voters particularly who are moderates, who don't support everything that is being talked about today."[4] This is a story about a man who was Republican—and, in many important ways, bipartisan.

"WE DREW ACES WITH OUR PARENTS"

Bill Ratliff's life began in the dark days of the Great Depression, but his story (like all of our stories) begins well before his own birth. Each of us is born into a special and unique set of circumstances. Our individual opportunities and successes depend on many factors within our individual lives and families. Our parents, siblings, extended family, schools, religions, and a myriad of other factors, including the makeup of the larger community that surrounds us, play a significant and often even a defining role in shaping our individual journeys and the impact we have on the world. Bill Ratliff was a fortunate child. As his older brother, Jack, would later say, "we were extremely lucky—in that we drew aces with our parents."[5]

Bill's parents, John Thomas Ratliff (Tom) and Bess Roark (called Bess, never Bessie), came from hard scrabble and humble homes in Texas and Louisiana. Bill's grandfather, John Lafayette Ratliff, was nicknamed "Fate" and was a gruff and hardworking Baptist preacher (who always wore a wool suit and tie—always, no matter the weather or calendar). Fate (born in 1880 to John Washington Ratliff and Elizabeth Rebecca Vernon) married Nora Ann Harrison and raised eight children while building houses to pay his way through seminary. Fate's son Tom (Bill's father) would learn the personal values of dedication to family, service to community, hard work, and integrity directly from a man who lived out those very values.

Tom

Fate Ratliff worked hard to make sure his children went to college. In 1926, his son Tom attended Baylor University and then the Texas Normal College (later named University of North Texas) in Denton where he would play football and baseball, as well as stand out in debate and acting. Tom was a member of the Alpha Psi Omega National Theatre Honor Society. While attending the University of North Texas, Tom was an active and award winning member the Historical Society, Alpha Psi Omega National Theatre Honor Society, Glee Club, Debate Team, and the Lillie Bruce Dramatic Club. Tom's participation in these clubs would have long-term and directly positive effects on his children and on many others.[6]

In January of 1927, the University of North Texas Lillie Bruce Dramatic Club staged George Bernard Shaw's comedy *Candida* in the college auditorium. Shaw's play questions the Victorian notions of marriage and sparked his audience to ask questions about traditional notions of desire and love. Tom was the president of the dramatic club and took the leading role of "clergyman James Morell." A rising star known as Rosebud (or just "Buddy" to her close friends) took the leading female role of Candida. Tom and Buddy's performances delighted the people of Denton and drew the largest crowds in the drama club's history. Tom spent substantial time with and became quite close with Buddy, whose full name was Rose Joan Blondell. After winning a beauty pageant in Dallas later that year, Blondell would embark upon a film career and appear in more than one hundred movies and television productions. Years later Blondell was nominated for an Academy Award for Best Supporting Actress for her work in *The Blue Veil*. Bess, in later years, would grow quiet at any mention of Blondell. Many years later, Tom's sons would follow their father's footsteps into debate and acting.[7]

After college Tom became an outstanding coach, but not the stereotypical Texas football coach. An unusual man for his time and generation, Tom coached teams in Sanger, Kemp, and Sherman, Texas, and in Shreveport, Louisiana. While he was highly successful, very popular, and a much beloved mentor, he was not the aggressive win-at-all-costs type of coach.[8] Tom never yelled at his players. He never berated or criticized his players (or his sons) for making a mistake or a bad play. Tom set very strict and quietly communicated rules on the young men in his charge, including his three sons.

Tom would not tolerate or accept displays of temper, unsportsmanlike conduct, and especially not cheating of any kind. Bill would later say that for Tom, "nothing was lower than a cheater."[9] His players and his sons were to keep cool and calm heads about them, even when others were losing theirs. Tom's players and sons never wanted to face him if they had so much as even slightly shown disrespect to an opponent or to an official. Tom coached his boys to work hard, to "keep their heads in the game" in every contest and in every other life endeavor. To a player who had not had a good game, Coach Ratliff would quietly say, "It looks to me like you didn't have your head in the game, son."[10]

Preparation was always key for Coach Tom Ratliff. Tom's teams and sons were always well prepared and ready to play. His players were drilled to do the hard and consistent work of preparing for the contest so that they would show hustle and be prepared. Tom's quiet praise and authentic admiration went to the "heads-up" players who were the best prepared, who played smart, were good sports, and who played by the rules. Tom's rules—be well prepared, be a person of impeccable honesty, be a person who is respectful of others, and be one who follows the rules—were the foundation for players on his teams and for his boys both on the field of play and in life itself. If Tom had a single guiding principle above all others, that fairness to all was a central and critical value.[11]

You Play by the Rules. You Hustle.

Jack would later say, "What Tom required was committed effort, attention to the game and, without fail, honesty and good sportsmanship. You have to break up a double play, but you cannot hurt anyone in the way you do it. You do not complain about bad calls. He called it "bellyaching." You congratulate your opponents. You play by the rules. You hustle. You give credit to your teammates. Always. He liked it when we won, but his praise was for the way we won."[12]

One summer when Tom's boys were about ten or twelve there was a polio scare across the United States. Tom and Bess decided to send the boys to stay with their grandmother in Shreveport. There Bill and Jack managed to get on an organized Pony League baseball team sponsored by the local glass manufacturing plant. But that team and experience was unsatisfying for the Ratliff boys. The culture of the "Shreveport kids was loud, brash, and unsportsmanlike."[13] According to Jack, they would keep up "chatter" in the infield during play. They would yell at the batter all the time. "Batter-batter-batter or No Hitter, No Hitter to distract him at the time the ball went over the plate they would yell in unison "swing batter!" Both Bill and Jack felt then that such chatter was wrong and was a pretty clear violation of Tom's rules of sportsmanship.[14]

Of course, the game was only a game, but Tom insisted that it must always be played with fairness and integrity, even when that meant losing. The opponents, rules, and officials must all be respected and treated fairly. This central rule of fairness permeated all of his actions in coaching, in business, and in his discussions at home and his actions in life and politics. There is little doubt that Tom's deeply held values and convictions became central in Bill's own moral compass, allowing him to face great pressure and courageously stand for right and fairness, even when it was extremely hard to do.

Bess

Bill's mother's early years were not nearly as stable as those of her husband nor did she have many of the unearned advantages that Fate Ratliff had bestowed on Tom. But somehow Bess (born on 30 September 1905) took her early life lessons and made the very best of them for her boys and for all those around her. Bess's earliest memories of her father (William Roark) and mother (Caddy) came in no small measure to also shape the nature, home, and the expectations she would come to have for her own children in the years to come. Bess always hated the nickname "Bessie" which well-meaning friends would sometimes use affectionately.[15] During her early teen years, that awkward time of growth for most children, she would on occasion knock something over and have to endure her father's cruel response, "there she comes, Bessie the cow."[16]

Bess never shared this memory with her three boys and possibly never even with her husband Tom, but in later years she confided to her daughter-in-law (Clare Ratliff) that her father was a brutally mean alcoholic who abused his wife, her, and her sister.[17] As Bess would decades later tell Clare, her earliest memory of her father, was that of she and her mother sitting on the floor in front of her intoxicated father who was rocking in a chair waving a loaded pistol at them and saying that he was going to kill Bess, her mother, and then himself. Bess and Caddy were crying and begging for their lives. Thankfully he didn't follow through with this threat. In Bess's early teen years her father would abandon his family, leaving Bess to be the sole supporter of the family until her younger brothers and sisters could finish high school and also contribute (Caddy was unable to work). Bess managed to finish high school and even attend secretarial school while she was not working at one of her many jobs to support her mother and sister.

Bess's life circumstances never allowed her the privilege of attending college which was something she always regretted. All of these disadvantages led Bess to a lifelong preoccupation with the acquisition of safety, security, knowledge, and even the social graces she missed in her formative years.[18] Bess sought these not only for herself but also for her three children. By all measures, Bess Roark would come to have and hold all those high attributes she missed as a child. It is often the case that men and women who have known great struggle are both the strongest and most interesting people. This is certainly the case for Bess Roark as she knew well both pain and struggle. She was a devoted and deeply caring mother.[19] She was deeply loving to her husband and children, and a graceful friend to many and a saint in the eyes of many others and was well respected in her community. From that unstable and difficult upbringing came a most remarkable woman who devoted her life to raising Bill and his brothers to know and have what she had not. Her son Jack would later write, "maybe it was because she never went to college or because she grew up poor, but she had some ambitious ideas for her children and devoted herself to seeing that we had advantages she didn't."[20]

In seeking to provide her sons with many of the advantages she valued, Bess consistently read to them. She created a "dictionary game" that constantly introduced new vocabulary; she drilled home the importance of education, taught them to dance, and was ever conscious of the need to provide them with the polish and social graces of gentlemen. As parents, Tom and Bess did the very best they could, which it turns out to have been extraordinary, to provide the best possible advantages and opportunities for their three sons. Thomas Ratliff and Bess Roark absolutely devoted their lives to Jack, Bill, and Shannon.[21]

PERSONAL AND SOCIAL RESPONSIBILITY

A brief look at great men and women across history will reveal that rather than focus on personal gain, those who we admire or celebrate as heroes often dedicated themselves to work for the benefit of their communities, their country, and our world. Great leaders—men and women of politics, science, as well as those of technology and industry—are those who focused on the needs of others rather than themselves. Great leaders—Thomas Jefferson, Abraham Lincoln, Theodore Roosevelt, Mahatma Gandhi, Winston Churchill, Franklin D. Roosevelt, Martin Luther King Jr., Ronald Reagan, Nelson Mandela, Bill Clinton, Aung San Suu Kyi, and Mary Robinson—all balanced (or still balance) a healthy sense of both personal and social responsibility. This is not to say that these leaders are perfect humans who never experienced failure. But it is the case that great leaders do manage to succeed in fulfilling their personal and social responsibilities.

Personal responsibility is the ability to connect personal choices, individual actions, and consequences to ethical decision making. Social responsibility includes intercultural competence, a knowledge of civic responsibility, and the ability to engage effectively in regional, national, and global communities. All great leaders, like Bill Ratliff, demonstrate a strong and successful implementation of an effective and engaged personal and social responsibility. Lesser leaders often fail to do this in one way or the other. If a leader fails in ethical decision making, she fails to understand how her personal choices and individual actions are critical to her success; there is a short circuit between what one professes and how one behaves. If a leader fails to understand that his leadership serves others, is focused on civic responsibility rather than promoting his own agenda and own personal gain he will fall short of serving greatly and will become merely a shell of a leader who is only taking for personal gain and not serving the larger regional, national, and global village needs. While it is entirely possible and even expected for great leaders to differ in scope, purpose, and policy, all great leaders exhibit a strong and effective implementation of both social and personal responsibility. Great leaders understand that personal choices matter. Great leaders understand and are keenly aware of their civil responsibility.

Those who lived during the years of the Great Depression and the great war that followed came to know a special perspective, an interesting understanding of what it means to be a conservative, and to have a special connection with the meaning of service and working together to overcome adversity. The people who experienced those years of American history saw firsthand the horrible injustice of racial hatred in Adolf Hitler and Nazi Germany and conversely, the critical need for democracy, and the value of working together to create a fairer and just society. Tom and Bess made sure that their three sons learned those lessons.

Selfish and short-sighted men and women may rise to some level of status and even to the highest leadership positions, they may even change the course of history, but almost without exception they are not among those we choose to celebrate. It is important to note perfection in leaders does not exist. In all great men and women, we are able to point to their flaws, mistakes, and often to many failures and shortcomings. It is despite those flaws, inefficacies, and struggles that great men and women have found both the discipline and inspiration to recognize and then rise to meet the challenges and needs of those around them. Bess found strength in hardship and challenges and shared that strength with her sons.

THE KINGFISH

The life circumstances of Tom, Bess, and their three boys were in no small part shaped by another American leader known to many as the Kingfish.[22] The Kingfish was a highly influential political leader in Louisiana from 1915 to 1935 who knew hardship, failure, and great success. In those twenty years Huey Pierce Long Jr. focused first on others, the poor, disenfranchised, and downtrodden, and then tragically became driven by ruthless ambition. Huey Long was born on August 30, 1893, about a decade before Tom and Bess, in Winnfield, Louisiana, a small, very rural community in the piney woods of north central Louisiana, about one hundred miles south of Shreveport.

Huey Long lived in Louisiana at a time when public schools were few to nonexistent. As public schools were simply not available in the early 1900s in Louisiana, most children were either educated at home by their parents or went without education. After years of being schooled at home by his mother, Huey was only able to start formal schooling in the fourth grade. Young Huey Long was an undisciplined and impatient student. He refused to suffer in an inept teacher's class and was inclined to skip school. It seemed he felt he had so very little time and needed to focus urgently on his life's work. Even so, his mother had well prepared her brilliant young student for school and he found he was years ahead of his classmates, and skipped grades. Huey excelled at debate in high school and even without earning a diploma was awarded a scholarship to Louisiana State University as a prize in a statewide debating competition. Sadly, neither Huey nor his family could·afford the textbooks or room and board necessary to attend the university.[23] Years later as Governor of Louisiana, Huey Long's personal strife and trials in education would come to change the lives of many Americans—including Bill Ratliff's father and mother.

Every Man a King

Huey Long was a gifted orator (like Tom and later the Ratliff boys) and stood out as a high school and college debater. After high school Long became a salesman. "I can sell anything to anybody," remarked Long, and proved this to be true on many occasions.[24] At age twenty-one, after only one year of law school at Tulane University in New Orleans, young Huey convinced an examining board to allow him to take the Louisiana Bar exam and he passed. Newly admitted to the Louisiana Bar, Long moved his family to Shreveport and opened a law practice, concentrating on law suits against Standard Oil and other big corporations. He primarily represented small plaintiffs against large businesses, including workers' compensation cases. He made a name for himself as an outspoken reformer by taking on the biggest businesses in the region and even lobbying the Louisiana state legislature for workers' compensation reform (social protection for workers was at the top of his agenda). Long was proud to say that he never took a case against a poor man. He claimed that he was a "defender of the friendless."[25] Ideologically, Huey Long was a populist. Some have argued that he was even an "extreme populist." Long declared loudly and often that he was the enemy of corporate interests and championed the "little man" against the rich and privileged. The Kingfish called for government programs to "Share Our Wealth." In 1918 at age twenty-five Long won a seat on the Louisiana Railroad Commission (later renamed the Louisiana Public Service Commission). He used his position on the commission to build a name for himself as a champion of the common man, fighting against utility rate increases and oil pipeline monopolies. He became chairman of the Public Service Commission in 1922 and won statewide acclaim after he sued the Cumberland Telephone Company for unjustly raising its rates by 20 percent and successfully arguing the case on appeal before the US Supreme Court.[26] The phone company was forced to send refund checks to eighty thousand overcharged customers.[27] In 1924, Long ran for Louisiana governor and lost, but won the praise of many and became a major player in Louisiana politics winning the governor's office just four years later with the campaign slogan "every man a king." Governor Long immediately worked with the Louisiana legislature to pass dozens of bills to build state infrastructure (schools, roads, hospitals, and bridges) and to provide all students with an opportunity to attend schools within walking distance of their home and with free schoolbooks. Long immediately faced significant and growing opposition over his legislative agenda and methods. In 1929 Governor Long managed to overcome an impeachment effort by opponents including Standard Oil, after trying to enact a new tax of 5 cents per barrel on crude oil refined in Louisiana to pay for the textbooks, new schoolss and hospitals, bridges, and roads.[28]

Tom and Bess Ratliff were both personally and professionally directly affected by the Kingfish's social revolution in Louisiana. In the same year Standard Oil sought to impeach Governor Long, Tom was hired as the coach at Shreveport, Louisiana's Fair Park High School. Tom coached all of the school's sports.[29] The year before, Governor Long had begun to champion the idea that education is every child's birthright and had pushed a bill through the Louisiana Legislature that provided a great expansion in public education for every Louisiana student. Coach Tom Ratliff found opportunity (and ultimately his reason for moving to Texas) in Huey Long's revolution to expand and build public schools in Louisiana. In his service to others, Governor Long made higher education possible for tens of thousands of students. Long also greatly expanded Louisiana State University and established many scholarships to support those who like himself, would not have been able to attend otherwise.[30]

Shreveport

After finishing secretarial school, Bess took a position in the new and expanding Shreveport public school system. She worked as an administrative assistant in the central administration building. In a strange crossing of paths, one rainy morning, Governor Long (who made it a regular habit to offer people rides in his limo) picked up Bess at bus stop and gave her a ride to work.[31] The governor and the school secretary chatted as the big car splashed through the rain-soaked Shreveport streets. Not long after the governor had given Bess a ride to work, a tall and handsome Tom Ratliff walked into the administration building and noticed the enchanting Bess working behind the front desk. After that first visit Tom regularly found reasons to need to be in that building. On Christmas Eve in 1930 Bess and Tom married in Dallas, Texas. In that same year, Coach Ratliff's Fair Park High School baseball team won the North Louisiana State Championship. The quiet and fair coach who was a compelling teacher of boys would soon have three of his own.

Tom and Bess lived in a modest apartment next door to Caddy's house about a mile from Fair Park High in Shreveport. Even in the middle of the Great Depression, the city of Shreveport was growing. In addition to Governor Long's new schools and other state infrastructure, a delegation of citizens from Shreveport traveled to Washington, D.C., to visit with officials of the US War Department to propose a new airfield just outside the city. In 1933, the year before the birth of Tom and Bess's first son, Jack, the citizens of Shreveport had celebrated the opening of the Barksdale Army Air Field. The dedication of Barksdale Air Field marked the culmination of a concerted community action that brought growth and significant commercial activity to the region. The children of the many men on women who worked on the Barksdale Air Force Base (named in honor of Lt. Eugene Hoy Barksdale, US Air Corps) were the students on Tom's teams in the Shreveport schools. Barksdale would later become a training base for bomber crews that would soon be flying in World War II European operations. The young Ratliff family was growing right along with the city.

In the early morning of August 16, 1936, she knew it was time. The summer heat had been hard on Bess, that day the thermometer would top one hundred humid degrees in the northwest corner of Louisiana. Having been through this once before, both she and Tom were excited but not in a panic as they drove to the nearby Shreveport neighborhood of Queensborough. They parked their dusty 1930 black Chevrolet just down the street from the Tri-State Hospital, and chatted about the coming school year as they walked up the curved sidewalk to the large wooden double doors of the hospital (Tri-State Hospital photo about here). The Shreveport hospital staff knew Tom and Bess well and were happy to see them. Bess's doctor and Tom's friend, Wyeth "Docky" Worley, greeted them not long after they were settled into a room. After a full and difficult day of labor Bess brought a healthy baby boy, William Roark Ratliff, into the world. Bess had such difficulty delivering the 11 pounds 5-ounce baby boy that afterward Docky warned her not to have any more children. A warning Bess would decide to ignore and Shannon, son number three, would celebrate. To avoid the noise and bustle of lots of family in Caddy's house (2909 West College Street) Bess and baby Bill (never Billy) were carried by two hospital orderlies dressed in white to Tom and Bess's apartment. As they got her to the landing outside the door a chorus of celebratory cheers was heard in the neighborhood for Bess, Tom, and baby Bill.[32]

As Tom, Bess, and Jack settled in to care for the new baby in Shreveport, Jesse Owens was competing in the summer Olympics in Berlin. Owens won four gold medals under Adolf Hitler's disapproving gaze. As Bill's parents took him home from the hospital President Franklin Delano Roosevelt (recently elected to a second term) was working along with then Senator Huey Long and the US Congress to fight the Great Depression that griped the country. Germany was bristling with Nazism and on the verge of waging world war. Bess seemed to understand the situation of money and banking better than most and suggested to Tom that they move their money from their bank account.[33] Tom suggested keeping it in a bank safe deposit box. Bess insisted that the cash be kept at home. It turned out that this move saved the Ratliff family from much of the hardship endured by many during the Great Depression. In fact, Tom and Bess were able to purchase very expensive and fine furniture during those days that still remains in the Ratliff family today.[34]

Bess was a deeply religious woman.[35] She was, however, a person who did not share her spiritual life with others—not even her family. Every day, without fail, Bess devoted some quiet time to reading and prayer and Bess would end every day reading from a small book of prayers. While her husband, Tom, was also a man of some faith (raised in the deep southern Baptist traditions) he did not share his wife's deeply spiritual side. And so the two young parents decided to allow their sons to be seekers, to find their own spiritual ways. And each in his own time would do just that. In 1938, Bess would bring her third son, Shannon, into the world also in the Tri-State Hospital in Shreveport. With the birth of Shannon, Tom and Bess's family was complete. Their three remarkable boys would all enjoy long and highly influential careers and their lives would in turn help shape the lives and opportunities of millions of Americans.

Columbia University

Not long after Shannon was born, Tom was appointed the principal post in one of Governor Long's small-town schools in Belcher, Louisiana. Tom's success in coaching and in teaching had earned him wide and growing respect in the Northwest Louisiana community and within the Shreveport public school system. As such he was both working toward and being groomed for the superintendent post of the Shreveport schools. Governor Long, whose reach of power extended deep into every Louisiana community, was very closely tied to the leaders of Shreveport Public Schools. In preparation for the Shreveport administrative post, Tom spent two summers away from his family in New York at Columbia University. At Columbia University, which was founded in 1754 by

George II of Great Britain, Tom would work hard and sacrifice to earn a Master's Degree in history.[36] Tom's education, employment, and civic engagement in Governor Long's schools would in turn come to profoundly affect the lives of his three boys and millions of Texans.

Jack, Bill, and Shannon's "aces of parents" spent many loving and gentle hours with them. From sports to dance, to singing and reading to the boys at bedtime, Tom and Bess both doted on their sons. At bedtime each night they would read from Aesop's Fables, Winnie the Pooh, Swiss Family Robinson, and many other classic books. Jack recalled his father and mother bending over Bill's old-fashioned crib and singing while rocking it. Sometimes when one of the boys was ill, Tom would put his hand on the boy's forehead and call him by a silly made-up name.[37] At those times, neither Tom nor Bess were strict or authoritarian, but simply loving, quiet, gentle, and concerned. This parental habit was a theme and a pattern of love and devotion throughout the boy's early childhood. The Ratliff boys had the advantage of wonderful, gentle, caring, and loving parents. But the political climate in Louisiana in those years was anything but gentle.

In the 1930s, Huey Long's focus shifted from being a champion of the people and serving the poor to a focus on personal ambition and power. Many of his critics accused him of seizing dictatorial-like powers in Louisiana. By the 1930s, Long controlled almost every aspect of the state's government. By the time Jack Ratliff was born, Huey Long had begun a reorganization of the state of Louisiana that all but abolished local government and gave himself the power to appoint all state employees which included the selection of the superintendent of the Shreveport schools. In a move that would change history, Senator Long gave his support to Weldon Jones—not Tom Ratliff. In light of Long's decision and this lost opportunity, Tom and Bess Ratliff decided to leave Louisiana and moved their young family to Sonora, Texas.[38]

More than anything else, Tom and Bess wanted to give their three sons a future. Jack, Bill, and Shannon grew up in a home and in an America that supported them and provided them with real opportunities to flourish. For many America is a place of progress and opportunity. American successes are nearly always stories of many men and women working together to support one another, to build and to create. The Ratliff boys (Jack, Bill, and Shannon) became great and wonderfully successful Texans not only through their own efforts, but also with the support of a host of characters, Tom, Bess, Docky, Huey Long, even George II of Great Britain also playing major roles in their success. It is important to acknowledge the earned and unearned privileges the Ratliff boys enjoyed. If we fail to understand advantages—both earned and unearned—we risk misunderstanding and underestimating their successes and failures. It was the hard work and investments of many others over the course of history who created the opportunity for the Ratliff success.

While the Ratliff story is a hopeful and optimistic story of hard work, perseverance, and ultimately great success it is also a story of the immeasurable advantages of a devoted family and community support.

MAILED MY RESIGNATION

On Thursday, July 8, 1943, Tom noted in his diary, "mailed my resignation, no longer a school teacher."[39] The Ratliff's moved to Sutton County, Sonora, Texas, that hot July (the county was named for John Schuyler Sutton, an officer in the Confederate Army). Sonora is in Southwest Texas, an area of the state that exhibits bicultural characteristics—it has a large Mexican-American population and as such has strong ties to Mexico. As Tom, Bess, Jack, Bill, and Shannon settled into the Sonora community, brown-shirted German Storm Troopers goose-stepped across Berlin. In the small central Texas town, Tom and Bess worked hard to settle in and provide a good solid life for their young family.

War Still

The Ratliff family lived in a very small two-bedroom frame house with a detached garage/washroom in the back. The boy's bedroom barely held all three single beds. Their room was so small that they had to crawl over other beds to reach the one on the far side of the room. As Tom took over the family dry-goods store that fall, Adolf Hitler was threatening, imprisoning, and already killing Jews, Roma, and many others. While the economic hardship of the Great Depression made living and parenting a struggle in the United States, evil arose in Germany. Tom clearly worried about national and international events and his family as evident in several notes like this one from May 10, 1943, "War still. Bill had his tonsils out. In the hospital, having a rough time—bad tonsils."[40] On Wednesday morning, May 12, 1943, as Bill was released from the Shreveport hospital, General Eisenhower and General Alexander of the Allied Armies in North Africa announced that the war in Africa was over.

While World War II was being fought, the small community of Sonora, the southwestern region of the country, and eventually the entire United States, was still being affected by the Great Depression. By the time the Ratliff family moved to Texas the depression had steadily worsened. Unemployment had risen from 8 to 15 million (roughly 1/3 of the non-farmer workforce) and the gross national product had decreased from $103.8 billion to $55.7 billion. Nearly half of the farms in the Dust Bowl were taken over by the banks.[41] Although the depression was prevalent worldwide, no other country (except Hitler's Germany) reached so high a percentage of unemployed. Huey Long's poor were hit the hardest. Farmers were doubly hit by the economic downturn and the Dust

Bowl. Bill Ratliff and his brothers would attend Sonora public school in those years, with shrinking budgets, poorly paid teachers, and shortened calendars. Years later Bill would marry a public school teacher and become a champion of public education for Texas children.

There was much debate regarding how best to respond to the economic crisis of the 1930s. Following the writing and suggestions of John Maynard Keynes, President Roosevelt promoted a wide variety of federally funded programs aimed at restoring the American economy. Senator Huey Long and others promoted even more radical changes and proposed a "Share Our Wealth Society" that would redistribute wealth by taxing the rich and giving to the poor. Long advocated free higher education and vocational training, pensions for the elderly, veteran's benefits and health care, and a yearly stipend for all families earning less than one-third the national average income. Long also argued that every American should have enough income to support a home, an automobile, a radio, and the ordinary conveniences.[42] Roosevelt sought to help relieve the suffering of the unemployed by reforming the economic system so that such a severe crisis could never happen again. However, most economists believe that government spending to fight the Germans and Japanese pulled the economy from the Great Depression.

During World War II, numerous challenges confronted the American people. The government found it necessary to ration food, gas, and even clothing. Americans were asked to conserve on everything. With not a single person unaffected by the war, rationing meant sacrifices for all. In the spring of 1942, the Food Rationing Program was set into motion. Rationing would deeply affect the way of life for most Americans. The federal government needed to control supply and demand. Rationing was introduced to avoid public anger with shortages and not to allow only the wealthy to purchase commodities. The Ratliff dry-goods store in Sonora, Texas, was deeply affected by rationing.

As a young boy, Bill learned the value of not only fair government policy but also personal sacrifice for the greater societal good. As a move toward that "good society" the US Supreme Court began to address the issue of racial segregation. The schools in Sonora were like the schools all across the United States—racially segregated. The US Supreme Court had made racial segregation legal in *Plessy v. Ferguson* (1896). In *Plessy*, the Court held that segregated public facilities were constitutional so long as the black and white facilities were equal to each other. Of course, segregated schools were not in any way equal.[43]

In the late 1940s, without the entertainment options available in larger cities, Bill (like many boys in rural America) followed and played baseball. Dreaming of one day playing ball in the Major leagues, during the hot summers the Ratliff boys and others would often go out to a dusty hardpan makeshift baseball diamond and play catch and take turns hitting and catching fly balls. The white community of Sonora did not have enough teenage boys to play an actual baseball game. [44]

Before Heman Sweatt's lawsuit (decided in June 1950 and eliminating racial bias as legal in the University of Texas School of Law admission process), [45] Gustavo C. Garcia (Gus), a Mexican American, was among UT Law's brightest stars. Garcia graduated from the law school a little more than a decade before the US Supreme Court forced UT to open its law program to blacks. Unlike black Americans, Hispanic Americans were able to attend UT's Law school from its inception in 1883. [46]

Latino and black Americans were kept separate and apart from whites in all aspects of daily life, including sandlot baseball games. In Sonora in the 1940s and 1950s, Mexican American children were almost never even seen by the white children. Unless they happened to tag along with a parent to do house or yard work for a white family, the Latino children never had any interaction with white children. In Sonora, like all towns across Texas, the Latino children did not attend schools with the white children but rather went to school in a collection of shacks across the Dry Devil's River. [47] Texas schools were segregated and afforded the white students a real and significant unearned advantage in life. In Bill Ratliff's teen years, lawyers were challenging the segregated schools in Texas. At the time, Texas law required "separate but equal" schools for Anglos and African Americans but not for Latino Americans. The segregation of Latino Americans was widespread across Texas, enforced not by written laws, as was the case for African Americans, but by a rigid social code. In 1938, the University of Texas Law School graduate Gus Garcia filed a legal challenge arguing that Minerva Delgado and twenty other Latino children were unconstitutionally denied the same school facilities and educational opportunities available to white children. The Texas courts agreed and began the process of ending the segregation of Latino and Anglo schoolchildren in Texas. [48]

Red and the Boys, Days of Endless Baseball

One hot day in late May 1948, Bill, his brothers, and several other white boys from Sonora looked up from their sandlot play to see a group of Latino teenagers approaching. Just beyond the fence of that hardpan baseball diamond, one of the Latino boys who wore a frayed red baseball cap, white T-shirt, and faded jeans approached the white Sonora boys. Because he wore a red cap the white boys called him "Red." [49] The boys observed the approach of the group of Latino boys cautiously, as the previous summer there had been a couple of racially charged encounters between the town's white and Latino boys. Jack and Bill Ratliff, as the oldest boys were the leaders on the dusty baseball diamond, both hated fighting and badly wanted to avoid a clash. [50]

After wary smiles and considerable stumbling with translations between English and Spanish it became clear that Red and his friends simply wanted to play ball. And so Jack, Bill, Shannon, and a handful of other white Sonora boys together with the Latino Sonora boys organized a regular and endless sandlot baseball game, a game that lasted countless innings and several seasons. With only a couple of exceptions, the Latino boys did not own baseball gloves and only one old beat-up baseball bat among them. Sharing of equipment became essential in order to play. So they shared. The boys had to improvise bases and the game had to be umpired by the boys themselves. They worked out a system of alternating behind the plate to call balls and strikes. Close calls were negotiated—between two languages—until they could all reach some kind of agreement. There were temper flares and a number of heated arguments—but never once a fight. In extreme cases, a "do-over" would be called, repeated turn at bat, or the runner whose tag at second was an issue would have to go back to first base. The crux that kept the never-ending game going was sportsmanship as well as a shared love of the game. Without each other, both groups of boys would be relegated to hitting fly balls and playing catch. The boys of Sonora, both white and Latino, learned a great deal about life from those endless innings of baseball. They learned about sportsmanship, fairness, leadership, and the fine art of negotiation. They also learned about each other, their cultural differences, and their innate similarities.

A Class Apart

While Bill and his brothers were playing the continuous sandlot baseball game with the Latino boys from across Dry Devil's River, a case was working its way to the US Supreme Court that would help bring an end to the discrimination Latino Americans faced in Sonora and across the state of Texas. On Saturday, August 4, 1951, about three hundred miles to the southeast of Sonora, in Edna, Texas, a farmer named Joe Espinosa, made a snide remark to Pedro Hernandez as they drank beer in Chencho Sánchez's café on Menefee Street. Pedro was a field worker with a bad leg and Joe said, "no woman is ever going to look at a cripple like you, Pedro. They're only interested in a real he-man like me." And with that remark, Pedro left the café walked home and got his rifle and came back to the café and killed Joe. An all-white Texas Jackson County jury found Pedro guilty of murder. Latinos were systematically excluded from jury duty. Attorney's Gus Garcia, Carlos Cadena, John Herrera, and James DeAnda challenged Pedro's conviction, arguing that the exclusion of Latinos from the jury violated Pedro's right to equal protection of the law guaranteed by the Fourteenth Amendment to the US Constitution. Gus Garcia argued the case before the US Supreme Court. Garcia argued that Latinos, although white, were a "class apart" and were suffering discrimination in Texas. The US Supreme Court agreed. In a unanimous opinion delivered by Chief Justice Earl Warren, the Supreme Court held that the Fourteenth Amendment protects those (such as the Latino-Texan) beyond the two classes of white or black.[51]

I Lobbied for Separate Bedrooms

As Tom and Bess's sons grew, their small two-bedroom house seemed to shrink. Baseball gloves, clothes, bats, dusty cleats, books, backpacks, and all the gear boys need on a daily basis filled the small spaces of their tiny bedroom. Bill grew frustrated with his brothers, as neither Jack nor Shannon were the neatest of boys.[52] Neither seemed to care about the mess. So, in the spring of 1950 Tom and Bess began to plan to build a new house. Bill would later kindly say, "my brothers were far from meticulous" so in planning for a new house, "I lobbied for separate bedrooms." Tom did not think he could afford three separate bedrooms for his growing sons, but he gave Bill the square footage and roofline that he could afford, and said if Bill could come up with a floor plan that accommodated bedrooms for each the boys he would build it. Bill was already exuding the neat and orderly characteristics and the mind of an engineer, and on his small drawing board he came up with a workable floor plan with a bedroom for each son. Tom and Bess had their new home built out on the edge of Sonora. The new home was not large by any standard, but offered each boy his own personal space. Young Bill had designed the center of the house with a relatively large living-dining room with a fireplace and picture windows looking out the back of the house onto the Sonora ranching country.[53] On one end of the house were three small bedrooms with built-in dressers and small closets for each boy. These three rooms were not large but were adequate for a single bed and a small pine desk. Bill kept his room picture perfect neat. At the other end of the house was the kitchen and Tom and Bess's bedroom. Both Tom and Bess had a walk-in closet (a real luxury for the time). Just out through the kitchen was a double carport. Day in and day out for years to come that home provided the Ratliffs with a space to love one another, share, grow, and learn.

THE RATLIFF FAMILY AND POLITICAL SOCIALIZATION

Bill and his brothers watched their father work long and hard to support his family. A few years after they moved to Sonora, Tom opened a dry-goods store. The boys remember him pushing himself so hard in his work that one night his hands shook as he was opening a box to restock the shelves. Bill watched his father work to complete a master's degree from Columbia University in New York while working as a principal and refereeing night basketball games at Centenary College because his princi-pal salary did not adequately support his education and the needs of Bess and the boys. While working hard during the day, Tom and Bess would drive their boys to football and baseball games in the evenings, some-times fifty or ninety miles away. Tom served as mayor of Sonora—with-out pay—and ran for and was elected to the office of county judge—an office with great responsibility and very little pay or reward.

"I Keep My Self-Respect"

Tom was a progressive liberal in a community that was largely con-servative. "Here's the thing," he told Jack, his oldest son, "Everybody in town knows my politics, I don't hide them. But it gets exhausting to be disagreeing and arguing with people every day. I mean, there are only so many people I can go to have coffee with in the morning. Nobody in the coffee group agrees with me. So here's my problem. If I go over to the drugstore for coffee, I am faced with a choice. I can just sit and be quiet while everybody cusses government programs and the liberals and Ralph Yarborough and then leave the impression that now I may be agreeing with them. Or I can get into a long argument every day. So I made this compromise with myself. About every two weeks or so I will say 'You know, don't you, that I've disagreed with almost everything you fellows have been saying about politics in the last two weeks.' And they accept that. They knew it already, of course. But it's a reminder. I keep my self-respect. I don't have to argue all the time and I don't have to feel like a hypocrite because I don't. It's like I say, you wouldn't like it."[54]

Bill's father, Tom, would often host political discussions at their home in Sonora.[55] He enjoyed playing dominoes and talking politics (usually at the same time). The area opinion leaders, local commissioners, and politi-cians—would gather in the Ratliff parlor to meet and discuss the issues of the day. Often people from the community would bring disputes to Tom who would work to settle the issues via mediation. Bill and his brothers learned much about politics and power while listening in on those long political conversations. As Mayor of Sonora and later County Judge, Tom always insisted on fairness and doing the right thing, even if that meant being unpopular. It was a common practice for the county commissioners to give and receive two different political favors for holding office. One favor was extended to the local landowners. The county would grade (maintain) private roads and provide long driveways to homes and ranches. The other favor was a gift of a golf/leisure trip paid for by the firms that sold equipment to the county to the county commissioner. Tom refused both of those favors for himself and others, and consequently lost his elected post to a man who some believed would continue using the county equipment for personal use and accepted the gift of the golf trip.[56] While Tom's loss stung, the life lessons taught by painful example became a strong and deeply ingrained value for Bill and his brothers. Taking and giving favors for political and personal gain was wrong. Years later Senator Ratliff would be asked to address this very ethical problem within the Texas Legislature.

A political ideology is a set of values and ideas about politics, the nature of humans, and the scope and purpose of government. Our own political ideology develops through years and years of political socialization. We first learn from our parents and then from ever expanding circles of influencers in our lives. From our teachers, to peers, to the media we come to know what we think is correct about politics, policy, and the scope and purpose of a legitimate government. Of course, one's ideology is not static. It can and does evolve in most people over time—as new information and ideas are experienced. Many different people, places, and circumstances shaped the early life of William Roark Ratliff and his brothers. From Fate Ratliff, to Huey Long, to Tom's debate club and coaching, to Bess's love and devotion, to playing cross-cultural baseball on a dusty diamond, these factors shaped advantages, opportunities, and his outlook on life. A myriad of factors shaped his ideology. Just as Huey Long's early life in Winnfield, Louisiana, shaped his ideology, the shaping of Bill Ratliff's life occurred in his formative years in Sonora, Texas.

Political scholars describe the political culture in Texas as a mix of the traditional and individualistic.[57] The traditional political subculture is one in which people view government as an institution that exists primarily to maintain the dominate social and religious values. This is evident today in the way many Texas political leaders promote specific religious values. On the other hand, the individualistic subculture dominates across the rest of the state—including Sonora, Texas. Bill Ratliff came to know and value the individualistic subculture and as such to view government as a practical necessity. For the Ratliff family, the purpose and role of government was and is to promote private enterprise—but also to play only a minimal or no other role in the daily people's lives. Bill would come to alter this point of view in later years.[58]

In Bill's life, fairness to others was a central value. Fairness was a core value reinforced over and over by his father in Bill's early years, from baseball to football to the way his family treated others. In Tom and Bess, the values of respect for others and honesty, strength when faced with adversity, and personal responsibility and integrity are ever present. Tom often and repeatedly let his boys know of his intolerance of hypocritical and dishonest individuals. Tom and Bess taught respect for opponents and the value of teamwork. On the football field and hardpan baseball diamond the boys learned that teamwork and working together (social responsibility) were central to play and to accomplishing tasks. The Great Depression and World War II taught the boys the value of conservation and sacrifice (both social and personal responsibility).[59] The Ratliff boys well learned the values of hard work, dedication, and preparation (personal responsibility). Tom and Bess taught by example the importance of being engaged citizens and the need for political participation in the Sonora community (social responsibility). Many people use their political ideology to make decisions about politics and policy. Using one's ideology as a guide, a person can shortcut to answer questions of politics and policy. Often—very often—those shortcuts provide only superficial and limited answers to the reality of governing in a complex and multidimensional world. Of course, one's values and norms inform how one approaches and defines a problem but ideology can and often does lead to misunderstanding the problem at hand and to unintended consequences.

In high school and then in college at the University of Texas at Austin, Bill and his brothers gained new and far reaching perspectives and decision-making skills. The combination of the solid foundation provided by family, Bess, and Tom along with the high school and college experiences would prove to shape the lives of many Americans for years to come.

NOTES

1. See the list of John F. Kennedy Foundation Profile in Courage Award Recipients. Profiles in Courage Award list includes President George H. W. Bush, President Gerald Ford, and Senator John McCain, just to name a few.

2. Bickerstaff discusses "Electing the Right Republican" in chapter 4 in *Lines in the Sand*.

3. See, for example, *Marco Rubio's Crisis of Faith: Why His Complicated, Unique Religious Journey is Causing Him Trouble with Voters* by Michael Kruse. http://www.politico.com/magazine/story/2016/01/marco-rubios-crisis-of-faith-213553. January 22, 2016.

4. In an interview in PBS's "Karl Rove—The Architect" (http://www.pbs.org/wgbh/pages/frontline/shows/architect/interviews/whitman.html).

5. Interview with Jack and Clare Ratliff, October 2014.

6. The information in this section came from interviews with Bill Ratliff, Shannon Ratliff, and Jack Ratliff.

7. Information for this section came from an interview with Jack Ratliff in October 2014 and from Lights! Camera! University of North Texas!: Joan Blondell (1906-1979) and blog post on the University of North Texas website (http://blogs.library.unt.edu/unt125/2015/08/27/joan_blondell/).

8. Interview with Bill Ratliff, Shannon Ratliff, and Jack Ratliff, 2013 and 2014.

9. Interview with Bill Ratliff, May 2014.

10. Interview with Jack Ratliff, October 2014.

11. Interview with Bill Ratliff.

12. Interview with Jack Ratliff, October 2014.

13. Ibid.

14. Interview with Jack Ratliff, October 2014.

15. Interview with Bill Ratliff.

16. Ibid.

17. Interview with Jack and Clare Ratliff, October 2014.

18. Interview with Shannon Ratliff, June 2014.

19. Interviews with Bill Ratliff, Jack Ratliff, Clare Ratliff, and Shannon Ratliff.

20. From Jack Ratliff's notes and interview in October 2014.

21. Shannon Ratliff recalled the dictionary game in an interview in June 2014.

22. The influence of Governor Huey P. Long on the Ratliff family was told and retold in interviews with Bill, Jack, and Shannon.

23. The information in this section about governor Huey Long came primarily from "Huey Long: The Man, Mission, and Legacy," http://www.hueylong.com/life-times/governor.php.

24. *Every Man a King: The Autobiography of Huey P. Long*, by Huey P. Long.

25. Ibid.

26. Ibid.

27. *Cumberland Tel. & Tel. Co. v. Louisiana Pub. Serv. Comm'n*, 260 US 212 (1922).

28. The information in this section about Governor Huey Long came primarily from "Huey Long: The Man, Mission, and Legacy," http://www.hueylong.com/life-times/governor.php.

29. Interview with Bill Ratliff, Shannon Ratliff, and Jack Ratliff, 2014.

30. *Kingfish: The Reign of Huey P. Long* by Richard White, September 19, 2006.

31. Interview with Bill Ratliff and Jack Ratliff, 2014.

32. Re-created from interviews with Bill Ratliff (2013) and Jack Ratliff (2014).

33. Interview with Jack Ratliff, 2014.

34. Ibid.

35. Interview with Bill Ratliff, 2013.

36. History of Columbia University. http://www.columbia.edu/content/history.html.

37. Interview with Jack Ratliff, 2014.

38. Interview with Bill Ratliff, 2013, and Jack Ratliff, 2014.

39. Calendar/journal entry provided by Jack Ratliff.

40. Ibid.

41. *History of Great Depression*. http://www.econlib.org/library/Enc/GreatDepression.html.

42. *Every Man a King: The Autobiography of Huey P. Long*, by Huey P. Long.

43. *Plessy v. Ferguson* (No. 210) 163 U.S. 537, May 18, 1896.

44. Interview with Jack Ratliff, 2014.

45. Richard Allen Burns, "Sweatt, Heman Marion," Handbook of Texas Online (http://www.tshaonline.org/handbook/online/articles/fsw23), accessed February 4, 2016. Uploaded on June 15, 2010. Modified on February 25, 2015. Published by the Texas State Historical Association.

46. Noted in Gustavo C. (Gus) Garcia Papers, Benson Latin American Collection, University of Texas Libraries, the University of Texas at Austin.

47. Interview with Jack Ratliff, 2014.

48. *Delgado vs. Bastrop ISD*, 1948.

49. Jack Ratliff did not have a record of Red's name—only his nickname. He did tell me that in later years he attempted to find Red—to learn his full name and about his life—but was unsuccessful.

50. Interview with Jack Ratliff, 2014.

51. Ian Haney-Lopez: *Hernandez v. Texas and Ruben Munguia*, A Cotton Picker Finds Justice: The Saga of the Hernandez Case (1954). http://www.law.uh.edu/Hernandez50/saga.pdf.

52. Interview with Bill Ratliff, 2013.

53. Ibid.

54. Quoted in Jack Ratliff's yet to be published book about Fate, Tom, and Bess, 2016.

55. Interviews with Bill Ratliff, Shannon Ratliff, and Jack Ratliff, 2014.

56. Interview with Bill Ratliff, 2013.

57. *Texas Politics: Governing the Lone Star State*, by Cal Jillson p. 8.

58. Interview with Bill Ratliff and many others, 2013, 2014, 2015, and 2016.

59. Core Commitments: Educating Students for Personal and Social Responsibility created and established by the American Association of Colleges and Universities (https://www.aacu.org/core_commitments).

TWO

The Engineer: Free of Egotism

Bill's father had been athlete, a champion debater, and had acted alongside the famous Joan Blondell. Bill's mother was an extraordinarily strong and driven woman—in Jack's word they were "aces." It was little wonder that both Bess and Tom had high expectations for their three sons. Their expectations were not only met but greatly exceeded. All three boys were outstanding students and athletes. Bill's older brother Jack, and his younger brother Shannon, were fond of and excelled at debate and enjoyed acting. Both Jack and Shannon won many regional, state, and national competitions.[1] Jack won first in state in "One Act Play" category, Shannon won first in state in Debate. All three of the Ratliff boys each made a major and significant impact on the lives of many Americans.

THE GUY YOU WANTED WITH THE BALL

In the early 1950s, Bill was a handsome student at Sonora High School. His brother Jack later said, "Bill was known as the guy you wanted with the ball when the game was on the line."[2] The Sonora Broncos basketball team had an outstanding season during Bill's senior year in high school.[3] Late into the playoffs the Broncos were scheduled to play the well-coached and winning Eldorado Eagles. The Broncos had a successful season and the Eagles had lost only a few games. A very large crowd filled the Sonora High gym. Lots of Eagle fans had made the drive to watch the playoff game. The pep band had the crowd in high spirits when the Broncos and then the Eagles burst from the locker rooms. On that glorious night in 1954, Bill made the Sonora community happy and proud. The score was close all throughout the game. The Broncos entered the locker room at halftime down by only one bucket. As the last seconds ticked off the clock in the fourth quarter, the Eagles had possession of the ball and were up by one point.

With the crowd in a frenzy, the Eagles were dribbling and passing down the court watching the clock tick off for the win, when suddenly Bill Ratliff burst across the hardwood floor and stole the ball. The crowd roared. As he raced toward his own goal to make the layup he was fouled from behind. The buzzer went off to signal the end of the game. The Broncos were down by one point but still had two free throw shots. The crowd was wild as Bill stepped to the free throw line.

Tom and Bess watched as Bill stepped to the line, bounced the ball twice, and with confidence and ease made the first shot. A hush fell over the crowd while the referee bounced the ball back to Bill. The game was now tied. With one more point, the Broncos would win. Calmly and quietly Bill again stepped to the line, bounced the ball twice, and with one fluid motion won the game for the Broncos. It was well known in the Sonora community that "Bill performed best when the pressure was the greatest."[4] The community of Sonora loved the Ratliff boys.

Sonora High—1949 to 1954

The high school years for the Ratliff boys held many successes in academics and extracurricular activities. Each of the Ratliff boys was— and still is—highly competitive. Bill held class leadership offices each year from eighth grade through his senior year at Sonora High.[5] The boys flourished with the warm loving support and nurturing provided by Bess.[6] Bess rarely let a day go by without telling each of her sons how much she loved them and how proud she was of them.[7] Although Tom was not as demonstrative, his sons benefited from his many strengths.[8]

As the oldest, Jack assumed a cautious and reflective role.[9] He was his brothers' protector and watched over his two younger siblings whenever he could. As the middle child, Bill was more reserved than his brothers.[10] While Jack and Shannon easily took to the "stage," Bill was a reluctant performer.[11] Jack and Shannon won award after award in debate, acting, and declamation (oratory competitions).

As a boy Shannon was and still is today the most competitive of the three Ratliff boys.[12] Jack and Bill always speculated that they pushed Shannon to be so very competitive by "never cutting their younger brother any slack" when they played games together.[13] Growing up, Shannon also had something of a redhead's temper, which seemed to fuel his competitiveness.[14] Shannon's tendencies lean toward boldness and ferocity. His father once wrote, "Shan is the pick of the town, but is getting too smart."[15] Once when all three boys were playing in the yard, they pulled out one of Tom's old golf clubs (Sonora didn't have a golf course, but the club was left over from the days in Shreveport).[16] Shannon decided that he was going to rare back and take a full swing at the ball, not checking what was behind him. He took a full swing and hit Bill just under his left eye, cutting a one-inch gash; the scar is visible to this day.[17]

Loathed the Limelight

In the 1949–1950 academic year Bill and Jack were elected members of the Sonora High student council.[18] Jack played the clarinet in the Bronco marching band. Bill and Jack were both members of the Drama Club.[19] In the 1951–1952 academic year, Bill served as the vice president of the sophomore class, and was a member of the Speech Club.[20] Bill wore jersey number 72, Jack wore number 68 in football,[21] and Shannon was president of the student council in the 1951–1952 year.[22] Both Jack and Shannon won the University Interscholastic League (UIL) declamation contest that year.[23] The UIL organization ran annual high school debate, speech, drama, and sport competitions. Both Jack and Shannon were champion UIL speakers. They both won Texas State competitions in debate and speaking declamation. While his brothers followed their father's example and became extraordinary speakers, Bill hated public speaking.[24]

Bill "loathed the limelight," and thus did not share his brothers' enthusiasm for debate, theater, and public speaking in the high school years.[25] Instead Bill was a champion of science and math.[26] He won "slide rule" competitions and excelled in the hard sciences. However, it would be incorrect to say that Bill was a misfit or an introvert; conversely he was well liked by his peers and according to his older brother he was a "ladies' man" in his high school years.[27]

Punching Huge Holes in the Prison Wall

Early Saturday morning, April 3, 1948, Bess set a big breakfast on the table for her boys. Tom was reading the *Devil's River News* when he suddenly put down his coffee and said, "What do you know, my old friend Ted Lyons will be in Del Rio next week!"[28] Tom and Ted Lyons had played baseball together under Coach Frank Bridgesat at Baylor University in 1923.[29] Lyons went on to pitch for the Chicago White Sox from 1923 to 1946 and was managing his old club. They were scheduled to play the Pittsburg Pirates in an exhibition game in Del Rio.

On Wednesday, April 7, 1948, Tom packed his three sons into his car and drove the ninety miles south to watch the game. In the seventh inning Bill and his brothers watched a foul ball fly high over them and out behind the stands.[30] Bill spotted where it landed and saw that no else had found it. After the game, the boys ran out in the parking lot and found that ball. With the fans almost all gone, Tom was down on the field visiting with Ted when his sons came back with the ball. Ted joked with the boys a bit, telling them tall tales about his playing career. Ted loved to joke. He often told the wild story of playing "in an exhibition game at Joliet state prison until the warden ordered him to the bench because his line drives were punching huge holes in the prison wall."[31] Bill and his brothers saw a legend that night in his last season in baseball; Lyons resigned as manager in October, 1948. Lyons was the face of White Sox baseball in those years and was inducted into the Baseball Hall of Fame as a player in 1955.[32] On that April night in 1948 down on that grassy infield, Lyons made a special memory as he signed that foul ball for the Ratliff boys. They still treasure that old baseball today.[33]

A MENTOR: MR. NORMAN DAVIS

With his senior year coming to an end, Bill contemplated his next move. Would he follow his older brother, Jack, to the University of Texas at Austin, and if so what career path would he take? Feeling somewhat lost, Bill decided to confide in one of his much-loved teachers, his plane geometry teacher, Mr. Norman Davis.[34] After school one afternoon, Bill walked into Mr. Davis's classroom. The late afternoon sun streamed on the teacher's desk where Norman was grading that day's papers. Bill and his teacher talked for some time about the decisions Bill's brothers made to be lawyers and their obvious talents in debate and theater. While Bill knew he wanted a professional degree and career he did not feel drawn to a law career.[35] Bill and Norman discussed a possible medical career, but the day-to-day work with sick people did not appeal to young Ratliff. Bill had always excelled in math and sciences. He was a wizard at using the mechanical analog device for multiplication, division, as well as for functions such as roots, logarithms, and even trigonometry.[36] He had won state in the statewide UIL "slide rule" competition. With such excellent math skills his mentor suggested a career in engineering.[37] Using his love of math to solve, build, and create was exciting to young Ratliff and an engineer was born.

Ratliff became an engineer during a wonderful time in American history. The 1950s were prosperous times in America and a time of infrastructure development, substantial economic growths and social reflection. In May 1954, US Senator Joseph McCarthy held hearings on alleged Communists in the US Army, at the time when Bill and his family were celebrating his graduation from Sonora High School. Also, the US Supreme Court was handing down landmark decisions that remade education and the very face of America. Having seen and defeated the hatred and racism in Adolf Hitler's Germany, Americans in the 1950s, were beginning to reflect on racial segregation at home. Under Chief Justice Earl Warren's leadership, the Supreme Court handed down what is now thought to be one of the all-time greatest decisions by the Court. In *Brown v. Board of Education*, the Supreme Court unanimously held that the racial segregation of children in public schools violated the Equal Protection Clause of the Fourteenth Amendment.[38]

In April 1954, the US Supreme Court unanimously ruled in favor of school integration.[39] It helped abolish de facto and de jure segregation that persisted throughout the United States. The twelve-page historic opinion was written by Chief Justice Earl Warren and overturned the 1896 decision of *Plessy v. Ferguson* that established a doctrine of separate but equal education.[40] The *Plessy v. Ferguson* decision had allowed that as long as accommodation existed, segregation did not constitute discrimination.[41]

At the time Bill Ratliff graduated from Sonora High School many Americans were cheering the US Supreme Court's decision. However, across the deep south many white people called the day (May 17, 1954) the Supreme Court handed down the decision "Black Monday."[42] All across the south—including Texas—organizations called "Citizens' Councils" (organizations of white segregationists and supremacists who opposed integration) were created. Led by Mississippi Circuit Court Judge Tom P. Brady, Citizen's Councils grew to encompass virtually all white businesses.[43] Council members published a book entitled "Black Monday" which outlined their simple belief—African Americans were inferior to whites and the races must remain separate. Judge Brady wrote "If in one mighty voice we do not protest this travesty of justice, we might as well surrender."[44]

A DEEP SENSE OF THE POWER OF EDUCATION

Bill graduated from high school in May of 1954. In the fall of 1954, he enrolled at the University of Texas at Austin and informed his friends and family that he was going to study aeronautical engineering.[45] The focus of his field of study quickly changed to civil engineering as he could not get his brain to register the dynamics that allowed airplane wings to sustain so much weight.[46] His early college years were not that different from those that many freshman and sophomores experience. He enjoyed the freedom and at times did not apply as much energy and time as his demanding coursework required. Bill followed Jack into the Phi Gamma Delta fraternity.[47] Hazing was (as it remains today) a significant problem in fraternities.[48] To protect Bill and to keep him safe, Jack took the leadership role of Bill's pledge class.[49] Fraternity life was (and is still) largely a training and socialization process for the social elite.[50] The norms and expectations of that social group, good and bad, are passed along to its new members.[51]

By the time Bill enrolled in the school of engineering, the department had earned a long and storied history. The University of Texas School of Engineering was established in 1882 and the very first engineering degree was awarded to William H. P. Hunnicut, B.S.C.E., in 1888.[52] When Bill attended the UT College of Engineering it had not yet been named for the late Ernest Cockrell Jr. of Houston. Ernest was a firm believer in and supporter of public education.[53] He had grown up during the Great Depression and benefited greatly from the public investment and public support of the University of Texas. Texas taxpayers had created an institution that paved the way for him to become a petroleum engineer; Cockrell graduated in 1936, a member of the engineering school's very first class of petroleum engineers.[54] Cockrell's son would later say, "I believe he was aware of what his engineering education had enabled him to do, and he felt he was pretty fortunate. Going to UT and acquiring that engineering background gave him a deep sense of the power of education."[55] The University of Texas Board of Regents renamed the engineering school in 2007 after the Cockrell family endowed $220 million for the engineering program.[56] Cockrell "recognized what only public universities could achieve: a broad-based education for a great many students," explained Cockrell Jr.'s son. "He recognized that the state had an obligation to fund the school adequately, but funding would be subject to budgetary pressures. He understood that there would always be a necessity for additional funding to support excellence," notes Ernest Cockrell Jr.'s daughter, Carol Cockrell Curran.[57] Like William Hunnicut in 1888, and Ernest Cockrell in 1936, Bill Ratliff (and years later Bennett Ratliff) benefited directly from the tax support of the people of Texas in the college of engineering at the University of Texas. These graduates and many others not only enjoyed successful lives but also greatly enriched all of Texas, the United States, and the world. There would be a day in Ratliff's future that he would help establish yet another University of Texas engineering school that today bears his name.[58]

During Bill's political life, he said, "it was a good thing college transcripts are not public record, because my college record would not have looked too good in a campaign."[59] Bill was ill prepared for the rigors of the UT engineering program by his Senora high school education; he was overwhelmed with the demands of his courses. He worked very hard and earned a 3.5 GPA (freshman honorary) in his first semester. Unfortunately, he decided that college wasn't so hard after all, and in the second semester he learned to play the guitar, and ended up on academic probation.[60] The following semesters, he rededicated himself to his studies and maintained minimally, a 3.0 GPA.

At the University of Texas School of Engineering Bill learned the intricacies of bridge and road construction and to think like an engineer. Engineers learn to combine knowledge of science, mathematics, and even economics and politics to solve problems that confront society.[61] Engineers are not only scientists but also practical real-world problem solvers. Where scientists are taught to seek to know, Bill and his fellow engineering students were taught to seek, know, and do. In the late 1800s, engineer A. M. Wellington explained the engineer's practical and scientific mind saying engineering is, "the art of doing well with one dollar, which any bungler can do with two."[62] The root of the word engineer derives from ingenious which comes from the Latin root *generare*, meaning "to create." Engineers create solutions; they are problem solvers by nature and training. At the University of Texas Bill was trained to be a problem solver.

The desired end result of an engineering effort is to solve a problem with a device, or structure, system, or process. At the University of Texas, Bill was taught careful and logical steps to address problems. All engineers learn to identify need. What is the real need? What is the real problem that we are seeking to address? Often the obvious surface level problem is only the symptom of a real latent problem. As such, problem definition is critical. Once a problem has been identified, engineers are taught to research it from all angles and to discover the constraints that might limit solutions. Engineers are taught to complete a thorough analysis and to seek alternative solutions to a problem before making a decision about how to proceed. And finally engineers are taught to clearly and effectively communicate these activities to others.

While studying engineering, Bill began to hone skills, knowledge, and patterns of thinking that would not only help him to become a highly successful engineer but would one day help him to be one of the most successful public servants to ever serve in the Texas Senate. While science is discovery—uncovering what exists, engineering is design or the creation of objects or systems that do not naturally occur. At the University of Texas School of Engineering, Ratliff learned to address problems with creative solutions. As an engineer Ratliff became skilled at describing problems and solutions with numbers and in certain numerical relationships or formulas. Engineers use mathematics to analyze and design solutions to problems. Many years later, Ratliff used the imagination of the engineer to make rational public policy choices to design solutions for many of the biggest problems facing the people.

THE RATLIFF BROTHERS

Bill Ratliff's story would be incomplete without an understanding of his two extraordinary brothers. Jack, Bill's older brother, and Shannon, his younger brother, are men of extraordinary success. Shannon became a renowned and successful lawyer serving in many leadership roles. Jack had not only a highly successful legal career but also was a much-loved tenured professor at the University of Texas School of Law.[63] All three of the Ratliff boy's lives came to wind in and around the pantheons of power.

On a cool and clear Monday morning, February 1, 1943, Tom sat at the kitchen table, while Bess washed the dishes, and jotted this simple note into his calendar: "Jack is nine, Bill is seven, and Shannon is five. Jack is not too happy—worries about friends. Bill is serious—focused. Shan still the pick of the town—but getting too smart."[64] In some ways this note sums up much about the lives his three highly successful sons. Jack would always be concerned about others—his life would focus on serving to make others happy.[65] Bill's life—of course, not always—has been serious and focused. Shannon remains highly competitive, driven, and the pick of the party—he is an extraordinarily successful lawyer.[66]

Stop In and Visit

In an interesting turn of events the Ratliff family story would become intertwined with President Lyndon Baines Johnson's story. In 1908, Lyndon Baines Johnson was born on a farm about a hundred miles east of Sonora. Johnson was a representative and senator from his home state of Texas before becoming vice president and president of the United States. LBJ was a highly gifted legislator, becoming the Democratic whip very early in his Washington career. In 1957, the year he became the Democratic Party leader, Senator Johnson's staff mailed a letter to the Ratliff home in Sonora.[67] It so happened that Shannon Ratliff won the Texas state championships in debate and declamation his freshman, sophomore, and senior years. The loss in his junior year turned out to be one of the best turn of events in his life.[68] The Sonora High School debate rules at the time did not allow the state champion to compete again in the same competition the following year. After his loss in his junior year, Shannon went on to win the Texas State Debate Championship in his senior year.

At that time, Senator Johnson had one of his staff members comb local Texas newspapers for successes like Shannon's championship and then write a letter of congratulation for the success. Senator Johnson signed the letters and sometimes handwrote, "stop in and visit me if you are ever in Washington" across the top or bottom of the letter.[69] On Shannon's letter was Johnson's handwritten invitation to "stop in and visit."[70]

As the winner of the Texas state debate competition, Shannon was invited to Washington to a national debate conference and awarded a $10,000 scholarship.[71] In early May 1957, Tom and Shannon drove the 1,657 miles from Sonora to Washington, D.C. Once checked into their hotel room, they phoned Bess to tell her that they had made it safely. Sitting on the bed, Tom said "So, do you want to stop in and see Senator Johnson?" Shannon said, "Yes sir, let's go."[72] So the two drove over to the Senate Majority Leader's office, which was located in S-211[73] at that time, in the northeast corner of the US Capitol, part of the 1851–1859 Senate extension designed by Thomas U. Walter.[74] Office S-211 is today called the Lyndon Baines Johnson Room.[75]

Together Tom and his high school senior son walked into the reception area of Johnson's office and were kindly greeted by the receptionist. Tom and Shannon let the receptionist know about the letter and invitation from the Senator (it is possible that they were the first to ever take Johnson up on his offer). They were told that the Senator was probably too busy to visit with them, but that they could wait if they wanted. After waiting for almost half an hour, Johnson strode into the office, greeted Shannon and Tom warmly and invited them into his office. The three men visited for a bit. Johnson wanted to know if Tom had voted for him. Tom answered honestly, he had not. Tom told Senator Johnson that he'd supported Coke Stevenson because "Stevenson was his friend and neighbor."[76] Undeterred and with genuine interest, Johnson asked Shannon about his debate successes, high school experiences, and his future plans. Shannon explained to the Senator that he planned to follow his brothers to the University of Texas. Toward the end of the conversation, Johnson looked at Shannon and said, "I want you on my staff, son, how would you like to work for me here in Washington this summer?" Without waiting for an answer, Johnson buzzed his secretary, Mary Margaret Wiley, and said, "Mary, send Walter in here a minute."[77]

The Last Person I Ever Directly Hired

Walter Jenkins was Senator Johnson's right-hand man.[78] Years earlier, in 1939, Johnson approached the president of the University of Texas at Austin, Dr. Homer Price Rainey, and asked him to recommend a good student to work for him in Congress. Jenkins was recommended and immediately began working for Johnson (Jenkins never went back to the University of Texas nor did he ever graduate from college). Johnson was so impressed with Jenkins that by 1941 he had Jenkins involved in dealing with leading figures of government.

A few minutes after Johnson called for him, Walter Jenkins walked into the Senator's office. "Walter, I want you to put young Shannon Ratliff on our staff for this summer," ordered the Senator. Johnson was known for being very direct. He continued, "Shannon is a bright young man with a very promising future and I'd like to have him on my staff." Walter nodded and said that he would get the paperwork started. But Shannon had already promised a local Sonora rancher that he would work for him that summer. Shannon insisted that he had to make sure he could get out of his previous commitment before he committed to work for Senator Johnson. Back at the hotel Shannon called the rancher and was released from his commitment—even though the rancher declared he held no admiration for the Democratic Senator from Texas. For many years afterward, Johnson would tell others, "Shannon Ratliff was the last person I ever directly hired."[79]

UNIVERSITY OF TEXAS PHI GAMMA DELTA PRESIDENCY

In the spring of Bill's sophomore year at the University of Texas, he served as chairman of his fraternity's homecoming float committee. Focused on fraternity life, Bill neglected his classroom studies yet again and received a stern warning letter from the dean. The letter had the intended effect—Bill settled down and earned respectable grades. Interestingly, Bill also began to wait tables at the fraternity house to pay for his board, and rather than distracting him further from his studies, the work seemed to help focus his attention on academic endeavors.[80] In Bill's senior year he decided to run for the presidency of his fraternity—a post that his brother Jack had held just a year earlier. Shannon, who was only a sophomore at the time, also decided to run for the post—against his older brother. It would be brother versus brother for the Phi Gamma Delta presidency. The ever competitive Shannon won the position.[81]

The Scholar

Ever the scholar, Jack Ratliff attended the University of Texas' prestigious Plan II Honors program.[82] To help supplement the Ratliff family budget, Jack chose to join the Navy ROTC while an undergraduate student. As such, the Navy paid for Jack's tuition, fees, uniforms, and allocated him an allowance for his room and board in Austin. In return, Jack committed to serve three years in the United States Navy.[83] Jack could have delayed active duty until he finished law school, but he realized that Shannon was about to enter the same university, which would mean that Tom and Bess would have three boys in college at the same time. Therefore, Jack decided, after his first year in law school, to go on active duty to relieve some of the financial load on his family.[84] Jack's best friend, Ben West, was on a similar path and the two of them arranged to serve on the same destroyer "plowing the Pacific" for two years.[85] Jack decided that he needed something more challenging, and transferred to Underwater Demolition Teams—the predecessor to the "SEALs." Jack spent a year with a SEALs team before he was honorably discharged. He then returned to the University of Texas to finish law school where he was an officer and comment editor of the *University of Texas Law Review*.[86, 87] By the time Jack returned to Austin, Bill was in his last semester of engineering and thus Tom and Bess did not have to support three boys at the university together for long. Jack would have remarkable private and public law practice followed by a long and distinguished career as a professor at the University of Texas School of Law. Shannon and Jack's experiences, service, and legal expertise comes to play important roles in the future of this story and for Texas.

BILL MEETS SALLY—1958

While Bill was learning to be a college student and an engineer, his future wife, Sally Sandlin, graduated from Mt. Pleasant High School and, like her sister before her, attended Stephen's College for Women in Missouri (founded in 1833). Sally spent two years at Stephen's College (unlike Bill, she achieved a very strong academic record), and then transferred to the University of Texas in 1958.[88]

In the fall of 1958, Bill's cousin, Ann Ratliff, was living with Bill's parents when she was not at school in Austin.[89] On Tuesday, November 20, just before the Thanksgiving holidays, Bill went to the Zeta Tau Alpha sorority house to pick up Ann for the drive to Sonora for the family gathering. Ann had several things she wanted to take to Sonora and sent Bill upstairs to collect her luggage for the trip.[90] He pushed open the door to Ann's room and there on the floor playing bridge sat the beautiful Sally Sandlin. Sally was waiting for her own ride to her East Texas home of Mt. Pleasant. Bill was smitten. It was love at first sight. On the drive to Sonora, Bill asked Ann to help him get a date with Sally. In the weeks before Christmas of 1958 the young couple saw as much of each other as they could and still did well on their final examinations. On a romantic Valentine's date on Thursday, February 14th, the following year, Bill asked Sally to marry him. Sally did not answer immediately. In fact, she made Bill wait just over two weeks before she accepted.[91]

Sally completed her bachelor's degree in Home Economics at the University of Texas at Austin, and went on to teach that subject in Big Spring, Texas, before she and Bill were married. Bill and Sally were married in the Presbyterian Church in Mt. Pleasant on Saturday, August 8, 1959 (Sally's family was Episcopalian, but the Episcopal Church in Mt. Pleasant was too small for the Ratliff-Sandlin wedding and thus they used the Presbyterian Church for the wedding.) Bill's older brother Jack was his best man.[92] Bill and Sally set out to make a life together.

I JUST WATCHED POLITICS DESTROY SOME PRETTY GOOD PEOPLE

As Bill and Sally set up a new home in Fort Worth, the country was in the midst of the 1960 presidential election. In July of that year, at the Republican convention in Chicago, Vice President Richard Nixon won the nomination for president. Nixon was then defeated by John F. Kennedy in the general election.[93] Then tragically, Lyndon Johnson had to assume the office of the president when President Kennedy was assassinated in Dallas, Texas, on Friday, November 22, 1963. In the transition, Johnson offered Shannon Ratliff a position as a junior staffer in the White House. But, Shannon told Walter Jenkins and the president that he could not accept. Instead he went back to the University of Texas and finished his law degree.[94] "It wasn't an easy job to pass up,"[95] Shannon said, "But at the same time, I guess I had always noticed one thing about D.C. A lot of the people that went there were going to serve a congressman or senator for a few years, go back to school and get a degree. They never made that second step. So from that day on, they were dependent upon somebody for a job."[96] Shannon Ratliff would later add, "I just watched politics destroy some pretty good people and I decided maybe that wasn't my game. I just didn't like some of the ways it messed up people's lives. And not just the person who's running, but his family and everybody else."[97] He did not know it at that time, but as Shannon left Washington after working for Johnson and with Walter Jenkins for five summers he would be returning just one year later.[98]

In August 1964, a United States Navy destroyer clashed with a Vietnamese attack ship in the Gulf of Tonkin.[99] As a result of that Gulf of Tonkin clash the US Congress passed the Gulf of Tonkin Resolution.[100] That joint resolution gave President Johnson the authority to increase United States involvement in the war between North and South Vietnam.[101] As American casualties in Vietnam soared, the decision to further involve the United States in that Southeast Asian war embroiled the country and the Johnson White House in a troubled and turbulent political nightmare. In those difficult days Shannon's friend, and President Johnson's closest advisor and friend, Walter Jenkins found himself in the middle of the public spotlight in a "scandal" that some analysts say may have changed the course of history for the United States and the people of Vietnam and Southeast Asia.[102] Walter Jenkins and the tragic event of "Jenkins's scandal" would also come to deeply affect Shannon's views and thoughts about politics.[103]

On October 7, 1964, Walter Jenkins went to a cocktail party at the Washington offices of *Newsweek*. On his way home he stopped into a YMCA where he was later arrested by the police after being discovered having homosexual sex in the men's room at a YMCA not far from the White House. The story eventually appeared in the *Washington Star* and Jenkins was forced to resign his position in the White House. Jenkins was dearly missed by Johnson.[104]

Bill Moyers, also former aide to Johnson, wrote in *Newsweek*: "When they come to canonize political aides, [Jenkins] will be the first summoned, for no man ever negotiated the shark-infested waters of the Potomac with more decency or charity or came out on the other side with his integrity less shaken. If Lyndon Johnson owed everything to one human being other than Lady Bird, he owed it to Walter Jenkins."[105] Former attorney general Ramsey Clark said that Jenkins's resignation "deprived the president of the single most effective and trusted aide that he had. The results would be enormous when the president came into his hard times. Walter's counsel on Vietnam might have been extremely helpful."[106]

Although the American public attitude on homosexual behavior is still divided it is rapidly changing. Historical surveys indicate that American opinion remained fairly constant until 1991.[107] Before 1991, about three-quarters of American's consistently reported that homosexual behavior was "always wrong" with only about 10 to 15 percent considering it to be "not wrong at all."[108] In October 1964, when Walter was arrested for homosexual behavior President Johnson said in a phone call to Ladybird, "When questioned, and I will be questioned, I'm going to say that this is incredible for a man that I have known all these years, a devout Catholic, a father of six children, a happily married husband."[109] Johnson added, "The average farmer just can't understand your knowing it and approving it or condoning it."[110] Walter tendered his resignation and immediately returned to Austin, Texas. Shannon Ratliff saw politics destroy a very good man.[111]

If the President Calls

Upon graduation from the University of Texas School of Law, Shannon accepted an offer to clerk with another native Texan, U.S. Supreme Court Justice Tom C. Clark.[112] A Supreme Court clerkship is a very prestigious position, serving as assistant to a Supreme Court Justice. Each of the eight Associate Justices can select up to four law clerks for each term of the court; the Chief Justice selects up to five clerks. Justice Clark was born in Dallas in 1899 and graduated from the University of Texas Law School in 1922 and is to date the only Texan to ever serve on the US Supreme Court. In his seventeen years on the Court, Clark employed two clerks each term. Shannon served with Michael Maupin who later practiced securities law in Virginia.[113] Shannon had barely begun working in Clark's office when Walter Jenkins reached out to him for the president. Not getting an affirmative answer right away from Shannon, President Johnson then called Justice Clark to request that Clark release Shannon to come work for his 1964 presidential campaign. Shannon was not sure what to do. "You know, we have a saying in Washington," Clark told Shannon. "If the president calls, you try to do what the president asks."[114] Shannon went back to work for Johnson.

Temporarily leaving the US Supreme Court, Shannon worked hard to elect his boss. Early, during the presidential campaign, Barry Goldwater appeared to be a strong contender. To counter the Goldwater campaign's gaining support, on September 7, 1964, the Johnson campaign broadcast the "Daisy ad." The ad, now famous for its negativity and the fear it portrayed, featured a sweet little freckled-face girl in a dress picking petals from a daisy, slowly counting (and miscounting) up to ten. Then a deep and dramatic voice took over, counted down from ten to zero and the the screen goes white with the explosion of a nuclear bomb.[115] The ad had a real impact on the race. In the closing weeks of the campaign, despite trailing in the polls, Goldwater decided not to use the Walter Jenkins incident in his campaign against Johnson. Later, in his autobiography, "The Conscience of a Conservative," Goldwater wrote, "It was a sad time for Jenkins and his family. Winning isn't everything. Some things, like loyalty to friends, or lasting principle, are more important."[116] Johnson won the 1964 presidency in a landslide with 61.05 percent of the popular vote. In the Electoral College, Johnson defeated Goldwater by a margin of 486 to 52.[117] Johnson won fourty-four states, compared to just six for Goldwater.[118] After that landslide win, Ratliff returned to his clerkship with Justice Clark. A year later when his time in the Supreme Court ended, Shannon went back to Austin, Texas, and to an extraordinary successful private law practice.[119]

THE CONSULTING ENGINEER

While Shannon was finishing up his clerkship, Bill's career was taking off and his family began to grow with the births of three children, Bess, Bennett, and then Thomas (all three born in Ft. Worth). In the early days of his engineering career, Bill was designated as the "City Engineer" for several cities (Euless, Bedford, and Colleyville) at the same time. These cities were too small to afford an on-staff engineer, so they contracted with Bill's firm to provide engineering services. These fast-growing cities needed solutions to infrastructure needs like a large, dependable source of water. Bill was in charge of putting together plans to contract with the Trinity River Authority (TRA) to furnish the needed water. He created the plans to construct a large water supply pipeline from the TRA's raw water supply line, across the Trinity River to his client cities. Bill and his firm also created the plans for the construction of water treatment facilities to supply treated water. These were multimillion dollar projects and, at the time, and were among the earliest of the water transfer agreements. The engineering firm Bill founded in Ft. Worth was doing so well by this time that it was attracting the attention of much larger firms across the state of Texas and beyond. Eventually the firm affiliated with Turner, Collie, and Braden (TC&B) in Houston.[120]

While Bill was with TC&B, he took a leading role with water concerns for the city of Dallas. At that time Dallas furnished water to many of the suburban communities in the Dallas and Fort Worth region. Ratliff was directly and deeply involved in litigation with many of those communities about the charges being levied for water supply from the city of Dallas.[121] Dallas retained Bill's firm, TC&B, to design a study of the costs associated with such supplies, and the manner of allocating such costs to Dallas's own retail customers, as well as to these customer cities. Bill was designated as the principal person in charge and spent years (along with one of the big eight accounting firms) in preparation of the report. This work required many adversarial meetings with the customer cities to arrive at a solution.

A Decade of Oil, Change, and Growth, 1970 to 1980

As Bill and Sally's three children grew into teenagers the world was plunged into an energy crisis. From the early 1970s to the early 1980s nearly every major country in the world faced substantial petroleum shortages. Gasoline—when available at all—was extremely expensive in relation to its previous cost. In October of 1973, the United States helped Israel in a war with its neighbors. Israel was at war with a coalition of Arab states led by Egypt and Syria. In early October 1973, President Richard Nixon ordered an American airlift to resupply the Israeli military and provide support for Israel in the war.[122] In retaliation for the United States' support of Israel the Arab members of the Organization of Petroleum Exporting Countries imposed an oil embargo against the United States.[123] The embargo banned petroleum exports to the United States and dramatically cut oil production. In order to get gas for their cars the Ratliff's had to wait in long lines with many other Texans at gas stations. Bill would sometimes go to fill up his car before dawn in an attempt to avoid the wait for gasoline. In Texas, odd-even rationing was introduced—if the last digit on your license plate was odd, you could buy gas only on odd-numbered days.

In January 1979, Bill and Sally's oldest son, Bennett, was a senior in high school when the Iranian Revolution ended. Their daughter, Bess, was in college, when the Shah of Iran fled his country on January 16, 1979. The new Iranian regime cut their oil output by about 5 million barrels per day and was very inconsistent with production which forced another gasoline shortage and an increase of prices in the United States.[124] Also that year, Texans elected a brash oilman William "Bill" Clements to be their first Republican governor since Reconstruction.[125] Bill Clements's election marked the beginning of a "sea change in Texas politics, preparing the way for Republicans to take the governor's office in Austin."[126]

With the United States once again in an energy crisis, President Jimmy Carter outlined plans to reduce oil imports, improve energy efficiency, and encourage Americans to reduce their use of energy.[127] The Ratliff engineering firm greatly benefited from the oil crisis of the 1970s as the price of Texas crude oil increased some 250 percent between 1978 and 1980. Houston, like all of the oil-producing areas of Texas experienced an economic boom and enormous population inflows.

After the Houston firm absorbed the Ft. Worth firm, Ratliff became the firm's vice president from 1975 to 1981, in the oil boom years in

Houston. Bill and his partners designed solutions and created large infrastructure projects, including the Houston Intercontinental Airport and
the modernizing of the Houston ship channel.[128] In this role Ratliff spent
a great deal of his time in public relations, politics, working directly with
the clients.[129] His strength of seeing the big picture, of persuasion, and
crystal clear presentations made him a significant and important influence in many municipal projects, both large and small across the state of
Texas and beyond.[130] Bill received many professional engineering
awards—both state and national—and testified before US Congressional
committees on a number of occasions, regarding the nation's infrastructure. In 1981 he served as president of the American Consulting Engineers Council headquartered in Washington, D.C.[131] In essence Bill was
involved in politics and policy all of his professional life.

For Bill Ratliff, a city park, a commercial zone, an airport, or a university building could be designed to be expensive, or affordable, or rugged
or functional—depending on need and on available funding. As the engineer, Ratliff came to know that those decisions and numerical relationships were not just matters of calculations—but rather involved choices.
A bridge can hold up its weight and carry the intended load with a
design that is costly or economical or ugly or elegant. It is often politics
(who gets what, when, and how) that makes decisions. Ratliff became
very skilled in politics. While engineering enhanced his natural problem
solving abilities his work honed his political skills. Upon graduation
from the University of Texas College of Engineering, Ratliff spent the
next forty years as a practicing consulting engineer solving problems in
Texas and throughout the United States.

Piling It Up Higher Is Not What Life Is About

The engineering years were some of the best years of Bill and Sally's
life.[132] At the top of the engineering profession and living a life of Houston commuting, high-level consulting, extended travel, and lots of income—Bill and Sally decided to reconsider the path of their lives and
their priorities.[133] Bill and Sally wanted something different for their daily lives and for the lives of their three growing children. Life in Houston
had become inhospitable for their family.[134] So they decided to make a
change—a big change. Bill left his thriving engineering firm and career
and moved his family to the small East Texas town of Mt. Pleasant, the
hometown of his wife. Mt. Pleasant, Texas may just be the polar opposite
of Houston, Texas. The populations alone are enormously different—
Houston had about 1.6 million people whereas Mt Pleasant was home to
only about 12,000 East Texans.[135] To ease this major life change, Bill had
reached a point of success in his career that allowed him to sell his share
of the Houston firm and still have enough financial security that he
would never have to worry about making a living again—if he and Sally

lived conservatively and managed properly.[136] Bill and Sally were focused on the quality of their lives and not the quantity of things.[137] They wanted to provide their three children with their time and "an appreciation for those things which are truly valuable, and for not chasing the all mighty dollar."[138] Bill went on to say, "Sally and I left at a time when we could have made a lot more money and we hoped that would illustrate to our three children that piling it up higher is not what life is about."[139]

Hard Work and Decisions

Back in 1954, Mr. Norman Davis was obviously on target with his advice for his student. Becoming an engineer not only suited young Ratliff very well—but it also provided him with a career that he loved and in which he flourished. As a college student Bill took advantage of the real opportunities provided by Tom and Bess, Ernest Cockrell, his bother Jack, his professors, the taxpayers of Texas, and many others. He dedicated himself to the tasks of a student and worked hard to learn the concepts and skills of an engineer. He earned his engineering degree. Then as a consulting engineer, Bill willingly engaged in the day-to-day hard work of finding solid solutions for his clients. He was a man people could trust and over time many came to depend upon him for counsel and solutions. The men and women in his profession chose him as their leader.[140] Bill Ratliff's education, experiences, and career well prepared him for the next chapter and the extremely complex challenges that were to come.

In politics as in engineering, the most difficult part of any given problem is precisely defining the problem itself. The very same can be said for many moral and ethical decisions. Lyndon Johnson and Barry Goldwater both faced decisions about how to react to the arrest of Walter Jenkins. Each man chose a different course of action—one focused on others and one focused on self. In the years ahead Bill Ratliff also faced these very challenging decisions. In making his decision he would employ the principles of integrity and fairness and the problem-solving skills of an engineer. A successful leader is one who will expend considerable effort at the beginning of the analytic process, in eliminating things that are unimportant or irrelevant, and focus on those people and things that are both priorities and at the root or heart of the real problem. As a youngster in Tom and Bess's care, as an athlete, student, and engineer, Bill was taught to do his homework. He learned to engage in honest, hard, and solid thinking and to reject easy answers and half-baked solutions. Too many leaders choose the shortcut of defaulting to the easy answer. President Johnson did not think about the life, health, and real struggles facing Walter Jenkins but rather focused on the election and his own personal gain and power. In the next chapter of his life, Bill Ratliff would say, "nothing is politically right that is morally wrong" and he would face challenges that put that statement squarely to the test.[141]

NOTES

1. Interviews with Bill Ratliff, Jack Ratliff, and Shannon Ratliff 2012, 2013, and 2014.

2. Interview with Jack Ratliff (2013).

3. *The Devil's River News*, Sonora, Texas January 1954.

4. This story was retold in an interview with Jack Ratliff in October 2014. Jack had newspaper clippings from the *Devil's River News* to support the story.

5. Jack Ratliff provided me with the Sonora yearbooks for these years.

6. Interviews with Bill Ratliff, Shannon Ratliff, and Jack Ratliff 2013, 2014, and 2015.

7. Ibid.

8. Interview with Shannon Ratliff 2014.

9. Interview with Bill Ratliff and Shannon Ratliff 2014.

10. Interviews with Bill Ratliff, Shannon Ratliff and Jack Ratliff 2014.

11. Ibid.

12. Interviews with Jack Ratliff and Bill Ratliff 2013 and 2014.

13. Ibid.

14. Reported in an email from Bill Ratliff 2015.

15. Jack Ratliff provided me with copies of Tom's calendars. Many days, Tom would make notes such as this.

16. Reported in an email from Bill Ratliff in 2015.

17. Ibid.

18. Sonora High School 1949-1950 Yearbook.

19. Ibid.

20. Sonora High School 1951–1952 Yearbook.

21. Both Jack Ratliff and Bill Ratliff are pictured in these jerseys with the football team in the 1951-1952 Sonora High Yearbook.

22. Sonora High 1952–1943 Yearbook.

23. Interviews with Shannon Ratliff and Jack Ratliff 2014.

24. Interviews with Bill Ratliff and Jack Ratliff 2013 and 2014.

25. Ibid.

26. Ibid.

27. Interview with Jack Ratliff 2014.

28. This story was pieced together from an email from Bill Ratliff and an interview with Jack Ratliff in 2014 and from newspaper accounts of the game and from MLB records of Ted Lyons.

29. 1923 Baylor University Baseball roster.

30. Reported in an email from Bill Ratliff 2013.

31. Ted Lyons by Warren Corbett (http://sabr.org/bioproj/person/b3442150).

32. Ibid.

33. Jack Ratliff has retold this in a forthcoming book titled *Tom and Bess* 2016.

34. Interview with Bill Ratliff 2013.

35. Later in his life Bill would attend South Texas School of Law—but was very frustrated with the inexact nature of law and law study.

36. Interview with Bill Ratliff 2013.

37. Ibid.

38. *Brown v. Board of Education of Topeka*, 347 U.S. 483.

39. Ibid.

40. *Plessy v. Ferguson*, 163 U.S. 537.

41. Ibid.

42. PBS *The Murder of Emmett Till* (http://www.pbs.org/wgbh/amex/till/peoplee-vents/e_councils.html).

43. Ibid.

44. Ibid.

45. Interview with Bill Ratliff 2013.

46. Ibid.

47. Ibid.

48. Interview with Jack Ratliff. In 2010, Jack Ratliff served on a committee that examined the hazing actions of fraternities and sororities at the University of Texas at Austin.

49. Interview with Jack Ratliff 2014.

50. Ibid.

51. Ibid.

52. From the History & Traditions pages of the University of Texas at Austin Cockrell Engineering College (http://www.engr.utexas.edu/about/history/200-cockrell-school-history).

53. Ibid.

54. The University of Texas at Austin Cockrell School of Engineering, History & Traditions Who Are the Cockrells? (http://www.engr.utexas.edu/about/history/83-the-cockrells).

55. Ibid.

56. Ibid.

57. Ibid.

58. The University of Texas at Tyler is housed in the Bill Ratliff College of Engineering.

59. Bill Ratliff noted this in several speeches given later in his career.

60. Interview with Bill Ratliff 2013.

61. *Exploring Engineering: An Introduction to Engineering and Design* by Philip Kosky, Robert T. Balmer, William D. Keat, and George Wise.

62. Ibid.

63. Jack Ratliff was honored with teaching and research awards.

64. Jack Ratliff provided me a copy of Tom's calendar in which he regularly made such notes.

65. In my interviews with Jack Ratliff this trait was very apparent.

66. *The Man Who Said No to LBJ*, by Carlos Harrison, published in: 2013 Texas Super Lawyers—October 2013 (http://www.superlawyers.com/texas/article/The-Man-Who-Said-No-to-LBJ/5187bd08-85a2-4f3f-af1f-81627136bfe9.html).

67. Interview with Bill Ratliff and Shannon Ratliff 2013 and 2014.

68. Interview with Shannon Ratliff 2014.

69. Ibid.

70. Ibid.

71. Ibid.

72. Ibid.

73. The Lyndon Baines Johnson Room (http://www.lbjlibrary.org/assets/uploads/lbj/Lyndon_B._Johnson_Room.pdf).

74. History of the U.S. Capitol Building (http://www.aoc.gov/history-us-capitol-building).

75. The Lyndon Baines Johnson Room (http://www.lbjlibrary.org/assets/uploads/lbj/Lyndon_B._Johnson_Room.pdf).

76. Interview with Shannon Ratliff 2014.

77. Ibid.

78. New tapes show LBJ struggled with aide's sex scandal CNN 1999. (http://edition.cnn.com/ALLPOLITICS/stories/1998/09/18/lbj.tapes/).

79. Interview with Shannon Ratliff 2014.

80. Interview with Bill Ratliff 2013.

81. Interview with Jack Ratliff October 2014.

82. Office of the Texas Attorney General News Release Wednesday, June 2, 1999 Ratliff Joins Cornyn Team.

83. Ibid.

84. Interview with Bill Ratliff and Shannon Ratliff 2014.

85. Interviews with Bill Ratliff and Jack Ratliff 2014.

86. Office of the Texas Attorney General News Release Wednesday, June 2, 1999 Ratliff Joins Cornyn Team.

87. After law school, Jack was a highly successful attorney with the El Paso firm of Ratliff, Haynes and Stadling. After twenty years of private practice, the practicing attorney became a professor and began a second career teaching at the University of Texas at Austin School of Law. Jack coauthored books with William Powers. In 1999, Texas Attorney General Cornyn appointed the professor to his staff to help with complex litigation for the people of Texas. Office of the Texas Attorney General News Release Wednesday, June 2, 1999 Ratliff Joins Cornyn Team.

88. Interview with Bill and Sally Ratliff 2013.

89. Ibid.

90. Ibid.

91. Ibid.

92. Ibid.

93. http://www.loc.gov/rr/main/republican_conventions.pdf.

94. Interview with Shannon Ratliff 2014.

95. Shannon told me this story in an interview; it has also been published in *The Man Who Said No to LBJ*, by Carlos Harrison in 2013 Texas Super Lawyers—October 2013. Shannon Ratliff chose politics over ranching, then law over politics.

96. Ibid.

97. Ibid.

98. Interview with Shannon Ratliff 2014.

99. The Gulf of Tonkin Incident, 40 Years Later Flawed Intelligence and the Decision for War in Vietnam (http://nsarchive.gwu.edu/NSAEBB/NSAEBB132/index.htm).

100. Tonkin Gulf Resolution (1964) (http://www.ourdocuments.gov/doc.php?flash=true&doc=98).

101. H.J. RES 1145 dated August 7, 1964.

102. Storm Center in Capital; Walter Wilson Jenkins Special to the *New York Times*, October 16, 1964.

103. Walter W. Jenkins, Top Aide to Johnson in the White House by Marjorie Hunter, Special to the *New York Times*, Published November 26, 1985 (http://www.nytimes.com/1985/11/26/us/walter-w-jenkins-top-aide-to-johnson-in-the-white-house.html).

104. LBJ's Gay Sex Scandal, by Al Weisel in *OUT* magazine December 1999 is a comprehensive work on Walter Jenkins.

105. Ibid.

106. Storm Center in Capital; Walter Wilson Jenkins Special to the *New York Times*, October 16, 1964.

107. Americans Move Dramatically toward Acceptance of Homosexuality (http://www.norc.org/NewsEventsPublications/PressReleases/Pages/american-acceptance-of-homosexuality-gss-report.aspx).

108. Public Attitudes toward Homosexuality by Tom W. Smith NORC/University of Chicago September, 2011 (http://www.norc.org/PDFs/2011%20GSS%20Reports/GSS_Public%20Attitudes%20Toward%20Homosexuality_Sept2011.pdf).

109. New tapes show LBJ struggled with aide's sex scandal CNN 1999 (http://edition.cnn.com/ALLPOLITICS/stories/1998/09/18/lbj.tapes/).

110. Ibid.

111. LBJ Aide Walter Jenkins Dies by by Bart Barnes, November 26, 1985, the *Washington Post* (https://www.washingtonpost.com/archive/local/1985/11/26/lbj-aide-walter-jenkins-dies/f993fac7-d7a9-47bb-a5fc-6f9204dad30e/).

112. The Papers of US Supreme Court Justice Tom Clark at the University of Texas School of Law, Tarlton Law Library (https://tarlton.law.utexas.edu/clark/clerks.html).

113. Ibid.

114. Interview with Shannon Ratliff 2014.

115. "Daisy" Attack Ad from 1964 Presidential Election on YouTube (https://youtu.be/dDTBnsqxZ3k).

116. The Conscience of a Conservative: Barry M. Goldwater, published by Princeton University Press and copyrighted 2007.

117. See the University of California Santa Barbara US Presidential Project (http://www.presidency.ucsb.edu/showelection.php?year=1964) 1964.

118. Ibid.

119. The Man Who Said No to LBJ, by Carlos Harrison, published in Texas Super Lawyers—October 2013 (http://www.superlawyers.com/texas/article/The-Man-Who-Said-No-to-LBJ/5187bd08-85a2-4f3f-af1f-81627136bfe9.html).

120. Interviews with Bill Ratliff and Don Edmonds 2014.

121. Interview with Bill Ratliff 2015.

122. October 9, 1973, conversation (6:10–6:35 p.m.) between Israeli Ambassador to the United States Simcha Dinitz, Henry Kissinger, Brent Scowcroft, and Peter Rodman. Transcript George Washington University National Security Archive (http://nsarchive.gwu.edu/NSAEBB/NSAEBB98/octwar-21b.pdf).

123. Oil Embargo, 1973–1974 (https://history.state.gov/milestones/1969-1976/oil-embargo).

124. The Second Shock: The Great Panic by Penn State Oil Evolution (https://www.e-education.psu.edu/egee120/node/292).

125. Bill Clements Dies at 94; Set Texas on G.O.P. Path, by James C. McKinley Jr. May 30, 2011.

126. Ibid.

127. Crisis of Confidence; Jimmy Carter delivered this televised speech on July 15, 1979 (http://www.pbs.org/wgbh/americanexperience/features/primary-resources/carter-crisis/).

128. Ibid.

129. Interview with Don Edmonds 2014.

130. Ibid.

131. See short bio in (http://www.utexas.edu/lbj/archive/news/images/file/bjf_program_2009.pdf).

132. Interviews with Bill and Sally Ratliff 2013, 2014, and 2015.

133. Ibid.

134. Interview with Sally and Bill Ratliff 2013.

135. 1990 Texas Census.

136. Ibid.

137. Ibid.

138. Ibid.

139. Ibid.

140. ill Ratliff served as president of the American Consulting Engineers Council.

141. At a political rally in Mt. Pleasant in September of 1988, Ratliff said, "Nothing is politically right that is morally wrong."

THREE

The Senator: Free of Ambition

FREE OF AMBITION

Ambition is a strong desire to do or to achieve something. Typically, ambitions require lots of determination and hard work. Achieving one of only thirty-one seats in the powerful Texas Senate takes serious determination and mountains of hard work by not just the candidate but also many others around him or her. Successful political campaigns have several common characteristics. Campaigns very often have managers (a person in charge of all operations), political consultants (usually high profile people that guide the look, feel, and strategies of the campaign), fundraisers (people who can help bring in much needed cash), office managers (people who handle the paperwork details and coordinate the staff and volunteers). The Ratliff campaign included all of these people. But one person—Mr. Don Edmonds—very ably took on a critical and important role—being *the* friend who was always there for Bill Ratliff.[1]

Considering the World of Politics

In March of 1987 Bill and Sally met their longtime friends Don and Bonney Edmonds at Lakeway tennis resort on Lake Travis not very far out of Austin, Texas. On Sunday afternoon before they were about to depart, Bill had a request, "Don, I want to visit with you privately for a few minutes." The two longtime friends sat on the patio of the condo they were sharing and Bill said, "I'm thinking about running for the state senate next year—District 1."[2] At that time, in 1987, Texas Senate District 1 covered the entire northeast corner of Texas and included fifteen counties—an area that is about the size of several other entire US states.[3]

Don Edmonds is tall, slender, and has an easy manner. He is open and friendly. People generally like Don immediately. Don and Bill became

45

friends early in their adult lives—when both were just out of college. Don worked to managed cities and Bill served as an engineer to several of Don's cities. Don would say, "Outside of family, Bill is the person I am closest to in my life."[4] It is clear that the two men are long and trusted friends.[5] They share many of the same characteristics but also complement each other's strengths and weaknesses well. Don is a sincere and devoted friend—as is Bill—only Don is not reserved about expressing his devotion.

A little shocked at his friend's news, Don replied, "District 1 isn't an open seat is it?" Don knew what political scientists have long known—it is extremely hard to beat an incumbent—even one with lots of troubles. Don knew that there are two critical factors in running for office: party identification and incumbency.

Don wanted to know, "So, who would you be running against?"

"A Democrat, a man named, 'Richard Anderson,'" Bill answered. The Senate seat Bill was thinking of pursing was held by Mr. Richard Anderson, an ambitious young lawyer. Anderson had attended Texas A&M University for his undergraduate degree in political science and then Baylor Law School.[6] He had been in Texas politics since being elected County Judge of Harrison County, in Marshall, Texas, in 1978. He was already an accomplished politician.

Don was supportive of his friend but was not sure Bill was making a wise choice in running as a Republican. Between 1931 and 1951 not one single Republican served in the Texas state legislature.[7] In the late 1980s East Texas was still only sending Democrats to Austin. Only months earlier in a 1986 special election, Anderson had easily beaten Texas A&M football star, Edward Hargett, a Republican, for his seat in the Texas Senate. Anderson won fourteen out of fifteen counties in the Senate district, including Hargett's home county of Cass.

Before Anderson, Senate District 1 had long been ably represented by Edward Howard, a Democrat from Texarkana who had become an influential lobbyist. Edward Howard was a highly respected and influential senator.[8] The Democrat, Anderson, would have a significant and real advantage over Don Edmond's friend.

In running against an incumbent Democrat, Ratliff would be defying the odds. Again, it is important to restate that the incumbent candidate—the person already in office who is up for reelection—is far more likely to win in the general election. Anderson would enjoy a number of advantages over Ratliff, the most important is that he'd already won the office. By winning Anderson had already created a campaign organization and he held the experience necessary to run a successful campaign. Also as the incumbent, Anderson was in a better position to raise money—as the likely winner the donations would be significantly easier for him to raise. Ratliff would need expert help with this ambitious run.

Meeting the Political Consultant

In the face of these long odds, on the last day of June 1987, Bill again called on his friend for support. "Don," Bill said, "I have an appointment with a political consultant named Bryan Eppstein. If you've got a few minutes tomorrow morning, how about meeting me in his office in Fort Worth? I have got to make up my mind about this senate thing. I'd like it if you'd sit in on the conversation."[9]

The next morning the two friends met just outside Bryan Eppstein's office on the sixth floor of a downtown Fort Worth office building. Eppstein was young (mid-thirties) but already had significant and successful campaign experience and according to Don, "lots of confidence."[10] Only a decade away from his Rice University graduation, Eppstein had not yet served as a consultant to a senate race, but he had worked several Texas House races, a number of county campaigns, and several small city-council races in Fort Worth.[11]

As Bill and Don walked into Eppstein's office they were greeted by a short, confident, and fast-talking man wearing jeans, ostrich skin boots, a white polo button-down shirt with red suspenders—no tie. To the two tall, older, more traditional men wearing suits and ties, Eppstein seemed a bit brash—perhaps too informal, but he also made a certain amount of sense. Eppstein had already earned a reputation in Texas Republican circles for accurate polling and aggressiveness in challenging Democrat incumbents. Don would later write that the diminutive Eppstein, "was the kind of guy you'd want on your side if you got into a fight in a dark alley—at least, if words and votes would help."[12]

Noting the honest and straight-talking gentlemanly approach of the fifty-one-year-old Ratliff, Eppstein directed the conversation to his strategy for winning a campaign. With a great deal of confidence and with much conviction he said, "Anderson is vulnerable. *But* you'll never beat him with a strictly positive, 'feel-good' campaign."[13]

Eppstein stressed that a successful campaign is one that relies on "negative campaigning."[14] If directed by Eppstein, the Ratliff campaign would attack Anderson's positions on issues and his personal character. Bill balked at the idea of attacking personal characteristics of his opponent.[15] "Winning," said Eppstein, "would take aggressive campaigning, and not just about the differences in policy."[16] Eppstein's role in Bill's campaign was to guide decisions about critical elements in campaign strategy. For Bill to reach rural voters and to win he would need to run a very effective campaign. Eppstein believed that negative campaigning in which Bill directly attacked Anderson's issue positions and his character would be most effective.

The aggressive campaign Eppstein wanted for Ratliff would take lots of money. Eppstein said, "Campaigns are expensive, you won't get close to him if you can't raise at least $300,000."[17] Ratliff would be not only challenging Anderson but also the Democrat Party even if they did not like Richard Anderson.[18] Many people would write checks to keep him in office. Eppstein said, "Of that $300,000, you will have to put up as much as $75,000 of your own," and then added, "If you're lucky enough to win, you will probably get that back at the end."[19] Bill was very concerned about the cost.[20] He had done very well as an engineer, but would be risking a significant amount of money that he and Sally had saved for their retirement to try to win a senate seat to serve the people of Texas. A 2016 candidate for Texas Senate in District 1 must raise and spend more than three times the amount Eppstein quoted Ratliff.[21]

Shaking hands with Eppstein, Bill said, "Let me think this over, Bryan, and get back with you." In the small open courtyard in front of Eppstein's office building Bill and Don sat down with a diet Coke to talk. They discussed Eppstein's character and the things they liked and did not like about his strategy and approach. Bill struggled with one central question: did he have "a decent chance to win?"[22]

Don interrupted Bill's focus on the chances of winning with a question of his own, "Sure enough, now Bill, why are you wanting to do this?"[23]

Bill paused and reflected for a few long moments.

On that hot first day of July, with the the sounds of the Fort Worth traffic in the background, Bill replied, "Oh, I don't fully know how to say it yet. I've had a successful engineering practice and I'm fairly comfortable now. There is probably a certain amount of ego in it, but I'd like to think I could make a small difference in the way things are going in Austin and across the state. It would be an honor to serve in the senate."[24]

"Well, then," Don said, "my suggestion would be this: if you are not too concerned about the potential cost, forget about winning and losing. Just do it for the adventure. You'll meet a lot of people, you'll have a number of crazy experiences, and you'll probably learn a few things about yourself along the way."

Bill replied, "thanks friend, you may be right."

Of course, Bill's brother Shannon who had been deeply involved in politics for many years had a more sobering response. In a phone call a few days later, Shannon gave Bill a note of caution saying, "I've seen politics destroy some awfully good men."[25]

I've Decided to Do It

A few days later Don's phone rang, Bill said, "I've decided to do it. I am preparing to formally announce my candidacy."[26]

As Ratliff was beginning his campaign in June of 1987, President Ronald Reagan traveled to West Berlin, Germany, and stood at the Brandenburg Gate and said, "General Secretary Gorbachev, if you seek peace, if you seek prosperity for the Soviet Union and Eastern Europe, if you seek liberalization: Come here to this gate! Mr. Gorbachev, open this gate! Mr. Gorbachev, tear down this wall!"[27] Reagan changed the perceptions of the Republican Party all across the United States—but the change was most pronounced in the South.

Riding this wave of popularity of President Reagan, Ratliff became the first candidate to announce for Texas Senate District 1. The 1988 race for District 1 would be a hot and closely fought race that would involve some of the biggest names in American politics. For some parts of the District this would be the first time a real challenge was made by a Republican. To win as a Republican would take lots of work, an extraordinary candidate, and lots of behind-the-scenes campaigning. The Ratliff campaign would need to shake hands, change minds, and win the hearts of the voters.

Upon hearing of Ratliff's candidacy, Anderson said, "Frankly it's not a surprise that they would target me. The Republicans are looking at redistricting after 1990 and gaining control of the Senate is one their primary goals."[28] Anderson's thought that Bill was seeking office because of redistricting was not the reason for Bill's challenge—but he was absolutely correct about the GOP looking at the number of seats held by Republicans in the United States House of Representatives and planning to increase those numbers by influencing the elections in the Texas Legislature.[29]

Winning Anderson's seat in the Texas Senate would require Bill to not only meet all of the legal requirements (to be a Texas state senator, an individual must be a U.S. citizen, a qualified voter, at least twenty-six years of age, and have lived in the state for the previous five years and in the district for one year prior to election) but also all of the informal requirements. Texas representatives very often fit rather neatly into specific demographic groups, occupations, and hold specific education and economic status.[30] Principal among the informal limitations is a candidate's party affiliation but it is easy to observe that being white, conservative, male, married, and middle-aged are also common informal requirements.

THE FIRST REPUBLICAN

With its election of Abraham Lincoln in 1860 the Republican Party had its first success. Of course, the party of Lincoln has seen significant ideological changes since the mid-1800s.[31] The Republican Party began when a small but dedicated group of abolitionists gathered to fight the expansion of slavery met in a little schoolhouse in Ripon, Wisconsin, in 1854.[32] This small group of passionate and dedicated people gave birth to a "Grand Old Party" dedicated to freedom and equal opportunity.[33] Lincoln added to that solid foundation of the new Republican Party in 1854 with a speech denouncing a law, written by a Democrat, that would allow slavery to expand into the western territories of the United States. Lincoln said, "The Republican Party holds that this government was instituted to secure the blessings of freedom, and that slavery is an unqualified evil."[34]

Opposing the Democrats from the South, Lincoln's party was aligned with the causes of civil rights for all Americans—today many Republicans do not value civil rights for all citizens—as seen in a number of new barriers to voting across the South.[35] As noted in chapters 1 and 2, Ratliff was well schooled and socialized into a party that was formed around the principles of liberty and freedom, the belief in hard work as a means of self-fulfillment, and a steadfast devotion to America's founding father's ideals and principles. Bill Ratliff and his Republican Party supported the values of equal opportunity for all, the inherent value in diversity, the idea of equality under the law, and a strong belief in rugged individualism and pragmatism. Lincoln's Republican Party was the natural home for Bill Ratliff in the late 1980s. But many in his party would change and many in the party challenge some of those values by the early 2000s and beyond.[36]

As early as the 1950s, conservative Democrats in Texas supported Republican presidential candidates. Beginning with the moderate and pragmatic Dwight David Eisenhower in 1952 and 1956, Richard Nixon in 1968 and 1972, and then Ronald Reagan in 1980 and 1984 many Texans split their tickets—voting for local and state level Democrats and for national Republicans.[37] Until the election of President Ronald Reagan in the early 1980s, Texas (like the rest of the South) had voted solidly Democratic in local and state races since the Civil War. Southern voters consistently voted against the party of Lincoln. In the 1980s, a momentous realignment took place in the South.[38] Ronald Reagan's presidency transformed the region's white electorate and made it possible for Republicans' to breakthrough in elections all throughout the South.[39] In 1987, however, Ratliff's district was still considered a Democratic stronghold even though its voters had helped elect Republicans President Reagan and Senator Phil Gramm. However, things were rapidly changing throughout the South.

George Smith writing in the *Marshall News* claimed that Ratliff had an "uphill battle for two reasons: 1) He's fighting a recognition factor, even though he is hitting the hinterlands with determination he still has a long way to go; 2) He's a Republican. That, in itself, is not a major negative—if you are running for the block chairman of Whaley Street in Longview. But when you are running all over the north and east part of Texas, there are some Democratic strongholds which reportedly lynch a Republican or two when the moon is full."[40] If he could defeat Richard Anderson, Bill Ratliff would be the first Republican to win Texas District 1.[41]

FAMOUS TANK RIDE

In the summer of 1988, as Ratliff and his campaign staff were working hard to make his name and ideas known, the American voters seemed ready for a change from the Reagan years.[42] On July 21 at the Democratic National Convention in Atlanta, Massachusetts Governor Michael Dukakis accepted his party's nomination and repeated an ancient pledge of the people of Athens saying, "We will never bring disgrace to this, our country, by any act of dishonesty or of cowardice. We will fight for the ideals of this, our country. We will revere and obey the law. We will strive to quicken our sense of civic duty. Thus, in all these ways, we will transmit this country greater, stronger, prouder and more beautiful than it was transmitted to us."[43] In the weeks following the Democratic Convention Governor Dukakis enjoyed polls showing him with a substantial lead over Vice President George H.W. Bush.[44] With so much enthusiasm for the Democrats, defeating Richard Anderson did not seem all that easy or obvious to the Ratliff campaign.[45] However, in spite of the early polls, the Republicans were not done. The Bush campaign launched a series of highly effective video ads. The "Willie Horton" and Governor Dukakis' famous "Tank Ride" ads would ultimately dramatically change things for Bush and the Republican ticket.[46]

"Democrats for Ratliff"

Although Ratliff filed as a Republican—was very active in the Texas Republican Party, and had actively supported both President Ronald Reagan and U.S. Senator Phil Gramm—he announced that he would run a bi-partisan campaign—and he did. Ratliff made a special note that his campaign treasurer, Joe Sandlin, was a Democrat.[47] This bi-partisan approach was a central and important theme throughout Ratliff's political career even in the face of tremendous Republican Party pressure.

Running as a Republican would mean that Ratliff would have to pull together a coalition of disgruntled Democrats (voters who were unhappy with Anderson), the Independents, and all the Republican voters in the district. Ratliff simply had to run across party lines to win. He created a "Democrats for Ratliff" campaign group with Vatra Solomon as the coordinator (Vatra would later become Bill's assistant).[48] Ms. Solomon said, "I have not left the Democratic Party. I still consider myself a Democrat. I voted on Super Tuesday as a Democrat. But in this particular race conscience becomes more important than the party issue."[49] Ms. Solomon has deep Democratic roots as her father, Neal Solomon, was a lifelong active member of the Democrat Party and had served in the Texas Legislature for eight years from 1965 to 1973 where he served as the chair of the House Banks and Banking Committee.[50]

"I'm simply running as a candidate who is concerned about taxes, jobs, crime, liability lawsuit problems, community values, education, and other state issues," said Ratliff, "my children are grown and my career is such that I can devote time to the office; I am a firm believer that if good people don't seek office they deserve what they get."[51]

Bill would later say, "I ran for the Senate for two major reasons. First, Richard Anderson had to be beaten. He was not a representative of the people—but simply a tool of the Texas Trial Lawyers Association. Mr. Anderson's personal life was a disaster at that time, from the day he was arrested for failure to pay child support to his arrest for DWI and resisting arrest to the misuse of state funds for his campaign—he was just someone who had to be beaten for the people of my district. Bill went on to say, "The second reason is ego, but not the power trip ego that many people think politician have in abundance, but the ego to think that I could do a better job for the people of my district." If elected Bill Ratliff would serve a four-year term in the powerful Texas Senate.

JOINING THE "CITIZEN'S LEGISLATURE"

The legislature of the state of Texas is a bicameral body composed of a 31-member Senate and a 150-member House of Representatives.[52] The Texas Legislature is an extremely powerful institution as the Texas House and Senate are not only responsible for legislation, policy, and oversight—but the leadership in those two houses also hold executive powers—that are shared with the Texas governor.[53] The men who drafted the Texas Constitution did not trust government to meet very often and as such the Texas Legislature only meets in regular session on the second Tuesday in January of each odd-numbered year. Moreover, Texas legislators are limited in regular legislative sessions to just 140 calendar days.[54]

The legislature was intended to be a "citizens legislature" not a professional legislature.[55] As such, the men and women who seek to serve must be independently wealthy enough to allow them to live in Austin and make ends meet on very meager public salaries.[56] Most of the members of the Texas Legislature are business owners/executives or lawyers—some years there are more lawyers than business owners and others not. The occupations of the members of the House and Senate are predominantly in law, business, real estate, consulting, ranching, and a few are in the medical and education fields. Rarely has a Senate seat been filled with an engineer.[57]

A Senator You Will Be Proud Of

Bill told the people of his district that he would make them one promise. Over and over he said, "I will be a senator you will be proud of."[58] Bill set out to serve the people of his community:

> Why should the people in my district vote for me? I believe my motives for serving are pure. I've finished two careers in engineering before I decided to run for office. I truly have nothing to gain by this office, and I simply want to look at issues and decide what is right and best for the people of my district. I may not put a chicken in every pot or agree with my constituents all the time, but I want them to be heard and be given a fair shake.[59]

In press releases Ratliff pointed at Anderson's failures saying that it was "simply ridiculous for the 71st Texas Legislature to pass more than 1,000 bills before adopting a budget."[60] George Smith in a *Marshall News Messenger* editorial wrote, "Ratliff may be a David in the East Texas version of Goliath's story. But he has already started gathering rocks."[61]

As the campaign rhetoric heated up that October 1987, the American and world economy saw the Dow Jones Industrial Average plunge 508.32 points, or about 22.6 percent, and closed at 1,738.40. The decline almost doubled the 12.8 percent loss in the 1929 crash.[62] The candidates were forced to answer many jobs and economic policy questions. Voters were worried. Ratliff was focused primarily on jobs saying, "my primary concern is the economy. I don't call it economic development or anything fancy," said Ratliff, "it's just jobs."[63] To create those jobs Ratliff said, "I'm not talking about federal grants or gimme programs to attract industry, but rather good financial policies that attract industry and growth to Texas communities."[64]

Democrats Are Split

Richard Anderson soon had more than Bill Ratliff and the Republican Party to worry about. In order to win his seat and return to Austin, Anderson had to first win the Democratic nomination in the primary election. In July 1987, Kilgore Mayor Mickey Smith announced his intention to challenge Anderson for the Democratic Party's nomination. Smith was a successful oilman and claimed to be the Democrat Party's conservative choice. As Smith jumped into the race, Ratliff was crisscrossing the monstrous fifteen-county Texas district to meet voters.

As Bill Ratliff made significant headway in the polls the Democrats began to worry about splitting the party with a heated primary campaign between Anderson and Smith. The Democrats saw Mickey Smith's announcement as a threat to holding off Ratliff and the Republicans. Lt. Governor Bill Hobby, the State Democratic Party Chairman Bob Slagle called Smith for a meeting.

Hobby and Slagle wanted to meet with Smith for two reasons. First, almost every county Democratic chairman in District 1 had suggested the meeting and second, party leaders wished to avoid the fragmentation of the party in the primary. The fragmentation of the party said Slagle, "Would open the door for a Republican candidate in the general election because of reduced resources (money) because of the primary fight."[65]

Mickey Smith was reluctant to meet with Governor Hobby and Chairman Slagle saying that he could defeat Anderson and that the voters should decide who they want as their senator. Bowing to party pressure Smith finally agreed to meet with Governor Hobby, Senator Richard Anderson, and Chairman Slagle. The meeting took place in room 184 of the Holiday Inn in Longview a few days before Christmas 1987. Anderson starting off the meeting saying, "The latest polls show me with a commanding lead. The possibility of you unseating me are very remote." Anderson went on to explain to Hobby, Slagle, and Smith that he wanted to "keep the election on the high road—as I have always done."[66]

Anderson paced as he talked, Smith sat and listened and then said, "I do not want to be a divisive influence on the Democratic Party."[67] The three party insiders suggested to Smith that he withdraw. Anderson pleaded with Smith saying "Withdrawing is the logical thing to do to save the Democratic Party campaign costs in the primary."

Smith replied, "It'll take more money to run my campaign if you guys are against me. I've always been a fighter, and I certainly don't feel like backing out now." Smith would not back out.

From January 1988 to March 8, 1988, Mickey Smith campaigned hard against Richard Anderson for the Democratic spot on the ticket. Of the 93,119 votes cast in the District Democratic primary that March, Anderson received 51,328 votes and Mickey Smith received 41,791 votes. After a bitter and costly fight, the Democrats had chosen Richard Anderson to face Republican Bill Ratliff in the general election.

CAMPAIGNING AND FUNDRAISING IN NEW BOSTON

Bill crisscrossed and recrossed his district many many times. Campaign stop after coffee shop after town hall meeting he worked to make his intentions and his name known to the people of his district. Much of the campaign was meeting solid good American citizens who cared deeply about their state and country, but Ratliff also had to deal with his share of those on the fringes of American political ideology and with those who have little understanding of politics and government. One night in the July before the election Bill and Don Edmonds were invited to an event in New Boston.[68]

New Boston was muggy that night. The late July temperatures had warmed up the humid deep East Texas woods. As Hamp Atkinson and his family prepared for the campaign cookout, the temperatures rose into upper nineties and an afternoon thundershower had pushed the humidity high. The air was stagnate. Hamp's land was somewhat flat with several wide open unwooded acres near a pond and a creek where they put the barbecue pittrailer next to an open camp house. Tables were set out. Coolers of beer were everywhere. Lawn chairs and camp stools were set about for the guests. All of the guests would be men—as the invitations stated, "stag affair."[69]

Hamp Atkinson—a lifelong Democrat—was supporting Ratliff that night. Atkinson had served four terms in the Texas House but on this night he was working to put a Republican in office. This stag affair was about cash—and having a good time—but mostly about cash. Men with cash to give to the campaign had been invited to a night of cold beer, strong whisky, and grilled meats. About fifty or so pickup trucks and a few cars lined Hamp's long red dirt driveway. Men in jeans and boots filed in the front door of the camp house dropping twenty, fifty, and hundred dollar bills into a big cowboy hat.[70]

The grill sizzled with sausages, steaks, and burgers. There was plenty of cold beer and lots of liquor. The candidate and his campaign manager, Don Edmonds, visited, ate, and drank their usual diet Coke all evening.[71] Facing about an hour drive back to Mt. Pleasant, on narrow winding two-lane roads, the candidate and his manager started walking toward their car at about 10:30. They were both exhausted from a long day of campaigning and felt they had stayed long enough. The stag affair would go on well into the small hours of the hot East Texas night. As they were just on the verge of escape, one of the drunken guests grabbed the candidate by the arm and slurred out his happy prediction that Bill would be elected. Following the candidate out the door and down the drive, the drunk man proceeded to proclaim that he'd never voted for a Republican before and then unloaded his views on every political issue that the senator might face in the next six sessions in Washington. Ratliff, of course, was not running for an office in Washington.

When the candidate and his manager finally closed the car doors leaving the drunk man swaying in the driveway, Bill slid down a bit in the passenger seat, put his head back on the headrest, and closed his eyes. "You know," he said quietly, "if it weren't for the drunks and the religious zealots, this wouldn't be such a bad business."

Starting the car, Don laughed, patted the bulge of cash in his pocket and said, "Yeah, but they both come with the territory. Don't bitch, we just picked up a few grand in cash tonight."[72]

ARE WOMEN ALLOWED?

Sally was very active in every Ratliff campaign. She would go into communities to visit with as many people as she could about their concerns for the future and to make sure they knew Bill's name and goals. Although she considers herself more of a "behind-the-scenes" person, she also does not hesitate to state that she believes her role is that of an "equal partner" in campaigning and in service.[73] Sally is and has been an equal partner in their marriage, in child rearing, in all decisions—including Bill's decision to run for the office of the senate.[74] It is very obvious that Bill and Sally have an extremely strong relationship.[75]

Sally would later say, "When Bill decided to run, we talked about it and decided we were either going to do it 100 percent or we weren't going to do it at all; and we were either both going to do it, or we weren't going to do it at all. I think, and he will tell you this, if I would have said, 'No, I don't want to,' he wouldn't have done it."[76]

In supporting her husband, Sally hit the campaign trail along with some forty other volunteers who became known as "Sally's Girls." Sally's Girls visited out-of-the-way places to campaign for Ratliff. In groups of two, three, or five, these women and Sally would travel from county-to-county, door-to-door, visiting country stores, barber shops, beauty shops, gas stations, and so on, to solicit votes in the very large sixteen-county district. Sally and her volunteers worked hard to campaign for Bill and the citizens of Texas.

One of the early Sally's Girls visits was in a tiny East Texas community. Sally's Girls drove the thirty miles of winding East Texas back roads to a small one-room wood-framed makeshift community center in Overton, Texas. The building sat up on blocks and two old dogs lay under the small porch in an attempt to stay cool. A group of old men were inside playing dominoes—a game called "Forty-Two."[77]

One of the men would later describe Sally's visit saying, "The ole 'girl' slowly opened the door," and, peering into the semi-dark roomful of men playing dominoes, Sally asked, "Are women allowed?"

One of the domino players replied with, "You don't see any signs, do ya?"

Sally said, "So, I went right on in and told them who I was and what I was doing and they were real friendly." Sally and her "girls" also visited garages, grocery stores, antique shops, craft businesses, and many other small places all across the district to "tell them about Bill," as she would later say.[78]

"Early on, when we'd go into these little stores and such, they'd sort of look at us like, 'Who?'" As time and campaigns went by, "I'd walk in and tell them who I am and that I'd like for them to vote for my husband and they just sort of brighten up," said Sally, "they'd all know his name."[79] With Sally's help, Bill had earned a solid reputation as a man of integrity who was clear and straight with his fellow citizens.

RATLIFF CLEARLY STATES HIS POSITION ON THE ISSUES

As the year came to a close in 1987, Ratliff said, "I feel pretty good about the campaign, it's a little hard to assess it so far, but I am getting good reactions. Almost to a person, people tell me that they're going to vote for the person rather than party." When asked about the strength of Anderson's incumbency, Ratliff said, "Anderson does not have the luxury of incumbency with the voters, he hasn't earned it yet."[80]

In an effort to be open and forthcoming, in August of 1988, Ratliff published his positions on a range of issues—eighteen issues of the time. Ratliff said, "I realize the publican of one's positions is not the political norm, since it is more difficult for a candidate to modify or evade a stance once it is made public in writing. It is my belief that the citizens of the First District have a right to know my thinking on these issues, whether or not those thoughts are politically popular with a particular interest group."[81]

On Guns

Anderson ran radio ads about his favorable NRA rating. Saying that Ratliff had an unfavorable rating because he supports measures to "take guns away from East Texans." Ratliff replied with a nonconventional stand that he favored a waiting period for handgun purchases, but did not consider that a pro-gun control stance because he supported the right to own guns.[82]

Trial Lawyers

Tort reform—I'm not a lawyer (though his two brother are) "it only takes eleven senators to block any measure they don't wish to reach the floor," Ratliff said, "I don't believe the people of the First District feel their senator can receive one-fourth of a million dollars ($273,000) from one lobby group (the state's trial lawyers) and still vote the convictions of his district." Ratliff pledged to take on the trial lawyers and to tackle tort reform and he did. "We don't believe anybody ought to be above the law."

In June of 1988, the campaigns were in full swing. Anderson was finding Ratliff to be a formidable opponent. In the heat of the battle Anderson's campaign made a costly mistake. The campaign used State of Texas offices and phones for calls to political consultants and for campaign operations. After it was revealed in the *Dallas Morning News*, Anderson repaid more than two thousand dollars for the telephone calls. [83]

The Ratliff campaign seized on the mistake to call for a more exhaustive investigation. [84] "We believe," said Ratliff, "that this kind of abuse of taxpayer money certainly justifies investigation by the district attorney of Travis County. We urge him to get to the bottom of this matter."

Public records revealed that Anderson's senate office had spent considerably more in operations than had the previous occupant, Senator Edward Howard. The Ratliff campaign revealed that Senator Howard had spent $118,880 and Senator Anderson had spent $196,127—a 65 percent increase. It appeared that Anderson was using state of Texas staff for his reelection campaign. [85]

Ratliff pointed out that the two thousand dollars in phone expenses may have been the lesser part of the abuse of state funds. Ratliff explained, "If we consider that there was a state staffer, sitting at a state desk, in a state-paid office at a state telephone making a two-hour telephone call to a campaign consultant, there's probably more abuse in that than there is in the cost of the telephone call itself." [86]

Ratliff argued that Senator Anderson's abuse indicated that the incumbent had larger character issues and stated, "We don't believe anybody ought to be above the law, and certainly not someone who wants to go to Austin to make the law." [87] The Ratliff campaign then began to follow the advice of the political consultant, Bryan Eppstein.

EPPSTEIN WINS AWARD FOR "SOFT ON CRIME" POLITICAL AD

In the 70th Regular Session in 1987, Bob McFarland (a Republican from District 10—at that time included parts of Dallas, Denton, and Tarrant counties) wrote a piece of legislation (SB 215) that would come to haunt those who supported it. McFarland's SB 215 bill was in response to court cases to an overcrowding problem in the Texas prison system.

On February 4, 1987, then governor of Texas, Bill Clements, sent the following message to the Senate of the 70th Texas Legislature, Regular Session: "Pursuant to Article III, Section 5 of the Texas Constitution, I hereby designate an emergency matter SB 215 by McFarland, relating to inmate population in the Texas Department of Corrections, good conduct time, and mandatory supervision." [88] With this message, Governor Clements signaled his support for and the urgency of the legislation.

The Texas Department of Corrections was under state court order to ease the overcrowding problems across the state's prison system. [89] McFarland's solution was for the Department of Corrections to emphasize probation and parole alternatives as opposed to more and longer incarcerations. Richard Anderson had voted for McFarland's bill. [90]

Texas has a culture that is "tough on crime" and has for years housed more prisoners than any other state in the United States.[91] According to the US Bureau of Justice Statistics there are 150,212 men and women in Texas' 109 prisons at the end of 2014.[92] Probation and parole options are, of course, far less expensive than incarceration. Richard Anderson's decision, in 1987, to support probation and parole over leaving people in prison for decades led to the creation of a "Willie Horton"-type political advertisement by the Ratliff campaign. The Horton saga began in 1972.

In 1972, the state legislature in Massachusetts implemented an inmate furlough program. Many states have laws enabling the use of furloughs, which allows an inmate to leave prison for a brief time and is designed to prepare the inmate for parole. When Michael Dukakis was the governor of Massachusetts he had supported his state's furlough program as a method of criminal rehabilitation.[93]

On Friday, April 3, 1987, William R. Horton (later nicknamed "Willie" by Lee Atwater[94]), a convicted murderer was furloughed from a Massachusetts prison for the weekend. That night, Horton broke into the home of Angela and Clifford Barnes. He bound and stabbed Clifford and then raped Angela.[95] The furlough of Mr. Horton was obviously a grave mistake. For his brutal attack on the Barneses Mr. Horton is now serving two life sentences plus eighty-five years in the state of Maryland. His story lives on in campaigns across America.

In June 1988, Republican candidate George H.W. Bush's campaign manager, Lee Atwater, seized on the Horton story to portray Michael Dukakis as soft on crime. Bush repeatedly used the Horton furlough in campaign speeches.[96] The issue worked so well in those speeches that Atwater created a campaign advertisement that morphed Governor Dukakis' face with that of Mr. Horton's face coming out of prison for a furlough. Atwater would say, "By the time we're finished, they're going to wonder whether Willie Horton is Dukakis' running mate."[97] Horton's mug shot photo was taped to the wall at Bush campaign headquarters.[98] Many scholars believe that Lee Atwater was instrumental in the George H.W. Bush victory. "You got to go negative," Atwater told then Vice President Bush.[99] "You just got to."[100] Atwater set out to completely change Bush's gentlemanly campaign style.[101] Atwater took a reluctant Bush campaign into the hard and harsh world of bare-knuckle politics.[102]

Bryan Eppstein used the same approach in a negative advertisement against Richard Anderson and that political ad played an important role in the outcome of the Ratliff campaign. In the Ratliff campaign ad, Eppstein cited Anderson's support for McFarland's probation and parole bill in a video portraying a burglar breaking into a lovely home all beautifully decorated for the holidays. A voice-over gave Richard Anderson credit for getting the felon "back home in time for Christmas."[103]

Negative campaign ads have been a part of American political culture since the early days of the nation. It is important to note that negative

does not necessarily mean bad. Negative ads can provide needed information to voters. Candidates must be able to critique the opposition.
However, Lee Atwater (and many others to follow) have taken the ma-
nipulation of information to new and unprecedented heights. In recent
campaigns analysts have noted that as many as 60 percent of the ads
were negative.[104]

In October of 1987, Ratliff said, "I feel pretty good about the campaign, it's a little hard to assess it so far, but I am getting good reactions.
Almost to a person, people tell me that they're going to vote for the
person rather than party." When asked about the strength of Anderson's
incumbency, Ratliff said, "Anderson does not have the luxury of incumbency with the voters, he hasn't earned it yet."[105]

The year 1988 was, of course, a presidential election year and as such
both Ratliff and Anderson expected a high turnout election. The Anderson campaign expected more than 185,000 voters to go to the polls in
District 1. Anderson and his staff assumed that a higher vote turnout
would spell victory for the Democrat as East Texas had historically voted
so solidly for Democrats since the Civil War in 1865.[106]

FIRST REPUBLICAN SINCE RECONSTRUCTION!

Election night, Tuesday, November 8, 1988, was tense and long for Bill
Ratliff's family and supporters. His campaign was concerned about the
national mood or what scholars call "presidential coattails." Even with
the early victory call for Republican president-elect George H.W. Bush
they waited anxiously. Bush soundly defeated Michael Dukakis 426–111
in the electoral vote. But as the Ratliff staff sat around several TVs watching the results come in, they worried about the popular vote—as it was
significantly closer, at 53 percent for Bush to 46 percent for Dukakis.[107]
Bush would not have long coattails—his election would not carry many
additional GOP candidates into office. The Ratliff campaigners had
worked tirelessly for many many months and all they could do was sit
and wait for the results of their work and the voters' decision.

Anderson appeared to be leading in the race through the late hours of
Tuesday night and into the early morning on Wednesday. It was not until
Wednesday afternoon that the people of East Texas finally learned that
Bill Ratliff had been elected to serve as senator of District 1. The down-to-
the-wire race was so close (Ratliff won with 52 percent of the vote) that it
was not decided until 2:30 p.m. on Wednesday when the last box of
absentee ballots were tallied in Harrison County.[108] Bill's sons, Bennett
and Thomas were home from college and had decided that they had to
get back to their respective schools when they were told the happy news.
They were both very delighted to turn around and drive back to Mt.
Pleasant to celebrate.[109] Ratliff carried only two of the fifteen counties in

District 1, but a strong showing in the more populated Gregg County and a surprise victory in Richard Anderson's home county were enough to give him a narrow victory in the bitterly contested race.

The newspaper headlines all across East Texas read, "First Republican Since Reconstruction! Ratliff Wins Senate!"[110] Overcoming tremendous odds, Ratliff defeated Anderson in an election that was about the men running for the office and not their parties. "It's a great day for Texas," said Mt. Pleasant Mayor Jerry Boatner shortly after the announcement that Ratliff had won.[111] Ratliff had unseated a Democrat to became the first Republican to win office in District 1 since Reconstruction. Ratliff's victory gave the Republicans eight seats of the thirty-one in the Texas Senate—up from six the previous election.[112] Late Wednesday afternoon the day after the election, Richard Anderson conceded, "The people of East Texas have spoken," he said, "I plan to return to my law practice, a practice I have neglected since serving in the Senate."[113]

Anderson Demands Recount

However, Anderson changed his mind later that evening and on Thursday demanded a recount.

Since voting is a human endeavor, vote counting tends to contain a good deal of error. Punch-card ballots used in 1988 were notorious for contributing to this error as the voter had to not only place the card correctly into a slot in the voting machine but also had to cleanly and completely punch a hole with a stylus next to the candidate name they intended to support. Estimates range from 1 to 3 percent of these were not done correctly in each election. This ballot issue became a central and critical issue in the Bush versus Gore presidential election in 2000. Texas law allows a candidate to request a recount if he or she loses by less than 10 percent. Anderson's loss was well within that margin. A recount must be paid for by the candidate requesting it. Ratliff was still the clear winner after the recount.

I AM GOING TO BE THERE TO REPRESENT THE PEOPLE

On January 10, 1989, Senator Ratliff began his career in the regular 71st Legislative session. Speaking that day, Senator Ratliff downplayed the fact that he was the first Republican from his district and even that he

Texas State Senate District 1—November 8, 1988

Bill Ratliff (Rep.)	....	86,682
Richard Anderson (Dem.)	....	84,333
Total Vote	....	171,015

was a Republican at all. "I just want to be a good senator," he said, "I'm not going to represent the Republicans. I am going to be there to represent the people of the first senatorial district."[114] When Bill was elected he was still a managing partner of an engineering firm that sometimes performed work for the state of Texas. So as not to have even the appearance of a conflict of interest, Ratliff sold his shares in that firm and took full retirement. The freshman senator made another financial decision that sent shock waves across the state.

Friendly Incumbent Rule

In the first few weeks and months after his election, Senator Ratliff made an important political and financial statement to powerful and large donors. As noted above, donors are more likely to support the incumbent rather than the challenger. Donors are typically reluctant to financially support a challenger because they fear that, if the incumbent is reelected, he/she might take retribution against the donor's legislative agenda. To protect their interests, donors follow what is known as the "friendly incumbent" rule. The friendly incumbent rule usually persuades contributors to give to the incumbent even when the challenger holds more like-minded views. The donor provides campaign funding to the incumbent even when the incumbent has been anything but friendly. It is a puzzle to many outsiders, but the friendly incumbent rule is a significant handicap to challengers, even when the donor supports the challenger's positions.

However, contributors frequently give money to the newly elected challenger *after* the Election Day. These donations are called "late train" contributions. Contributors reason that, after the challenger is elected, she/he will be overjoyed to be the winner, will probably need funds to repay campaign debts, and will willingly accept late train money. By making major contributions—even though late—contributors hope that the successful challenger will not hold grudges and will forget and forgive the contributor's lack of support during the election.

In Ratliff's run against Anderson, he supported reforming the states tort laws (see chapter 7 for tort reform). Anderson was opposed to tort reform. Because of Ratliff's support for tort reform policy, all of the major business interest groups in the state were hoping that he would win. But they only hoped, they did not contribute funding support to his campaign. Consistent with the friendly incumbent rule, the vast majority of the major business groups supported Senator Anderson with very large campaign contributions. Business organizations such as Texas Medical Association, Texas Association of Business, Texas Automobile Dealer's Association, and the Texas Realtors Association all supported tort reform, and yet they made major contributions (tens of thousands each) to Senator Anderson's campaign under the friendly incumbent rule. While

Ratliff was forced to raise funds in small personal contributions, Senator Anderson was receiving tens of thousands of dollars in support from not only the Texas Trial Lawyers Association, but also from all of the leading business groups.

After Ratliff won, the late train checks began to pour in from the business groups. Senator Ratliff made a surprising and very unusual decision. "I wrote each of these major lobby organizations a very nice letter," said Ratliff, "I enclosed their uncashed check and explained to them that I felt if I accepted their large contributions, my small contributors would feel that their small support for me would be overshadowed and somehow diminished in importance." Sending shock waves through the Austin lobby Senator Ratliff returned nearly $100,000 in late train contributions. With Sally by his side, Bill would independently and fully enter public service—his ambition was to serve and promote the welfare of others, his constituents, his state, and his country—not the lobby.

MANY PEOPLE SAY THAT ABOUT THEIR SPOUSES

Sally's partnership and support for her husband cannot be overestimated. "Many people say that about their spouses," Bill said, "but in my case it is true. Not only is she my wife but she is my best friend."[115] Bill and Sally rented an apartment in Austin and she accompanied him every legislative session—without exception. Sally sat as a quiet ever-present observer in the Texas Senate Gallery 100 percent of the time while Bill was on the Senate floor.[116] Bill went on to say, "It is a fact that I couldn't have done that job if she were at home and I were in Austin. My relationship with Sally is all of life."[117]

Senator Bill Ratliff would become so respected and revered in the Texas Legislature, in Austin, across the state of Texas, and in his district that some of his colleagues would later describe him as "bulletproof."[118] He would continue to win his seat for as long as he wanted to serve. Never again in his career did Bill Ratliff face a serious challenger for his Senate seat.[119] However, the challenges and personal tests that lay ahead for the engineer turned senator were enormous.

Bill Ratliff now held the powers of a Texas senator. With those powers and the guiding principles of intellectual honesty, fairness, and integrity he would courageously face many of the most daunting challenges of our time. From fighting the interests of big money, to finding support for Texas schoolchildren, to worker's compensation, to tort reform, to ethics reform, to redistricting, and finally to a personal moral challenge the Senator from East Texas would be tested. He'd won the election, but the real challenges for the man who *Texas Monthly* claimed was "a man free of ambition" had only just begun.

NOTES

1. Noted in numerous interviews with many people interviewed for this book.

2. This section was derived from interviews with Bill Ratliff (2013) and Don Edmonds (2014). Don has written extensive notes and memoirs of his life and graciously shared those with me.

3. Using mapfrappe.com simply mark out the shape of District 1 in Northeast Texas, and then superimpose it anywhere via a Google Maps API.

4. Interview with Don Edmonds 2014.

5. Learned through interviews with Bill Ratliff, Sally Ratliff, Jack Ratliff, Don Edmonds, Bonney Edmonds in 2013, 2014, 2015.

6. See the Texas Texas Senate 70th Legislature (http://www.lrl.state.tx.us/scanned/members/texas_senators/Public/Texas_Senate_70.pdf).

7. Steve Bickerstaff, *Lines in the Sand: Congressional Redistricting in Texas and the Downfall of Tom Delay*, p. 17.

8. Interview with Bill Ratliff 2013.

9. Interview with Don Edmonds 2014.

10. Ibid.

11. Ibid.

12. Don Edmonds unpublished memoirs.

13. Ibid.

14. Ibid.

15. Interviews with Don Edmonds, Jack Ratliff, Vatra Solomon, and Bill Ratliff 2013 and 2014.

16. Don Edmonds 2014.

17. Interviews with Bill Ratliff and Don Edmonds 2014.

18. As evidence see Lt. Governor Bill Hobby's personal involvement in this race.

19. Interview with Don Edmonds 2014.

20. Bill Ratliff, Sally Ratliff interview 2013.

21. Fundraising to replace Sen. Eltife nears $1 million, published on Saturday, January 23, 2016 by Adam Russell (http://www.tylerpaper.com/TP-News+Local/230212/fundraising-to-replace-sen-eltife-nears-1-million).

22. Interview with Don Edmonds 2014.

23. Don Edmond's unpublished memoirs.

24. Interview with Don Edmonds and Don's memoirs.

25. Interview with Shannon Ratliff 2014.

26. Don Edmond's unpublished memoirs.

27. *The Reagan Era from the Iran Crisis to Kosovo* edited by Rodney P. Carlisle J. Geoffrey Golson.

28. *News Messenger* July 6, 1987.

29. Interview with Bill Ratliff and Steve Bickerstaff, Lines in the Sand.

30. *Texas Politics: Governing the Lone Star State* by Cal Jillson p.

31. "Dog Whistle Politics: How Coded Racial Appeals Have Reinvented Racism and Wrecked the Middle Class," by Ian Haney-López 2014.

32. See the historical timeline and description at https://www.gop.com/history.

33. *Lincoln's Dilemma: Blair, Sumner and the Republican Struggle over Racism and Inequality in the Civil War Era* by Paul D. Escott, University of Virginia Press 2014.

34. *Lincoln: Political Writings and Speeches*, edited by Terence Ball 2012.

35. The New Attack on Hispanic Voting Rights after the Supreme Court Decision That Gutted the Voting Rights Act, tactics to suppress minority voting are flourishing—especially in states where Hispanic voters are reshaping the electorate. Part of a series by Jim Rutenberg December 17, 2015.

36. See: Yes, Polarization Is Asymmetric—And Conservatives Are Worse, by Norm Ornstein in *The Atlantic*, June 19, 2014.

37. Steve Bickerstaff, *Lines in the Sand* p. 19.

38. See Earl Black and Merle Black, "The Rise of Southern Republicans."

39. Ian Haney Lopez, *Dog Whistle Politics* 2014.

40. *Marshall News* on Sunday November 15, 1987.

41. Ibid.

42. PBS The American Experience George H.W. Bush (http://www.pbs.org/wgbh/americanexperience/features/transcript/bush-transcript/).

43. Michael S. Dukakis: "'A New Era of Greatness for America': Address Accepting the Presidential Nomination at the Democratic National Convention in Atlanta," July 21, 1988. Online by Gerhard Peters and John T. Woolley, The American Presidency Project. http://www.presidency.ucsb.edu/ws/?pid=25961

44. Poll Shows Dukakis Leads Bush; Many Reagan Backers Shift Sides by E. J. Dionne Jr. New York Times Published: May 17, 1988.

45. Interview with Don Edmonds 2014.

46. PBS, The American Experience George H.W. Bush (http://www.pbs.org/wgbh/americanexperience/features/transcript/bush-transcript/).

47. *New Messenger* August 1987.

48. *Paris* August 1987.

49. *Longview News Journal* August 4, 1987.

50. Interview with Vatra Solomon 2014.

51. *Longview* 1987.

52. See the state of Texas constitution at http://www.constitution.legis.state.tx.us.

53. Ibid.

54. See the University of Texas School of Law Tarlton Law Library Texas Constitutions page for excellent historical discussions (http://tarlton.law.utexas.edu/constitutions).

55. Ibid.

56. Texas senators and representatives earn only $7,200 per year, or $14,400 for a two-year legislative period.

57. In a speech in April of 2001, Ratliff mentioned his pleasure when Jon Lindsay was elected as state senator from District 7. "It was a big day when Jon came to Austin. I was no longer the only engineer in the group. I suffered through the legislative process for a while with him because it took us a long time to realize that logic plays no part in the process." Lt. Governor comes and speaks to North Houston Association by Cynthia Calvert (http://www.yourhoustonnews.com/archives/lt-governor-comes-and-speaks-to-north-houston-association/article_c672f9ea-818e-55af-b03f-ac4b8491a70a.html).

58. *Longview News Journal* 1987.

59. In undated twenty-one pages of notes found in the UT Tyler archives Bill Ratliff wrote questions he might be asked and then responded to those questions. Sally Ratliff saved those notes in her scrapbook collection. That collection includes every single article published about Bill, every single letter, photo, invitation, and memento from his entire political career. His notes are raw, honest, and thoughtful. They express his inner feelings—not polished political consultant answers.

60. Press releases are found in the University of Texas at Tyler Library archives.

61. *Marshall News Messenger* October 1987.

62. Dow Jones 100-Year Historical Chart (http://www.macrotrends.net/1319/dow-jones-100-year-historical-chart)

63. *Mount Pleasant Daily Tribune* December 12, 1987.

64. Ibid.

65. In a series of articles in the *Mount Pleasant Daily Tribune* 1987 and 1988.

66. Ibid.

67. Ibid.

68. Printed invitation is in the University of Texas at Tyler archives.

69. Ibid.

70. Interview with Don Edmonds 2014 also retold in Edmond's unpublished memoirs.

71. In several interviews I was told this was almost all Ratliff and Edmonds ever drank.

72. Ibid.

73. Interview with Sally Ratliff 2014.

74. Interview with Bill Ratliff 2013.

75. Noted over many interviews 2011, 2012, 2013, 2014, 2015.

76. Interview with Sally Ratliff 2013.

77. Reported in the *Mount Pleasant Daily Tribune* 1988.

78. Interview with Sally Ratliff 2014.

79. Ibid.

80. *Marshall News Messenger* October 1987.

81. *Texarkana Journal*, August 14, 1988.

82. *Longview News Journal* Saturday, October 29, 1988.

83. *Dallas Morning News* June 1988.

84. *The Victoria Advocate* June 24, 1988.

85. Ibid.

86. Ibid.

87. Ibid.

88. Journal of the Senate of the State of Texas Regular Session of the 70th Legislature (http://www.lrl.state.tx.us/scanned/govdocs/William%20P%20Clements/1987/mess3.pdf).

89. Legislative Library of Texas SB 215, 70th Regular Session Relating to inmate population in the Texas Department of Corrections and to sentencing and administrative and information provisions that affect that population providing for appropriations.

90. Ibid.

91. United States Bureau of Justice Statistics http://www.bjs.gov/content/pub/pdf/cpus14.pdf.

92. Ibid.

93. *New York Times*, "Prison Furloughs in Massachusetts Threaten Dukakis Record on Crime," by Robin Toner July 5, 1988.

94. Lee Atwater, changed William Horton into "Willie Horton." Horton had never gone by the nickname. "My illness helped me to see that what was missing in society is what was missing in me: a little heart, a lot of brotherhood," Atwater wrote in Life magazine before his death, at age forty, of a brain tumor. "In 1988," he continued, "fighting Dukakis, I said that I 'would strip the bark off the little bastard' and 'make Willie Horton his running mate.' I am sorry for both statements: the first for its naked cruelty, the second because it makes me sound racist, which I am not." Quoted in the Marshall Project online (https://www.themarshallproject.org/2015/05/13/willie-horton-revisited#.WpZXndfCQ).

95. *New York Times*, "Prison Furloughs in Massachusetts Threaten Dukakis Record on Crime," by Robin Toner July 5, 1988.

96. The Marshall Project (https://www.themarshallproject.org/2015/05/13/willie-horton-revisited#.WpZXndfCQ).

97. Quoted in "Road Show," by Roger Simon, published by Farrar, Straus & Giroux 1990.

98. The Marshall Project (https://www.themarshallproject.org/2015/05/13/willie-horton-revisited#.WpZXndfCQ).

99. Quoted in PBS, The American Experience, George H.W. Bush (http://www.pbs.org/wgbh/americanexperience/features/transcript/bush-transcript/).

100. Ibid.

101. Ibid.

102. From historian John Robert Greene in PBS, The American Experience, George H.W. Bush (http://www.pbs.org/wgbh/americanexperience/features/transcript/bush-transcript/).

103. Noted in Justice under Pressure: A Comparison of Recidivism Patterns among Four Successive Parolee Cohorts, by Sheldon Ekland-Olson, William Kelly, and H.J. Joo 1993.

104. Erika Franklin Fowler and Travis N. Ridout, "Negative, Angry and Ubiquitous: Political Advertising in 2012," *The Forum, A Journal of Applied Research in Contemporary Politics* 10, no. 4 (2012): 51–61.

105. *Marshall News Messenger* October

106. *Panola County Post* Sunday, November 13, 1988.

107. http://www.presidency.ucsb.edu/showelection.php?year=1988.

108. Interview with Bill Ratliff 2013.

109. Interview with Sally Ratliff 2014.

110. See for example the *Panola County Post* Sunday, November 13, 1988 (http://www.panola.edu/library/panola-watchman/document/1988/11-13-88.pdf).

111. *Mount Pleasant Daily Tribune* November 1988.

112. Ibid.

113. Ibid.

114. *Dekalb Newspaper* Thursday, January 5, 1989.

115. Interview with Bill Ratliff September 2014.

116. Interview with Bill Ratliff and Sally Ratliff 2014.

117. Ibid.

118. Steve Bickerstaff, *Lines in the Sand* 2007, p. 177.

119. This is not to say that he did not face challengers. He did. Bobby Akin (see chapter 4) for example would mount a challenge, but Ratliff continued to enjoy wins with 70 percent plus of the voters of District 1.

Free of egotism. Senator Ratliff serving as president pro tempore of the Senate (1989). The president pro tempore presides when the lieutenant governor is not present. Photo credit to Texas Senate Media Services.

Free of ambition. Senator Ratliff and Lt. Governor Bill Hobby (1989). Photo credit to Texas Senate Media Services.

Governor George W. Bush and Senator Ratliff (1995). Photo credit to Texas Senate Media Services.

Free of partisanship. Senator Ratliff and Lt. Governor Bob Bullock (1995). Photo credit to Texas Senate Media Services.

Free of the lobby. Senator Ratliff and Senator John Montford (1995). Photo credit to Texas Senate Media Services.

Mrs. Sally Ratliff (1995). Photo credit to Texas Senate Media Services.

Senator Ratliff explains the Texas Education Code (1995). Photo credit to Texas Senate Media Services.

Senator Ratliff and Senator Rodney Ellis (1997). Photo credit to Texas Senate Media Services.

Senator Ratliff in a committee hearing (1997). Photo credit to Texas Senate Media Services.

Senator Ratliff votes no (1997). Texas Senators indicate their vote by raising 1, 2, or 3 fingers. One finger means yes, two means no, and three means present but not voting. Photo credit to Texas Senate Media Services.

Bill and Sally on the Senate floor (1997). Sally never missed a day when Bill was working on the Senate floor. She always watched from the Senate gallery. Photo credit to Texas Senate Media Services.

Ratliff (1997) was free to act as every senator should, but few actually do. Photo credit to Texas Senate Media Services.

Ratliff famously said, "I am a Republican for the same reason I am a Methodist—I agree with them at least 51 percent of the time." Photo credit to Texas Senate Media Services.

On December 28, 2000, with Sally holding Sam Houston's Bible, Ratliff was sworn in as the forty-first Texas lieutenant governor by Chief Justice Tom Phillips. Photo credit to Texas Senate Media Services.

Bill Ratliff, the forty-first Texas lieutenant governor (2001). Photo credit to Texas Senate Media Services.

Left to right: Mr. Don Edmonds, Lt. Governor Ratliff, Ms. Vatra Solomon, and Mr. Eric Wright (2001). Photo credit to Texas Senate Media Services.

"Senator Shaplieh, You Are Not Recognized for That Purpose" (2001). Photo credit to Texas Senate Media Services.

Lt. Governor Ratliff calls the Senate to order (2001). Photo credit to Texas Senate Media Services.

Like Lt. Governor Bill Hobby before him, Lt. Governor Ratliff "Let the Senate work its will" (2001). Photo credit to Texas Senate Media Services.

Ratliff said, "I do not love politics, especially the kind involved in running a $10 million campaign. I don't think you can be as independent, as fiercely independent, as I have been in these last twelve years and be successful" (2001). Photo credit to Texas Senate Media Services.

Finding pennies for Thomas (2001). Ratliff was well known for working long hours for the people of Texas. Photo credit to Texas Senate Media Services.

Free of Partisanship (2003). Ratliff told reporters, "I have advised Lieutenant Governor David Dewhurst that I am in possession of a statement signed by ten senators stating their unalterable opposition to any motion to bring redistricting to the Senate floor. I have advised the lieutenant governor that I am adding my name to the statement." Photo credit to Texas Senate Media Services.

The Texas Senate from the view where Sally Ratliff watched Senator Ratliff work. Photo credit to Texas Senate Media Services.

FOUR

Robin Hood: A Totally Free Man

THE AMERICAN DREAM

Tom and Bess Ratliff had big dreams for their three sons. Their "American dream" was for their three boys to grow up to be strong and successful men. Those dreams were in no small way realized. Jack and Shannon became highly successful and influential lawyers and Bill became a highly successful engineer and senator. All three men and their wives established and nurtured beautiful and successful families. By any standard they achieved the American dream. From the small public schools of Sonora to the University of Texas, the Ratliff boys made their American dreams a reality through hard work and dedication. Education was a central and important part of the Ratliff family's success. Education has been seen as the great equalizer in America—as it seeks to provide real opportunity to all American children. Senator Ratliff spent the vast majority of his legislative career working to create opportunity for the children of Texas. He worked tirelessly for more than a decade to bring fairness and integrity to the highly complex budget issue of funding Texas public schools, colleges and universities. Just as Bill sought to be fair on the baseball diamond in Sonora, he also sought the same simple fairness for all Texas children.

Senator Ratliff based his work on a long and deeply held American value—that an equal opportunity for a solid and good education is a public good, and paying for it is a social responsibility. Bill Ratliff believes in hard work, in investing in education, and he worked (and continues to work) for an equal and real opportunity for the American dream for all Texas children. To achieve these ambitions, the engineer turned freshman senator set out to learn the operation of the levers and pulleys in his new position of power.

Will It Cost Money?

One January 8, 1989, Bill Ratliff told the *Paris News*, "You'd be amazed how many people, entities, and so forth there are in the first district who wanted to tell me their story before I left home. So I've been pretty busy just trying to understand the concerns of all those various people and listen to their issues." Senator Ratliff was sworn into office on January 10 with Sally right by his side.

In the opening weeks of the session, freshman senators all must pass through a mild initiation process.[1] On the Senate floor, Senator Ratliff introduced his first bill (SB 193—a simple bill that updated an existing job training law in the workforce development program) would have normally been passed without any discussion—but since it was his first bill it was anything but simple. Senator Ratliff's colleagues, tongue-in-cheek, rapidly fired questions about his first bill.

"Will it cost money?" asked Senator Carlos Truan (D-Corpus Christi). Senator Truan was a lifelong champion of education.[2]

"Shouldn't the bill be expanded to include training?" asked Senator Gonzalo Barrientos (D-Austin).

"I wonder if you'd accept an amendment that would open up Bishop College?" asked Eddie Bernice Johnson (D-Dallas). Senator Johnson was the first black female chair of a major Texas Senate committee.[3]

Senator Hector Uribe (D-Brownsville) said, "I don't know if it is a good bill. But since you're my desk mate, I think I ought to vote for at least one of your bills—then I want to talk to you about my lottery bill."

And on and on went the questions for the freshman senator from East Texas. When it came time to suspend the Senate's regular operating rules so that his bill could be voted on the senators voted 4–18 against taking up the bill for consideration. So Ratliff's first bill was left pending on the Senate agenda awaiting consideration yet another day and with that the freshman senator from East Texas was initiated into the strange and other world of politics and power.[4]

The unpretentious senator was a quick and hardworking student of the Senate and of his new position. If he didn't know something Ratliff would say so. As a freshman senator "Ratliff did not boldly or brashly set out to change the face of the Senate. Rather he set out to learn the job, the Senate, and to focus his lawmaking efforts and abilities where they mattered most—education and economy."[5]

In the 71st Legislature—Ratliff's first session—he authored twenty-eight bills—ranging from the regulation of the sale of milk (SB 1524) to the regulation of professional engineers, to medical and hospitalization (SB 737), and the self-insurance plans and insurance for counties (SB 936).[6] Most of Ratliff's bills which were simple resolutions congratulating special people, awards, and teams in his district. In the third special session, Ratliff authored and the Senate passed SR 64 congratulating his father, Tom Ratliff, on the occasion of his eighty-seventh birthday.[7] Much of the legislation sponsored by the freshman senator from the rural district was successfully sent to Governor Clements desk for signing. Ratliff was focused on making a difference not on authoring a great number of bills.[8]

The 71st Legislative session included no less than six special sessions called by Governor Bill Clements.[9] "Specials sessions" are only "special" in that they are not "regular" sessions. They have largely the same structure as the regular session—but only thirty days in length rather than one hundred forty days. The Texas governor can call a special session at any time. In 1989, Governor Bill Clements called six special sessions for the legislature to address fifty-nine different proposals. Clements kept lawmakers in Austin from the first day of the regular session on January 10, 1989, to the last day of the sixth called session on June 7, 1990.

In Ratliff's first weeks in the Senate, Lt. Governor Bill Hobby appointed him to the Economic Development Committee, Natural Resources (including the Subcommittee on Water) and Intergovernmental Relations committees. As a new member of the Senate, Ratliff sought to understand. He read and observed. He listened and took notes. He studied the habits, actions, likes, and dislikes of the leadership and of his colleagues.[10] He learned over time who he could trust and who not to trust. Trust and integrity were his guiding principles. He learned the ground rules of the Senate—both written and unwritten. He studied and learned from Lt. Governor Bill Hobby.[11] Hobby was a seasoned, revered, and experienced politician and announced at the beginning of the 71st session that he would not be seeking reelection. Bill Hobby was widely respected, *Texas Monthly* reported, "He has never cared about anything but what is best for Texas, he has run the Senate for seventeen years without a hint of corruption, and he has brought Texas government into the modern age. What will we do without him?"[12] Ratliff closely studied Hobby.[13]

WE HAD THE WORST EDUCATIONAL SYSTEM THAT YOU COULD POSSIBLY HAVE

The Sonora school Bill and his brothers attended in the 1940s was starkly different from the school Red and his friends attended just across town.[14] Like many towns and cities in Texas the two schools operated on remarkably different budgets. The school Bill and his brothers attended was much better funded and equipped to educate.[15] While Bill and his brothers were playing that continuous sandlot baseball game with their Latino friends from across Dry Devil's River, the Texas Legislature was at work seeking a remedy to funding disparities and to provide educational opportunities for all Texas public schools. Underfunding or no funding at all during the Great Depression and during the years of World War II had left many Texas schools in very poor condition. Of Texas schools at the time, Representative Reuben Senterfitt[16] said, "We had the worst educational system that you could possibly have."[17] In the late 1940s, the task of rebuilding Texas public schools, preparing for the coming baby boom generation (born between 1946–1964), and addressing the inequalities in education was led by Texas senator Alexander Mack Aikin Jr. In 1947, Senator Aikin called for a full and complete reevaluation of Texas public schools.[18]

The Father of Modern Texas Education

Long before Senator Ratliff defeated Richard Anderson for Senate District 1, Senator Aikin held that very same seat from 1937 until 1979.[19] Before being elected to the Senate, Aikin (D-Paris) had served two terms as a State representative — giving him the longest tenure of any legislator in Texas history.[20] Like so many others in the late 1940s, Mack Aikin and his wife, Welma, had a four-year-old son. The Aikin's son, A.M. "Bobby" Aikin III, born July 12, 1946, was part of the baby boom generation.[21] As birth rates soared in Bobby Aikin's generation, his father, who had a lifelong interest in public education, knew that something had to be done to prepare for his son, and all the other baby boom children, who would soon need quality public schools. So, in 1947, Aikin chaired an eighteen-member committee, composed of educators and legislators, to explore systems of funding schools that would guarantee at least a minimum educational offering to each child and that would help overcome inter-district disparities in taxable resources.[22]

As a young boy growing up in the deep East Texas woods not far from Mt. Pleasant, Mack Aikin struggled to get an education. From 1910 to 1920 Aikin attended a very tiny country school in the community of Milton just outside of Paris, Texas. Milton's school only had three teachers for the grades one through ten.[23] Since the village of Milton did not offer grades eleven and twelve, a determined student, Mack rode on horseback the five miles from Milton to Deport, Texas, each schoolday until he graduated from high school.[24] After high school Mack attended Paris Junior College.[25] While studying at Paris Junior College, he worked on a local dairy milking cows to earn room and board.[26] After graduating from Paris Junior College he worked in a department store in Paris, to earn enough money to attend Cumberland University in Lebanon, Tennessee, where he graduated with a bachelor of law degree in 1932.[27]

Like Huey Long, and many others mentioned elsewhere, Mack Aikin credited his lifetime interest in education to the early personal difficulties he encountered in acquiring his own education.[28] Legislative records indicate Aikin's passion, he played an important role and/or guided every piece of school legislation that was passed during the forty-six years he served at the Texas Capitol.[29] Aikin is known as "the father of modern Texas education" and is best remembered for the legislation he cosponsored with Representative Claud Gilmer titled the Gilmer-Aikin Laws.[30]

I Came Here Thinking a Child Ought to Get an Equal Educational Opportunity

Passed in 1949, the Gilmer-Aikin Laws established the Texas Minimum Foundation School Program. In Aikin's program state and local funds were earmarked specifically for teacher salaries, operating expenses, and transportation costs.[31] The state financed approximately 80 percent of the program and the local school districts were responsible for providing the remaining 20 percent.[32] The districts' share of state funding, known as the "Local Fund Assignment," was apportioned among the school districts under a formula designed to reflect each district's relative taxing ability.[33]

Senator Aikin said, "I came here thinking a child ought to get an equal educational opportunity whether he was born in the middle of an oil field or in the middle of a cotton field."[34] Senator Aikin, like Ernest Cockrell, knew the importance of the opportunity to receive an education and worked hard to provide that for others. For Senator Aikin, a child's opportunity for a quality education did not depend upon where he was born or where his parents could afford to live. To pay for that opportunity, in 1949, Senator Aikin, Representative Claud Gilmer, and a conservative Texas Legislature raised taxes to improve schools for all Texas children.[35]

The effects of the Gilmer-Aikin laws on Texas children, families, the state, and the United States were remarkable.[36] School—an education—became a reality for many Texas children for the first time in history. Also, over the next decade, from 1950 to 1960, the state of Texas saved millions of dollars by consolidating 6,409 Texas school districts into 1,539.[37] Schools like the one young Mack Aikin had attended in Milton—just three teachers of the first ten grades—were replaced with schools employing teachers who held bachelor's degrees for each grade.[38] Because of Aikin's work, Texas students were guaranteed 175 days of hopefully quality instruction over nine months each academic year. Gilmer and Aikin raised taxes on the citizens of Texas to increase teacher's salaries across the state and to provide teachers with additional training opportunities.[39] Teachers also received a bonus for each year of teaching experience.[40] Not only did the Ratliff boy's teachers in Sonora see a real and significant pay raise in 1950 (and each year afterward), so did the teachers in the Latino school across Dry Devil's River. Red and his friend's Latino teachers as well as the teachers in the predominantly black schools across the state saw the very same pay raise.[41] Thus, the Gilmer-Aikin laws[42] were a step toward equality a full four years ahead of the United States Supreme Court's unanimous decision stating that "separate educational facilities are inherently unequal."[43] As noted earlier, the United States Supreme Court, in *Brown v. Board of Education*, unanimously held that the racial segregation of children in public schools violated the Equal Protection Clause of the Fourteenth Amendment.[44] In that decision, Chief Justice Earl Warren wrote: "It is doubtful that any child may reasonably be expected to succeed in life if he is denied the opportunity of an education. Such an opportunity, where the state has undertaken to provide it, is a right which must be made available to all on equal terms."[45]

Born in a Cotton or Oil Field?

From roughly the 1840s to the 1940s Texas was predominantly rural and agrarian with both the population and property wealth spread somewhat evenly across the state. After World War II both commercial development and industrial activity began to concentrate in specific school districts across the state.[46] This concentration of economic activity created sizable differences in the value of property between Texas school districts.[47] Some school districts saw significant economic growth and activity while others enjoyed little or none. These economic disparities led to significant differences in the amount of money collected through local property taxes. In turn, the local property taxes created significant disparities in the amount of support each school district could provide each student. Over time this disparity in local spending and the unequal access to an education stimulated legislative attention. The Gilmer-Aikin laws were the first significant legislative steps toward increasing state funding to help offset these disparities. However, as significant as this first step was, disparities increased over time. By the 1960s, substantial differences in spending per student across school districts became the norm throughout the state. As such, the children born in Senator Aikin's "cotton and oil fields" did not have nearly equal educational opportunities.

EDGEWOOD AND ALAMO HEIGHTS SCHOOLS

About 175 miles to the Southeast of Sonora, Texas, is the school district of Edgewood, located in the greater San Antonio city area. The citizens of Edgewood (who are predominantly of Mexican-American descent) care deeply about education. They cared so deeply, in fact, that in the early 1970s they burdened themselves with one of the highest proportions of bonded indebtedness in the greater San Antonio region to pay for capital improvements and for a quality education for their children.[48] The residents of Edgewood voted to pay high local taxes in order to support their children.[49]

Not far from the Edgewood school district—just about ten miles across the city—is Alamo Heights school district. In the late 1960s, Alamo Heights was the most affluent school district in San Antonio. The Alamo Heights schools were situated in a residential community quite unlike the Edgewood District. Family income in Edgewood was less than half the family income in Alamo Heights. Property values were roughly six times higher in Alamo Heights. Tax rates were far *lower* in Alamo Heights—but the Alamo students enjoyed a per-student spending rate that was *twice* as high as the per-student spending rate in Edgewood.[50] The amount of funding shaped every aspect of these schools—from the actual learning space and conditions, to student-to-teacher ratios, to books, to counseling services, and even dropout rates were dramatically different.[51] The conditions for success were stacked in favor of the students who attended Alamo Heights.

On May 16, 1968, the students at Edgewood High School walked out of their classes in protest. The students marched to the district administration office demanding that a list of grievances—ranging from insufficient supplies to the lack of qualified teachers—be addressed. In the following weeks, Demetrio P. Rodriguez, a San Antonio sheet metal worker, and other parents from Edgewood filed a federal lawsuit challenging the fairness of the Texas school finance system.[52]

Rodriguez and the other parents considered their lawsuit to be the next step toward equality in American education. Financial disparities in school funding prevented Edgewood students from receiving the opportunity for an education on "equal terms." Demetrio Rodriguez's suit claimed that the Texas system of financing education discriminated against students in low-wealth districts.[53] Rodriguez's lawyers argued that the Texas system of finance led to better education for students in wealthier school districts and worse education for students in poorer districts and thus a violation of the equal protection clause in the Fourteenth Amendment to the U.S. Constitution.[54] The case made its way to the United States Supreme Court in March 1973. The Court agreed that students in poor districts received an inferior level of education compared to the students who lived in wealthy school districts.[55] However, the Court's ruling stated that a state's system of school finance must be judged on the individual state's constitution rather than the U.S. Constitution.[56] The Court ruled that there is not a right to equal funding in education under the U.S. Constitution.[57] In a strong dissenting opinion, Justice Thurgood Marshall wrote, "I cannot accept such an emasculation of the Equal Protection Clause in the context of this case."[58]

The Supreme Court's opinion encouraged Texas legislators to create a more equitable system, which the Court did not mandate.[59] Determined, the parents and families of Edgewood continued their legal fight in the Texas State courts.[60] After years of litigation, on October 2, 1989, the Texas Supreme Court declared the Texas public school finance system to be unconstitutional (stating that it violated the Texas Constitution) by a vote of 9–0. The Court ordered the Texas Legislature to completely overhaul the public finance system by May 1, 1990.

UNDERSTANDING THE FORMULAE

In 1989, Texas leaders (and freshman Senator Ratliff) knew that a decision from the Texas Supreme Court in the Edgewood case was imminent. Wanting to be prepared, Ratliff began doing his homework.[61] In the months before the Texas Supreme Court's final decision he began gathering facts, figures, and studying the complexities of the problem. He plugged the entire public school finance system into his laptop.[62] He needed to know how it all worked and whose interests were at stake. Ratliff met behind closed doors with teachers. He also met with public school administrators and board members—the press was not welcome in many of these meetings so that everyone could speak candidly.[63] Bill later wrote, "In my first term, the major challenge before the legislature was (as is still the case today) the unconstitutional school system. When I was first elected, I decided that, as an engineer, I could study the system and try to understand the various formulae."[64] Well before the Court's decision in October, Ratliff was prepared with a rough statistical model on which he could run many new funding plans.[65] Being prepared and doing the hard work of study and understanding opened the doors of opportunity for Senator Ratliff. He soon took a central and critical role in the statewide public school finance debate.

The Legislature Fails, 1990–1991

Governor Bill Clements opened the 71st session with the "State of the State" address in which he endorsed proposals affecting public education spending, college tuition, the expansion of the University of Texas into South Texas, and bonds to support the building of new educational space across the state. Senator Ratliff said that he supported the governor's call for a $39 million education incentive package aimed at lowering the dropout rate.[66] But the question was—as is always the question—how to pay for it? Governor Clements was opposed to any new taxes. In fact, while the Governor wanted to cut taxes, Ratliff was open to exploring all options. "A lottery won't create enough money," Ratliff said, "an income tax would, but either would take two to three years to get off the ground."[67] In the problem, the engineer saw an opportunity, "We are not talking particularly about just school finance so much as we are about school reform. On the theory that if we could remove a lot of the extraneous rules from schools, the same amount of money could go further."[68] At the end of Ratliff's first session, as promised, Bill Hobby and Bill

Clements both retired. New leadership inherited the quagmire of public school finance.

In 1990, the Republicans nominated rancher Clayton W. Williams Jr., for governor and the Democrats nominated Ann Richards. Richards narrowly defeated Williams on November 6, 1990, by a margin of 49 to 47 percent.[69] However, Governor Richards, Lt. Governor Bob Bullock, and Senator Carl Parker, who had chaired the Senate Education Committee for many years, were unable to create or pass a funding system which met the Texas Supreme Court's approval. The Texas legislature was not willing, or was perhaps unable to make the bold structural changes required to meet the approval of the Court. The Court ruled that the 1990 and 1991 Texas legislative attempts to reform the public school finance system were unconstitutional. Ratliff's first term came to an end and he faced his first reelection challenge.

AIKIN CHALLENGES RATLIFF

In 1992, Senator A.M. Aikin's son, Bobby, decided to challenge Senator Ratliff for the seat his father had held for forty-four years. By 1992, Bobby Aikin had served one term in the Texas House from 1987 to 1989[70]—in the 70th Legislature—one year before Ratliff was elected to the Senate.[71] In Texas House Resolution No. 91, from the summer of 1989 is a humorous glimpse into Bobby Aikin's life. His forty-first birthday, on July 12, fell during a special session that summer. The Texas House passed Resolution 91 to mark the occasion.

House Resolution No. 91

> WHEREAS, On Sunday, July 12th A.M. Aikin III, State Representative at Large and scion of the merchant princes of Paris, celebrated his 41st birthday in a clandestine bash catered by St. Nick; and
> WHEREAS, A.M.'s poor but honest parents could not afford to provide him with names, and he was forced to get by with mere initials; and
> WHEREAS, He is now known affectionately (or so we think) as Bobby Aikin; and
> WHEREAS, Bobby was bred to his work like a fine Arabian stallion (or, for that matter, like a mean ol' stump-pullin mule), as a son of the legendary Senator A.M. Aikin, and as a former senate mascot; and
> WHEREAS, Bobby is living proof that the legislature was wise to multiply Gilmer-Aikin by H.B. 72; and
> WHEREAS, His training and background have equipped him with the rare ability to schedule eight simultaneous meetings in the three widely separated locations without missing a beat; and
> WHEREAS, Bobby Aikin sacrificed a promising career in show business as Ed Sullivan's straight man to serve the people of this great state; now therefore be it

RESOLVED by the honorable House, That his hair remain fluffy and his shoes be retired to a home for aged footgear, and (in the language of those Star Treks to which he makes constant and aggravating reference) may he Live Long and Prosper.
Written by Rep. Paul Michael Colbert.[72]

A State Income Tax?

Name recognition alone would help Bobby Aikin in Senate District 1. He easily won the Democratic primary defeating Steve Gamble (Aikin 70 percent, Gamble 30 percent). Aikin then went directly after Ratliff on the school funding issue and the state income tax issue. Ratliff had not proposed a state income tax but only mentioned it as one of the several options for increased school funding. As the campaign heated, Ratliff repeated, "I could almost play you a tape, I've said it so many times before, that the legislature would never mandate a personal income tax and I will never vote for one. If a state income tax is chosen in place of a property tax, then that decision will come from the people of Texas."[73]

Responding to charges leveled by Aikin that Ratliff wanted a state income tax, the Ratliff campaign produced a tape of an April 1991 testimony when Bobby Aikin, as a member of the State Board of Education, indicated to the Senate Finance Committee that he would support an income tax for public education. "Bobby's big whopper is that I have supported a personal income tax in Texas," Ratliff said, "I will never vote for a personal income tax. That remains my position. I've said that Legislature will never vote for it, that if one is ever enacted, the people will have to vote for it."[74] Ratliff did acknowledge that property, sales, and business taxes could not be raised enough to adequately fund Texas public schools and that the people may someday have to decide whether an income tax is needed.[75] Looking for solutions, Ratliff thought it interesting that Aikin was criticizing the current taxation and funding of public schools without any of his own clear solutions.

"Bill is desperately trying to run from his record," Aikin said, "Ratliff says he's against a personal income tax and that the only way we would have it is if the people of Texas voted for it. But the only way the public will have a vote to pass an income tax is if the Legislature and Bill Ratliff vote to put it on the ballot. As a state representative, I voted for the opposite. I voted to put on the ballot a constitutional ban on personal income tax. I'll protect you from an income tax; he'll consider a personal income tax. Those are our positions."[76]

"In Bobby Aikin's case, it also happens to be hypocritical because on April 8, 1991, under sworn testimony before the Senate Finance Committee, Aikin said the only way to finance needed public school programs was a person income tax," Ratliff responded, "Aikin went on to say that he and a majority of the State Board of Education would support an income tax for that purpose."[77] The people of Texas are generally not supportive of taxes and this debate reflects those values.

You're the First Republican I Ever Voted For

Don Edmonds who was again heading the Ratliff campaign later wrote, "After the first election Bill was congratulated by numerous Democrat regulars who admitted, "you're the first Republican I ever voted for in my life."[78] "Now in 1992, we're convinced that Bill's re-election bid requires an ongoing and expanded appeal to Democrats and Independents."[79]

Two significant factors worked in Ratliff's favor and against Bobby Aikin. First, the differences between the Republicans and Democrats no longer appeared clear to the voters of East Texas.[80] Ratliff had shown himself to be a free-thinking, independent Republican who looked at all sides of issues before coming to a conclusion. Second, the GOP was beginning to make some significant gains across Texas in the early 1990's. In 1990, for example, the Republicans won three important statewide races. Republican Rick Perry was a surprise victor in the race for Agriculture Commissioner, Kay Bailey Hutchison won the post of State Treasurer, and John Cornyn was elected to the Texas Supreme Court.[81] It was fast becoming difficult for Democrats to be elected in Texas—even Democrats with the last name Aikin. The July 20, 1992, *Kilgore News Herald* headline told the story, "Democrats endorse Ratliff."[82]

Ratliff was also endorsed in his bid for reelection by two very prominent Democrats. The recently retired, Lt Governor Bill Hobby and former District 1 State Sen. Ed Howard wrote, "When Bill talks, the Senate (on both sides of the aisle) listens. Bill Ratliff always does his homework on the issues and is a no-nonsense leader."[83] Ratliff said, "It is very gratifying to have two such well-known and respected Democrats as Bill Hobby and Ed Howard endorse my performance in the Texas Senate. I am extremely pleased to have the support of these two men."[84] Senator Phil Gramm, a Republican, also endorsed the incumbent Ratliff.

In August 1992, the Republican Party held its National Convention in the Astrodome in Houston, Texas. The convention nominated President George H. W. Bush, and Vice President Dan Quayle for reelection.[85] Sally and Bill attended the Convention. Bill later wrote about Barbara Bush's speech at the Convention, "What struck me perhaps the strongest was the picture she painted of the president. She was telling us that 'you can't be one kind of a man and another kind of president,' and I think that kind of sets the tone for the election—does for me anyway."[86] Barbara Bush's husband ran against two other major candidates: Democratic Arkansas Governor Bill Clinton, and an independent Texas businessman, Ross Perot.[87] Both Bill Clinton and Bill Ratliff won on November 3, 1992. Forty-eight percent of the voters in District 1 supported Bobby Aikin while

Ratliff won with 52 percent of the 200,760 citizens who voted in that election.[88]

LIEUTENANT GOVERNOR BOB BULLOCK

Once back in Austin, Ratliff was appointed chairman of the Senate Education Committee by Lt. Governor Bob Bullock. As Bill Hobby prepared to step into retirement he held a series of meetings with Bob Bullock. In those discussions, Hobby told Bullock that Bill Ratliff was knowledgeable about school finance.[89] So, in the summer approaching the 1993 session, Bullock reached out to the Republican from Mt. Pleasant, indicating that he wanted Ratliff to chair the Education Committee.[90]

Bullock was by then a notorious politician. When Bullock died his obituary in the *New York Times* would described him as "the last of the earthy, string-pulling, hard-living political giants who used to sprout in Texas. Blunt, mercurial and often fearsome, Mr. Bullock, a Democrat, was an iron spine wrapped in a drawl. He had been at the center of Texas politics for forty years and dominated many of them, particularly in his two terms as lieutenant governor beginning in 1990."[91]

In 1992, Bullock traveled to New Boston, Texas, to help support the Democrats for Ratliff in the campaign against Bobby Aikin. Afterward Bullock sent a handwritten note to Sally Ratliff.

> Dear Sally,
> Jan and I were truly honored to be with you and Bill in New Boston.
> Sally, without the love, support, and dedication of our families, Bill and I would not be able to serve in public office. No one knows better than I the sacrifices that you and your family have made. Bill and I are truly blessed with beautiful families.
> Again, thank you and I look forward to seeing you both in Austin next month.
> With warmest regards, I am
> Sincerely,
> Bob[92]

Texas Governor George W. Bush later said, "Bob Bullock was the largest Texan of our time."[93] Bill Ratliff described Bob Bullock as "every bit the mercurial and cantankerous public figure that his reputation painted him. His management style was the exact opposite of Hobby's in that he tried to micromanage all the legislation coming through the Senate. That is, he tried to do so until, after about two sessions, he learned that he simply could not do so."[94]

In 1990, Robert "Bob" Douglas Bullock was easily elected lieutenant governor and succeeded the retiring Bill Hobby on January 8, 1991.[95] "As lieutenant governor, colleagues remembered, Mr. Bullock played the legislature like a steel guitar, threatening, cajoling, keeping encyclopedic track of every important piece of legislation, handing out favors, with-holding others and generally presiding over the whole messy affair like a circus ringmaster."[96]

According to Ratliff, Bullock was not quite the ringmaster in his first few sessions.[97] Ratliff recalled Bullock's first session in the Senate, "when Bullock was first elected, he 'busted' all the Republican chairmen, and ran the Senate in a totally partisan manner. However, after his first session, he found that he needed lieutenants chairing the committees and managing the floor debates and he needed some of the Republicans to make the body function."[98] Learning from his mistakes, "Bullock," Ratliff said, "then became the bipartisan lt. governor that history is now painting him."[99] In the first months of the 1992 session, Bullock had a distant relationship with Ratliff. Bullock kept their relationship "very much at arm's length" until he realized that he had to have the support of at least some Republicans in order to make the Senate function.[100] Bullock was also facing the very difficult and daunting task of meeting the State Supreme Court's school finance demand.

Ratliff wrote, "Even in his later years, Bullock attempted (and mostly succeeded) to manage the Senate by intimidation. His temper was legend, and the public temper was not nearly as volcanic as the one he would exhibit behind closed doors. However, I discovered that Bullock's temper was a tool that he used, and not simply a volatile personality."[101]

A Drive-By Ass Chewing

During the 1993 session, Ratliff was working fourteen-hour days trying to gather all the input and soliciting all the ideas he could to develop an education funding system that would meet the Texas Supreme Court's criteria. One day not long into the session, Bullock called Ratliff into the spacious lt. governor's office. Ratliff described the meeting, "he gave me (as Senator David Sibley once described) a 'drive-by ass chewing.' I don't know what the subject was, but I know it was the first time I had ever been subjected to such a tirade."[102] The senator was not willing to accept such abuse.

"When I left his office," Ratliff said, "I went to find Senator Bob Glasgow (considered to be Bullocks top lieutenant at the time) and I told Glasgow that he could deliver a message to the lt. governor for me. He could tell Bullock that I was fifty-plus years old. That I would 'bust my butt' trying to accomplish whatever was needed, but that if he ever wanted me to work with him in the future, I would never be talked to in that fashion again. From that time forward, he never raised his voice to me, nor was I ever again subjected to one of his temper fits."[103]

Many people over the years were victims of Bullock's drive-by ass chewing.[104] This episode convinced Ratliff "that Bullock was totally able to contain his temper when it suited him, and he was totally capable of unleashing it as a tool whenever he decided to do so."[105] By the time Bullock retired, he and the Republican senator from East Texas had become good friends.[106]

OX IN THE DITCH

Bill was not sure he was the person for the Herculean task of overhauling the Texas public school finance system. "I explained," said Ratliff, "to Bullock that I didn't know anything about the public school system in Texas (other than that I had gone through it as a student) and didn't think I was the person to chair Education."[107] Bullock replied, "Bill, that finance system is the ox in the ditch, and you have to take the job and fix it."[108] Ratliff took on the job.

In fact, in 1993, Bob Bullock stacked the Senate Education Committee with a number of very knowledgeable leaders. The *Dallas Morning News* once described senators Bivins, Sibley, and Ratliff as the "College of Cardinals" in the Texas Senate. Ratliff would explain, "that was because, with the possible addition of Senator John Montford, we were the three to whom Bullock turned for solutions to the state's problems."[109] All four senators of the "College of Cardinals" were on the Education Committee of 1993.[110]

The General Diffusion of Knowledge

The Texas State Constitution provided for the establishment of a system of efficient and free schools. In Article 7, Section 1 of the Texas Constitution required, "Support and Maintenance of System of Public Free Schools: A general diffusion of knowledge being essential to the preservation of the liberties and rights of the people, it shall be the duty of the legislature of the state to establish and make suitable provision for the support and maintenance of an efficient system of public free schools."[111] In 1989 the Texas Supreme Court focused on that section of the Texas Constitution in its ruling in *Edgewood ISD v. Kirby*.[112] The Court found that the school finance system violated the Texas Constitution.[113]

The Texas Senate Education Committee 1993

Bill Ratliff (R), Chair

Bill Haley (D) , Vice Chair	Gonzalo Barrientos (D)
Chris Harris (R)	Teel Bivins (R)
John T. Montford (D)	Gregory Luna (D)
David Sibley (R)	Florence Shapiro (R)
Judith Zaffirini (D)	Jim Turner (D)

The financing system was not efficient and it failed to deliver a general diffusion of knowledge. The Court ruled that the legislature had a constitutional mandate to create an efficient system.[114] After two failed attempts at creating a solution to the public school finance problem, Ratliff and the Senate Education Committee tackled the problem again in the Spring 1993. Bill Ratliff did not intend to become the champion and the central architect of public school finance—but he did. The issue found him and he accepted the challenge. The Texas Supreme Court placed a clear expectation on the legislative leaders of Texas—the court ordered the legislature to devise a new plan by June 1, 1993.[115] "The judge hung a sword over everybody's head and said, 'okay guys, work this out,'" said Ratliff.[116]

Ratliff knew that Senator Aikin's public education finance code was in need of a complete overhaul and so he met with state leaders, school administrators, teachers, parents, and even students. He gave speeches all across the state saying, "Because of the constraints placed on the legislature by the Texas Constitution (as interpreted by the Texas Supreme Court), there are only two types of solutions available to us. We must either pass a constitutional amendment removing the Supreme Court from the equation, or we must provide for a redistribution of funds from the haves to the have-nots."[117]

Ratliff did not think removing the Court from the process was in the best long-term interest of the citizens of Texas. He argued, "many members of the legislature agree with the Court that the current system of financing schools is unfair, there is insufficient support for an amendment to the Texas Constitution limiting the Court's authority. Also, protecting the role of the courts is in all of our interests."[118]

The engineer considered all alternatives—even taxes. Ratliff argued that a statewide property tax would require a constitutional amendment, which he believed Texas voters would not ratify. He dismissed the adoption of a state personal income tax saying "it is widely believed that Texans are against such a tax at this time."[119] He was also opposed to an increase in the sales tax. Ratliff said, "an enormous increase in the sales tax would be required to meet the need of the poor schools—the Texas sales tax rate is already among the nation's highest—and would have to be raised from 8.25 percent to at least 11 percent."[120]

Some were calling for a "massive consolidation of school districts." Ratliff did not think that would be a real solution either, "consolidating school districts," Ratliff indicated, "would more equally distribute wealth between poor and rich districts, but it would also lead to the creation of some huge, inefficient mega-districts."[121] Ratliff argued that there must be a redistribution of funds from the wealthy to the not-so-wealthy. He told the Longview City Council, "While some of these methods are more deserving of the 'Robin Hood' label than others, they are all simply different approaches to sharing the wealth."[122]

Senate Bill 7 — 1993

State District Judge Scott McCown, in whose court the lawsuit originated, made it very clear that if the legislature did not adopt a constitutional plan for school funding by June 1, 1993, he would cut off school funding. Ratliff said, "It is unthinkable that the great state of Texas would allow its schools to close. We cannot afford to be viewed as a kind of third-world country, unable to set aside individual self-interest for the greater common good of the state and its children."[123]

Governor Ann Richards, lt. Governor Bob Bullock, Speaker Gib Lewis, and Senate Education Chair Bill Ratliff were all collectively in the hot seat. The engineer from East Texas went to work on creating a solution. The draft of a bill originates in one of two ways: either a legislator personally drafts it or has it written by the professional staff of the office of the Texas Legislative Council.[124] SB 7 was received by the Secretary of the Senate on January 19, 1993. Ratliff's solution for the children of Texas was written in 21,764 words and was sixty-nine pages long.

Ratliff and the Education Committee held hearings on the bill from May 3 to May 11, 1993.[125] Republicans in both the House and the Senate said that they would not support any plan that redistributed property taxes. Ratliff insisted that some property tax income must be redistributed for the state to erase spending differences among districts and to have a constitutional funding system. "As I have presented my proposal for addressing the public school funding crisis, there has been no shortage of critics. Unfortunately, few of those criticizing have presented a workable alternative. Most have proposed only vague notions of 'restructuring the tax system' or have simply suggested, 'there had to be a better way.'"[126]

About midway through the session," Ratliff said, "when many ideas had been floated and rejected in an attempt to fulfill this charge, the idea of 'recapture' (not too fondly branded 'Robin Hood' by the wealthy districts) was brought forward."[127] After weeks of public testimony and private meetings, Ratliff reached out for "input from every legal expert we could call upon."[128] After several amendments and weeks of more public hearings in late May, the legislature passed Ratliff's Senate Bill 7 and Governor Ann Richards signed the bill into law on May 31, 1993. The Robin Hood law required school districts above a certain wealth level to transfer fund to poorer school districts. The law, which is still in effect today, gives property-wealthy school districts several options for sharing local property tax revenue with poor districts. In short, the Texas Education Code now requires wealthy school districts to share their wealth with school districts that are poor. In 1995, the justices on the Texas Supreme Court held SB 7 to be constitutional.[129] The system of public school finance was finally deemed to be efficient both financially and in providing for the "general diffusion of knowledge" for the children of

Texas. The Robin Hood law has been continuously challenged in Texas courts since 1993.[130] Many people who live in wealthy school districts, that spend lavishly to educate their children, argue that the Robin Hood law is wrong.

Like the Gilmer-Aikin laws, the Robin Hood law came to have a long-term impact on Texas schoolchildren. However, Senator Ratliff well understood that as a representative of the people he was responsible to and for all of the people in his district. That made the Robin Hood law difficult to celebrate. Ratliff said, "Few people realize that in the 1st District, 81 percent of the students are classified as poor—that is less than average wealth per student. That's a higher percentage than in the valley. What that means is that the Robin Hood redistribution of school money is going to benefit most the school districts in the 1st District. Again, however, it's a little hard to take too much advantage of—because the four or five school districts that are wealthy [in District 1] suffer under Robin Hood and they hold a higher percentage of my supporters than do the others; so it's difficult to take much credit for helping the poor districts through Robin Hood without running the risk of major downside in the wealthier districts of the 1st Senate District."[131]

The Robin Hood legislation received a great deal of press and criticism. "With all of the bad PR that Robin Hood has gotten. I am very proud of the Senate Education Committee for facing up to the fact that they needed to do this," Ratliff added, "When these critics have come forward with a plan and have provided enough details to evaluate it, those plans have inevitably fallen victim to the same limitations, either constitutional or political, which we have been battling for years. This is not surprising since the options open to the legislature are very limited."

PENNIES FOR THOMAS

After working long days in the Senate, Bill and Sally arrived late to their Austin apartment. The senator from District 1 would often have trouble sleeping. As the Chair of Education and later as Chair of Senate Finance Committee, Bill worried about finding funding for schoolchildren all across the state. He later said, "it's not a matter who deserves the funding, but rather who doesn't get funding."[132] Unable to sleep, he would walk the floors into the small hours of the night. Sally would wake up to find the Senator tapping away on his laptop or working with pencil and paper. One night, Sally asked, "it's late, what are you so focused on," Bill replied, "I have to find pennies for Thomas." The senator was "trying to determine how he was going to fund programs for children with special needs—like their grandson, Thomas."[133] However, even with the success of SB 7, Senator Ratliff was not yet finished with reestablishing the Gilmer-Aikin public school system. He had succeeded in creating a finance

system that was more equitable but the forty-five-year-old Texas education code was in dire need of a complete overhaul.

SENATE BILL 1—THE RATLIFF-SADLER ACT 1995

At the close of the 1995 Legislative session *Texas Monthly* declared, "Her-
cules slew the Hydra, cleaned the Augean stables, and brought back
Cerberus from the underworld. Big deal. Bill Ratliff and Paul Sadler rewrote Texas education laws from top to bottom, slew the stand-pat special interest groups, cleaned stultifying state regulations from the books,
and—maybe, just maybe—found a way to bring public schools back from
the dead."[134] All that success began just after the passage of the Robin
Hood legislation. In the months after the 1993 session and passage of SB
7, Ratliff went to Bullock and told him that they needed to look at the
entire education code because, "having had to work deeply within it, I
felt it was a mess."[135] Bullock agreed and he and Speaker Pete Laney
appointed a joint interim committee [co-chaired by Rep. Elizabeth Ann
"Libby" Linebarger (D-San Marcos)] to look into the code (other than
finance).[136] This interim committee held hearings all over the state, asking for and receiving input from all segments of the public on things
needed and things not needed in the Texas education code.[137]

The Texas Commissioner of Education, Dr. Lionel "Skip" Meno,
brought an issue to the attention of the interim committee. Meno argued
that because the legislature was not getting the satisfactory results from
Texas schools it had resorted to micromanaging the schools of the state
by the Texas education code.[138] Furthermore, since the previous session
the legislature had adopted an accountability system, the legislature
should be able to stop its top-down style of oversight, and simply judge
the school system by its results.[139] Meno presented the committee with a
simple test for items contained in the education code. First the state
should establish *what* public school students should know, and when
they should know it. Second, the local school districts should be held
accountable for reaching those results. Using Commissioner Meno's simple test, Ratliff "began to scrutinize the code."[140] "In shorthand," said
Ratliff, "the state would establish the 'what and when' and the local
districts should be free to establish the 'how.'"[141]

In the fall of 1993, while the interim committee held statewide hearings, George W. Bush won the election for Texas governor beating
Governor Ann Richards with 54 percent to 46 percent of the vote.[142]
Governor Bush had developed some positions on education for which he
wanted to advocate, and Ratliff's committee received input from the
Bush educational advisors. "Although," Ratliff said, "he only had a few
matters on which he pressed and was, for the most part, simply supportive of the committee's overall efforts."[143]

After holding hearings in the fall of 1993 and through the summer of 1994, Bill took the hearing materials and transcripts home with him to Mt. Pleasant over the 1994 Thanksgiving holidays. Before leaving Austin, he downloaded the education code on his Apple laptop. "The code was so large and my little Apple was so limited in space, I had to break it down into 3 or 4 files."[144]

While Sally and all of the family bustled about during the holiday, Bill began to page through the massive education code line-by-line, page-by-page, and section-by-section, applying Commissioner Meno's "what, when, and how" test.[145] "When I came upon a section or subsection which did not meet the test, I would strike through that section. When I recalled testimony with which I agreed about a need for additional code guidance, I would look through the materials for information on that item and then add that feature in underline. I went through the entire code in this manner. There were also many times where I felt that the structure (location of items) of the code did not make sense, and I would make changes in that structure."[146] "Sally," Bill would later say, "has never quite forgiven me for spending the entire holiday holed up on the Apple."[147] At the end of the Thanksgiving holidays Ratliff took the new draft of the education code to his committee staff and had them go through and make editing corrections as well as suggestions as to structure and, at times, as to substance.[148] This 1,100-plus-page draft then was taken to the Legislative Council for final drafting.[149] Thus, Ratliff rewrote the basic education laws Senator Aikin had drafted some forty-five years earlier. "The document was not the usual hodgepodge of recommendations designed to appease particular interests ("He kinda ignored us all equally," said one education lobbyist)."[150]

Next the bill went for approval by the full Senate and the House. Speaker Pete Laney turned to Paul Sadler to get SB 1 to the floor of the House and approved. Paul Sadler (D-Henderson) had first won a seat in the Texas House of Representatives in 1990 and represented the East Texas district in and around Henderson. For eight years he chaired the House Public Education Committee. Sadler had long been a champion of Texas public schools and teachers. In one session he fought for a teacher pay raise when he met resistance, Sadler said to the Texas House, "I ask the question, when will we stand up and do what is right for education in this state. For what group of children will we answer that question? For mine? For yours? For our grandchildren?"[151] With Sadler's help in the House, SB 1 was signed by Governor Bush on May 30, 1995. Bill later remarked, "Sometimes it is easier to pass a massive bill because the members look at the size and just throw up their hands. In such a case, I think they tend to look at the author and give him/her the benefit of the doubt."[152] Senator Ratliff not only worked to bring quality education to Texas children but also to college students.

SENATOR RATLIFF'S "FUNDING FORMULA"

Enrollments grew rapidly when Senator Aikin's postwar baby boom children reached college campuses in the 1960s. In 1965, to coordinate and meet this growing demand, Governor John Connally and the Texas Legislature established a coordinating board with certain regulatory powers.[153] The mission of the Texas Higher Education Coordinating Board (THECB) is to coordinate the complex system of higher education in Texas. It struggled against regional political power in trying to achieve its mission. As a part of that overall coordinating effort the board developed a formula funding system used to allocate state funds to Texas colleges and universities. Indeed, Governor Connally hoped that the Coordinating Board would take some of the politics out of the higher education funding process.[154] Until 1965, funding for colleges and universities in Texas was not planned or even coordinated across the state but rather left to legislative action or inaction on behalf of individual institutions. The Coordinating Board formulas were intended to fairly distribute funding across the state and to place it where it was needed. Over time those formulas became increasing complex and unwieldy.

By 1990s, there were more than a dozen different funding formulas used in appropriating funds to colleges and universities, including four separate formulas used to pay for facilities operations and maintenance. Recognizing significant problems and weaknesses in those formulas, Senator Ratliff, as chair of the Senate Education Committee took up the task of simplifying and reducing the number of formulas. In 1997, with the help of Coordinating Board staff, Ratliff rewrote, significantly reduced, and re-created the funding formulas to promote efficiency, fairness, and other priorities in Texas higher education.[155] For example, Ratliff's legislation included a formula which allocates more funding to an institution when a class is taught by a full-time terminally degreed professor rather than a teaching assistant. Senator Ratliff's "funding formula" is, as one would expect from an engineer, a mathematical relationship between different types of educational activities and the necessary resources required for those activities.[156] For example, it does not cost as much to teach Texas government as it does to teach Biology. Much like the public school funding, there were some institutions that did not fare as well as others under the new formula. For the most part, the higher education institutions that did not fare as well were the larger ones that, because of their disproportionate legislative and/or alumni influence, were doing far better than most other colleges and universities under the previous funding system. In 2016, with only small adjustments here and there, the formula and funding methodology Senator Ratliff wrote in 1997 has not been significantly changed. The methodology has stood the test of time.

I Knew from the Beginning That It Was a Bad Model

Governor Connally also charged the Coordinating Board with over-seeing the development of new colleges and programs across the entire State. Community leaders and college administrators have many different reasons for promoting the establishment of new institutions and new programs. Sometimes those reasons are at odds with larger State interests. The East Texas community of Tyler provides an excellent example. Community leaders in Tyler sought to establish an institution in opposition to what many argued was best for the overall state.

As the demand for higher education grew, in 1971, Senator Peyton McKnight (D-Tyler),[157] and other community leaders, founded Tyler State College in East Texas. At that time two other, long-established institutions, Tyler Junior College (founded in 1926), and Stephen F. Austin State University (founded in 1923), served the East Texas community. To get the legislation passed, Senator McKnight promised his colleagues in the legislature and State leaders that the new college would never become a four-year institution.[158] Instead, he said, it would only serve upper division (junior and senior) and graduate students. The new institution, McKnight said, would not ever compete with either Tyler Junior College or Stephen F. Austin State University. Tyler State College held its very first graduation on May 14, 1974. Introduced by Senator McKnight, Senator Aikin, the father of modern Texas education, delivered a stirring commencement address about equality and opportunity in Texas education. The college was renamed Texas Eastern University the following year and again renamed the University of Texas at Tyler, in 1979 when it joined the University of Texas System.

In the early 1990s, Senator McKnight's promise that the institution would never compete with other regional institutions became a hotly debated topic when Tyler community leaders sought to expand the campus to include freshmen and sophomore students. The change in the University of Texas at Tyler's mission and downward expansion of the campus divided leaders all across the region and State.[159] Regional community and academic leaders including Stephen F. Austin State University president, Dr. William R. Johnson,[160] and Tyler Junior College president, Dr. Raymond Hawkins, voiced strong opposition to both the model[161] (only serving junior and senior students) and later to downward expansion of the the University of Texas at Tyler.[162] UT Tyler's model of serving only upper division students was not sustainable. President Johnson later said, "I knew from the beginning that it was a bad model."[163]

In 1992, Senator Ratliff believed he should not violate Senator McKnight's promise. "I think politicians have enough problems with credibility without going around reneging on promises just because I am not the one who made it."[164] However, over time, Senator Ratliff was persuaded by the rationale used by Tyler leaders and University of Texas administrators to support the expansion. "Their argument is that expansion will attract economic development to the area and that they need a four-year higher education institution that can offer four-year degrees in engineering and sciences," Ratliff said.[165] With area community leaders, UT Tyler's president, Dr. George Hamm, and Tyler Junior Colleges' president Hawkins, all in agreement, Senator Ratliff sponsored Ted Kamel's (R-Tyler) House bill which allowed the University of Texas at Tyler and Tyler Junior College to create a partnership and for the University of Texas at Tyler to become a full four-year institution. On May 21, 1997, Governor George W. Bush signed the bill into law authorizing the the University of Texas at Tyler to expand to include freshmen and sophomore students. In 1999–2000, the University of Texas at Tyler admitted its first class of freshman students. In 2006, the the University of Texas at Tyler celebrated the opening of the Bill Ratliff Engineering and Sciences Complex.

ROBIN HOOD

Ratliff later said, "Probably the most dramatic accomplishment of my public service career came while I was chair of the Senate Education Committee. I truly believe that work will impact generations of Texans."[166] Ratliff also sought a quality and equal education for Texas children. The people of the United States have long supported the value of equality. In the United States all people are said to have an equal opportunity to become successful—to live their individual American dreams—or not. Americans do not generally support the notion that there should be an equality of results. The spirit of equal opportunity includes the notion of fairness. It was not possible to look objectively at the school districts across the state of Texas and say that all Texas children had an equal—or even nearly equal—opportunity at the American dream. Ratliff saw this clearly and sought to create a fair—or at least a fairer—system. Guided by the principle of fairness and the value of equality, Ratliff asked, "What is a minimum education, a basic education, or quality education? Who defines the terms? Is the quality of education based solely on dollars and cents? These are good questions, and we need some good answers to go with those questions. Is every child in Texas entitled to an equal, minimum education, or a quality education? Most people would say 'a quality education'—but then who pays for that quality education?"[167]

Senator Bill Ratliff fought for those who were not able to fight for themselves. He fought for "pennies" for schoolchildren.[168] He fought for those who had no power or voice—because it was the right thing to do—even if that meant losing major supporters. He fought for children and for the poor in the deep backwoods of East Texas. He worked hard for fairness and a more equal shot at opportunity in life for all Texas children. So it is only fitting that Ratliff's critics dubbed him and still today call him "Robin Hood."[169] There are many different stories about the legendary Robin Hood, but they all share a similar theme of fairness, righting of wrongs, and justice. In the ballads, books, and movies about Robin Hood and his merry band are men of principle and are seen acting within a very strict set of rules governing their behavior. They fight only for just causes. They always fight fair and deal honorably and respectfully with their opponents. They refuse to take advantage of their opponent's weaknesses. While they do indeed steal from the wealthy—it is not for self-gain—but for the poor. Bill Ratliff's work (SB 1 and SB 7) earned him this nickname and that work continues to shape the decades-long battle between the rich and the poor of the state of Texas. Many are troubled by the effect of the Robin Hood legislation and have criticized the Republican from East Texas for not being true to his party. But, perhaps like the legendary Robin Hood, Ratliff held to a higher authority— the principles of integrity and fairness. *Texas Monthly* exclaimed that Senator Ratliff was "a totally free man, free to act as every senator should, but few actually do."[170] Ratliff shouldered the difficult task of writing a fair law. It is certainly not a law that pleased all nor is it a perfect law but it was written by a "totally free man" who wrote it to improve the lives of those he served. As Herculean as the education law tasks were, the challenges yet to come were even greater; perhaps because they were challenges to his core principles and ethics.

NOTES

1. Reported by Debbie Graves in the Longview News Journal (February 3, 1989),
2. See: Carlos Flores Truan (http://www.cemetery.state.tx.us/pub/user_form.asp?step=1&pers_id=7137).
3. See Black Women in Texas History, 2008. In 1989, Johnson was chairing a special committee studying the feasibility of establishing a state-supported institution on the site of the former Bishop College. Bishop College was a historically black college that had closed the year before when a financial scandal caused it to lose accreditation.
4. Ibid.
5. The Texarkana Gazette's Melanie Poppiewell July 4, 1989.
6. Bills authored counted on Texas Legislature Online (http://www.capitol.state.tx.us/Members/MemberInfo.aspx?Leg=71&Chamber=S&Code=A1480)
7. Ibid.
8. Interview with Bill Ratliff 2013.
9. Ibid.
10. Interviews with Bill Ratliff 2013, 2014, and 2015.
11. Interview with Ratliff February 2016.
12. 20 Sessions: A brief history of every Legislature we've ever covered. July 2011 by Paul Burka and Nate Blakeslee Texas Monthly (http://www.texasmonthly.com/politics/20-sessions/).
13. Email from Bill Ratliff January 2016.

14. Interview with Jack Ratliff 2014.

15. Ibid.

16. Obituary (http://www.legacy.com/obituaries/lubbockonline/obituary.aspx?pid=168130484).

17. The House Will Come to Order: How the Texas Speaker Became a Power in State A Power in State and National Politics by Patrick L. Cox, Michael Phillips page 56.

18. Legislative Reference Library Texas Legislators: Past & Present A.M. Aikin, Jr. (http://www.lrl.state.tx.us/mobile/memberDisplay.cfm?memberID=350).

19. Ibid.

20. A.M. Aikin, Longest Tenured In Texas Legislature, Is Dead, New York Times October 26, 1981

21. Obituary of 'Bob' Aikin Jun 15, 2012 (http://www.heraldbanner.com/obituaries/bob-aikin/article_de764a90-6ae3-5b0c-8bc2-be58f0ecf9bf.html#sthash.fj3gDOHi.dpuf).

22. The Gilmer-Aikin Law by Archie P. McDonald.

23. The Aikin Archives (http://www.aikinarchives.org/index.php/main/about/about-the-aikin-archives).

24. Ibid.

25. Past Cumberland University alumni also include United States Secretary of State, Cordell Hull, who also was awarded the Nobel Peace Prize in 1945; James Lafayette Bomar, president of Rotary International; Thomas P. Gore, United States senator; more than eighty congressmen, including Albert Gore, Sr.; two justices of the U.S. Supreme Court, Howell Edmunds Jackson and Horace Harmon Lurton; thirteen governors, including Frank G. Clement; three ambassadors, including Edward Albright, U.S. Ambassador to Finland; scores of local, state and federal judges, including Charles Dickson Clark; and fifty college/university professors, including the "Father of Political Science", John Burgess." (http://www.cumberland.edu/about/).

26. The Aikin Archives (http://www.aikinarchives.org/index.php/main/about/about-the-aikin-archives).

27. Ibid.

28. Ibid.

29. Legislative Reference Library Texas Legislators: Past & Present A.M. Aikin, Jr. (http://www.lrl.state.tx.us/mobile/memberDisplay.cfm?memberID=350).

30. The Aikin Archives (http://www.aikinarchives.org/index.php/main/about/about-the-aikin-archives).

31. See 411 U.S. 1 San Antonio Independent School District v. Rodriguez (No. 71-1332) March 21, 1973.

32. Ibid.

33. Ibid.

34. Education Reforms from Gilmer-Aikin To Today by Marilyn Kuehlem (http://historicschools.org/pdf/tps_gilmer_aikin.pdf).

35. The House Will Come to Order: How the Texas Speaker Became a Power in State A Power in State and National Politics by Patrick L. Cox, Michael Phillips 2010.

36. The Gilmer-Aikin Law by Archie P. McDonald. (http://www.texasescapes.com/AllThingsHistorical/Gilmer-Aikin-Law-Texas-Educational-Reform-104AM.htm).

37. Ibid page 57.

38. Ibid.

39. Ibid.

40. Ibid.

41. Ibid.

42. Noted in The House Will Come to Order: How the Texas Speaker Became a Power in State A Power in State and National Politics by Patrick L. Cox, Michael Phillips 2010.

43. *Brown v. Board of Education of Topeka*, 347 U.S. 483. May 17, 1954.

44. Ibid.

45. Ibid.

46. San Antonio Independent School District v. Rodriguez 411 U.S. 1. March 21, 1973

47. Ibid.

48. Ibid.

49. Ibid.

50. Ibid.

51. Ibid.

52. Ibid.

53. Ibid.

54. Ibid.

55. Ibid.

56. Ibid.

57. Ibid.

58. Ibid.

59. Ibid.

60. For an excellent overview of this entire legal battle see The Educator's Guide to Texas School Law: by Jim Walsh, The University of Texas Press (2014).

61. Interviews with Bill Ratliff, Eric Wright, Vatra Soloman, 2013, 2014.

62. Ibid.

63. Marshall News Messenger (February 11, 1990).

64. Email Bill Ratliff February 2016.

65. Ibid.

66. Paris News. Feb 2, 1990.

67. Ibid.

68. Ibid.

69. See Let the People In: The Life and Times of Ann Richards by Jan Reid The University of Texas Press 2012.

70. During that legislative session Bobby Aikin worked closely with Stephen F. Austin State University President, Dr. William R. Johnson. I am grateful to Dr. Johnson for his support and for the detailed editing of this book.

71. Legislative Reference Library Texas Online.

72. H.R. No. 91 1989 (http://www.lrl.state.tx.us/scanned/members/honorary/70/Aikin_Bobby_HR91.pdf)

73. Longview News Journal February 21, 1992.

74. Paris Review November 17, 1992.

75. Interview with Bill Ratliff 2013.

76. Longview News Journal March 12, 1992.

77. Ibid.

78. Don Edmonds unpublished memoirs 2014.

79. Longview News Journal 1992.

80. Interview with Don Edmonds 2014.

81. See Era of Breaking Records Texas GOP online (http://www.texasgop.org/about-the-party/overview-and-history/).

82. The Kilgore News Herald July 20 1992.

83. Ibid.

84. Ibid.

85. The American Presidency Project at UCSB (http://www.presidency.ucsb.edu/showelection.php?year=1992).

86. Noted in the UT Tyler Archives Bill Ratliff papers 2012.

87. The American Presidency Project at UCSB (http://www.presidency.ucsb.edu/showelection.php?year=1992).

88. Texas Senate District 1 Election 1992.

89. Ibid.

90. Ibid.

91. Bob Bullock, a Titan of Texas Politics, Is Dead at 69 by Rick Lyman, Published: June 19, 1999.

92. Letter from Bob Bullock to Sally Ratliff dated October 21, 1992 is a handwritten note in the Ratliff papers in the University of Texas at Tyler's Archive.

93. Ibid.

94. Bill Ratliff email January 2016.

95. Texas Legislature Online (http://www.lrl.state.tx.us/legeLeaders/ltgovernors/ltGovPage.cfm?ltgovID=38).

96. Bob Bullock, a Titan of Texas Politics, Is Dead at 69 by Rick Lyman, Published: June 19, 1999.

97. Bill Ratliff email February 2016.

98. Bill Ratliff email January 2016.

99. Ibid.

100. Ibid.

101. Ibid.

102. Ibid.

103. Ibid. This encounter has also been retold in Bob Bullock: God Bless Texas by Dave McNeely published February 1, 2008

104. Ibid.

105. Bill Ratliff email February 2016.

106. Ibid.

107. Ibid.

108. Ibid.

109. Interview with Bill Ratliff 2014.

110. Ambassador Teel Bivins dead at 62 by Paul Burka October 26, 2009 (http://www.texasmonthly.com/burka-blog/ambassador-teel-bivins-dead-at-62/#sthash.lP9L7sAY.dpuf)

111. See the Texas Constitution online (http://www.constitution.legis.state.tx.us/).

112. Edgewood Independent School District v. Kirby 777 S.W.2d 391 (Tex. 1989).

113. Ibid.

114. Ibid.

115. Ibid.

116. Mt. Pleasant, Longview, and Paris newspapers January 27 1993.

117. Ibid.

118. Ibid.

119. Ibid.

120. Ibid.

121. Ibid.

122. Ibid.

123. Ibid.

124. See the Guide to Texas Legislative Information Prepared by the Research Divisionof the Texas Legislative Council published by the Texas Legislative Council (March 2015).

125. Texas Legislature Online (http://www.capitol.state.tx.us/BillLookup/Actions.aspx?LegSess=73R&Bill=SB7).

126. The Kilgore News January 22, 1993.

127. Bill Ratliff email February 24, 2016.

128. Ibid.

129. Edgewood Independent School District v. Meno 893 S.W.2d 450 (Tex. 1995).

130. See A timeline on the Texas school funding battle Texas State Teachers Association 2016.

131. Personal notes from the Ratliff papers in the University of Texas at Tyler Archives—these notes are not dated.

132. Interview with Bill Ratliff 2015.

133. Interview with Vatra Solomar 2015 and an email from Vatra Soloman February 2016.

134. A Perfect Team Bill Ratliff and Paul Sadler Texas Monthly The Best and the Worst Legislators 1995 July 1995 by Paul Burka and Patricia Hart (http://

www.texasmonthly.com/politics/the-best-and-the-worst-legislators-1995/
#sthash.uZYyZTYk.dpuf)

135. Bill Ratliff email February 24, 2016.

136. Ibid.

137. Ibid.

138. Ibid.

139. Ibid.

140. Ibid.

141. Ibid.

142. See chapter six for a full discussion. PBS's Karl Rove: The Architect: The Rove's east Texas campaign chairman, State Senator Bill Ratliff, accused Richards of hiring avowed and activist homosexuals to high state offices. Gov. Ann Richards (D-Texas 1991-'95) The issue of homosexuality was very much an issue. It was very much involved in that campaign. Narrator: Rove released a statement distancing the Bush campaign from Senator Ratliff's comments. Wayne Slater: But in every case, what I found was a duplication of the exact pattern of every Rove race, that Rove's opponent is attacked, often by a surrogate or anonymous group, whisper campaigns, direct mail pieces or other kinds of personal attacks, in a way that Rove can't be directly, clearly seen with his fingerprints, but that Rove's candidate benefits from. Narrator: In the end, the thoroughness of the Rove plan—anger, focused issues, attack, attack, attack — proved too much for Ann Richards. In 1994, George W. Bush won handily.

143. Bill Ratliff email February 24, 2016.

144. Ibid.

145. Ibid.

146. Ibid.

147. Ibid.

148. Ibid.

149. In an email Bill Ratliff noted: "One of the things that made this effort different was that the Legislative Council felt the normal procedure was not well suited to this effort. Because there were so many deletions, it made the bill terribly long, with many pages of strike-throughs. They made the suggestion that we simply delete the entire public education code (except for the school finance portions which had just been adopted) and then re-adopt the unchanged portions and adopt the new languages as well. This made the bill much easier to comprehend and made the bill many hundreds of pages shorter than it would have been under the normal procedure. This is the reason that, if one reads the public education code today, the large majority of the code will show that it was originally adopted in 1995, when much of it had originally been adopted prior to that time, but those portions had been deleted and re-adopted in this bill."

150. A Perfect Team Bill Ratliff and Paul Sadler Texas Monthly The Best and the Worst Legislators 1995 July 1995 by Paul Burka and Patricia Hart (http://www.texasmonthly.com/politics/the-best-and-the-worst-legislators-1995/#sthash.uZYyZTYk.dpuf)

151. Ibid.

152. Interview with Bill Ratliff 2015.

153. Charge to The Coordinating Board Texas College and University Systemby Governor John Connally, September 20, 1965, online at (http://www.thecb.state.tx.us/reports/PDF/0002.PDF?CFID=40927664&CFTOKEN=36115836).

154. Ibid.

155. SB 380, 73rd Regular Session, Relating to the distribution of state funds appropriated for elementary, secondary, and higher education. Author: Bill Ratliff, Session Law Chapter: Acts 1993, 73rd R.S.,ch. 27, General and Special Laws of Texas

156. Ibid.

157. McKnight's legislative career began in 1949 at the age of 23, when he was elected to the Texas House while attending the University of Texas at Austin Law School.

158. See Ratliff Opposes UT Tyler Expansion in Panola County Post September 27, 1992, p. 1.

159. See UT Tyler expansion still divides East Texas, Longview News Journal, 10 July 1992, p. 1.

160. See William R. Johnson Personal Papers, 1976-1990 in the East Texas Research Center online (https://library.sfasu.edu/findingaids/?p=collections/controlcard& id=431).

161. Email from Dr. William R. Johnson April 19, 2016.

162. Resolution by the Board of Regents of Stephen F. Austin State University: U.T. Tyler: Resolution of Opposition. WHEREAS, Stephen F. Austin State University is committed to helping meet the public higher education needs of East Texas this mission is accomplished through the cooperation of East Texas State University (at Commerce and Texarkana), Sam Houston State University, Stephen F. Austin Slate University and regional community colleges the Stale of Texas is facing a revenue gap of more than $5 billion in the next biennium the use of scarce state revenue for the downward expansion of U.T. Tyler will result in needless duplication of service this duplication will cost taxpayers between $50 and $100 million space exists for more than 4,000 additional students at East Texas Slate University, Sam Houston State University and Stephen F. Austin State University enrollment projections by the Texas Higher Education Coordinating Board indicate slow growth for Stephen F. Austin State University, Sam Houston State University, and East Texas Slate University during the next decade the driving force for this effort is based upon a desire for economic development rather than higher educational need Tyler Junior College, Panola Junior College, Kilgore Junior College, North East Texas Community College, the Deep East Texas Development Association, and the Kilgore Chamber of Commerce have already stated their opposition in newspaper editorials in The Houston Post (9-14-92) stated that "It's time to slop our college building binge and make sure the ones we have arc used efficiently." Former Senator Peyton McKnight, who authored the creation of U.T. Tyler, has stated that the legislation would never have passed without a promise that U.T. Tyler would not expand downward. The downward expansion of U.T. Tyler is not a local issue, but a regional and state educational and taxpayer issue. Studies by the Texas Higher Education Coordinating Board have concluded that U.T. Tyler is "to complement not compete with" other higher education institutions. The Texas Research League has studied the issue thoroughly and concluded that it should not be done. Local property taxes will be increased when the regional community colleges lose freshman and sophomore students. The Coordinating Board has dropped more than 80 Ph.D. programs in the past eight years "to stop duplication and waste." East Texas has a fully developed system of higher education already in place. There are important mandates regarding higher educational expansion that must take place in South Texas. The downward expansion of U.T. Tyler would have a significant and harmful impact on Stephen F. Austin State University, Sam Houston State University and East Texas Stale University. Texas Higher Education Coordinating Board Commissioner, Kenneth Ashworth, has noted that "To talk about further dilution at a time when colleges have been told to get by on less money than they have now is ridiculous." Such downward expansion would be a costly duplication, create negative competition, and unreasonably stretch limited stale resources. NOW THEREFORE BE IT RESOLVED, that the Stephen F. Austin State University Board of Regents does not support and will vigorously oppose the downward expansion of U.T. Tyler. The Board of Regents, Stephen F. Austin State University. October 20,1992. p. 21.

163. William R. Johnson email to the author April 19, 2016.

164. October 11, 1992 Longview News Messenger. p. 1.

165. Ibid.

166. . Interview with Bill Ratliff 2013.

167. The Bee newspaper January 17, 1990.

168. Interview and email from Vatra Soloman 2014 and 2016.

169. 'Robin Hood' Ratliff says money's the answer by Clay Robison, Houston Chronicle Published 5:30 am, Sunday, August 21, 2005.
170. The Best and The Worst Legislators The Best: Bill Ratliff October 1991 page 151.

FIVE

Obi-Wan Kenobi: Free of the Lobby

HOW AM I GOING TO LOBBY HIM?

Senator Ratliff understood that his first and primary responsibility was to serve the people who had elected him. He attempted to act as the representative of the people of his district—not just some of the people—not just the big donors—not just the poor—but *all* of the people. This is extremely difficult to do. Ratliff believed and acted as if the government in which he served rested upon the people. Another famous Republican, Abraham Lincoln, was of the same opinion, "our government," said Lincoln, "rests on public opinion. Public sentiment is everything. With public sentiment, nothing can fail. Without it, nothing can succeed."[1] Like Lincoln, Ratliff believed strongly in "government of the people, by the people, and for the people."[2]

Ratliff believed that his role was to be responsive to the will of the people of his district, that each citizen had an equal voice, and that the collective voices of his constituents must not only be heard but also should guide his actions. Ratliff never wavered from this principle. It was this—in fact, his unyielding stand on this principle—that ended his career in public service.

Vatra Solomon, Ratliff's long and trusted assistant, was once asked, "Your boss doesn't eat lunch, drink, or play golf, how am I going to lobby him?" Solomon's reply was, "Why don't you make an appointment?"[3] Ratliff was open to meeting and hearing from his constituents (from lobbyists) and set out from the beginning to be responsive. "The biggest shock is the volume of constituent requests, especially during the sessions. So many people want to make their point. I guess I knew it was going to happen," said Ratliff, "I have a commitment to myself that if

anyone contacts me, personally—not by form letter—they deserve a response."[4]

Lobbyist

Like much of American law and political structure, the term and verb
"lobby" originated in England.[5] The original lobby, in a political sense,
first referred to the large room or lobby found outside the House of
Commons in the British Parliament.[6] The lobby was the place where the
British public could gather to speak with their member of Parliament.
The *Oxford English Dictionary* cites the example of citizens lobbying members of the British Parliament as far back as 1640.[7]

Lobbying is citizen participation in politics and government. Any person or organization may lobby the government in the United States. A
letter, email, or phone call, or voice message is a form of lobbying—as is a
personal visit to share information with a representative. James Madison,
writing to support the new United States Constitution in 1787, understood that lobbying the government would play an important role in
politics and policy making. Madison wrote, in the *Federalist Papers No. 10*,
that people would join together in interest groups to represent the widely
diverse social and economic interest in the United States.[8]

Organized special interest groups have indeed become common and
they do, in fact, send armies of lobbyists to influence policy. This is not in
and of itself a negative practice. In fact, the Founding Fathers of the
United States established a government that would be responsive to the
people and fully intended for individuals and interest groups to seek to
influence and participate in governing.

The First Amendment to the United States Constitution protects "the
right of the people to peaceably assemble, and to petition the government
for a redress of grievances." The Framers of our nation's basic law understood that citizens would need to seek out others who had similar interests and to form groups to promote and protect those interests. This right
of association is today taken as the right to lobby—the right to try to
persuade an elected official to adopt or reject a specific course of action.
Almost any and every kind of issue or group—from economic, political,
business, trade and professional, environmental, labor unions, to colleges
and universities engage in lobbying. For example, University of Texas
officials—lobbyists—regularly and often visit with legislators on matters
of concern for their institutions and students. The wide variety of interests make the job of a legislator very challenging.

Free of the Lobby

Texas Monthly wrote that Ratliff was "free of the lobby."[9] In one sense
this is not accurate. Nearly every single day of Ratliff's career he was

lobbied by many different individuals and many different interest group organizations. While Ratliff was steadfast in his commitment to the people of his district, even those he never spoke with, he also understood that policy making required the input of those with authority and expertise over in different policy areas. Ratliff sought expert opinions on nearly every major policy decision he made. He maintained that contrary to popular belief, "lobby is not a bad word. We couldn't function without the lobbyists because we couldn't research everything we need to know. They perform a valuable service, and some are very honorable, such as Ed Howard, the former state senator."

Senator Ratliff believes in the "pluralist system" of policy making. In this system the legislator spends time with and listens to the competing interests of individuals and or groups as they share the issues that are most important to them. However, Ratliff also knew that it was important to make good sound judgments on policy without the undue influence of one specific stakeholder or donor or lobbying effort. Ratliff said, "I am a 'free man' of lobbyists and special interest groups in trying to determine what is best for the people of Texas."[10] In that important sense *Texas Monthly* was correct—he was a man "free of the lobby." He was free to act as every representative of the people should be. As noted previously, he worked to craft a fair public school finance law—not based on just the needs of his wealthy supporters—but based on the needs of all of the children in his district and in the state of Texas. Ratliff was also quick to spot the difference between an industry lobbying campaign and that of an individual and he gave special care and consideration to the individual constituent who reached out.

Tobacco Industry Blows Smoke

For example, lobbying efforts by the tobacco industry intensified in 1990.[11] "It is amazing," Ratliff said, "how sophisticated some of the lobbying groups have become." The lobbying efforts of the tobacco industry were well coordinated and planned in its request that Ratliff and the Senate respect the "rights of voters." Ratliff said, "a lot of time has gone into the lobbying efforts on behalf of the tobacco industry," Ratliff said. Ratliff received letters requesting that he vote against any tax increase on tobacco. Each letter was "beautifully typed, on different stock papers and all personally signed, have different styles, and give the appearance of being individually generated," said Ratliff.[12] "They even have return addresses in different places and even have slight variations in the address: Legislative Building, Capitol Building, and Senate Building."[13]

But Ratliff asserted, "they all have certain unmistakable similarities: they all are grammatically correct; they all quote statistics that the average voters wouldn't know in a million years; many use words like 'excise tax' which is not common for the type of letters and requests I receive;

and most are on high grade colored paper stock and I don't know of many people who have that type of stationary just lying around the house." [14] Ratliff called the tobacco industry's effort the "most organized grassroots lobbying effort I've ever seen or heard of, but it is definitely pushed by the tobacco industry. Several of the letters included the phrase, "$400 million is contributed to the Texas economy," said Ratliff. [15] "How many people know that figure?" [16] Ratliff made every effort to answer personal letters, but did not answer or respond to "fill-in-the-blanks" generated letters.

Because I Care

Another excellent example involved, Mr. Bryan Quinn of Longview, Texas. In 1990, Mr. Quinn needed a bone marrow transplant but he did not have a match within his family. Quinn was suffering from leukemia. While Bryan was waiting for a transplant, he decided to write a letter to his senator about a need for donors. Bryan wrote to Senator Ratliff and explained "the critical need for the increase in the number of people who are willing to put their tissue tests in a databank of bone marrow donors." [17] The Senator wrote back to Bryan asking for more information. Ratliff recalled, "after I corresponded with Bryan a couple of times, we started drawing up a program similar to the one he suggested that the state of Minnesota has. Bryan also put us in touch with officials from the National Bone Marrow Donor Program and they helped us put the bill together." [18] As a result of Mr. Quinn's lobbying efforts, Senator Ratliff introduced SB 84. The Senate Health and Human Services Committee voted six to one in favor of the bill on February 5, 1991. [19] Senate Bill 84 called for the Commissioner of Health to implement a program to educate the public about the need for bone marrow donors and the procedures required to become registered. [20] The bills strongest provision allowed the state to pay laboratory fees for state employees who volunteered to be tissue typed as potential marrow donors. [21] Ratliff was proud of the bone marrow legislation. [22] While leukemia eventually took Bryan's life, his efforts with Senator Ratliff and the efforts of his mother, Anita Quinn, who started "Because I Care," a volunteer recruitment group, have helped over 24,000 patients find donors. [23]

While scholars today debate the role and influence of lobbyists on legislators and policy, Bill Ratliff provides us with a model of exemplary leadership. Ratliff was "free of the lobby, free to act as every senator should: to look at every issue from all sides, and decide what is right." [24] It is obvious that being "free of the lobby" is not a simple task. As such most states and the national government have attempted to implement laws to achieve Ratliff's independence from lobbyists, by regulating financial contributions to legislator's campaigns and direct lobbying. Ratliff sought to make informed decisions that were in the best interest of and were fair for the people he represented.[25]

THE WILL OF THE PEOPLE

The task of serving to representing "the will of the people" is not simple. Each representative is expected to represent a large number of people. Each of the 31 Senate districts in Texas is made up of about 806,000 people. In any given policy decision two important factors must be present for a representative to act for the people. First, the people must care, know, and have an opinion about the issue or decision to be made. But, many legislative decisions go unnoticed by many people. Second, the representative must know "the opinion" of his or her constituents. Obviously, not all 800,000-plus people will have the same opinion. Thus, given these constraints, the representative must decide whether to act as a "delegate" for the people: meaning he/she simply follows the expressed preferences of the people or to act as a "trustee," meaning that he/she follows his/her own best judgment to make the best decision for the people represented. James Madison argued that a representative should follow the delegate conception of representation.[26] According to Madison, a representative should simply follow the expressed preferences of their constituents.[27] Others have argued that, once elected, the representative is then to make the best decision for constituents—even if it is not their preference.[28] The real world is far more complex as representatives are rarely able to act solely as delegates with a mandate from their constituents. Constituents often do not express clear mandates. Nor can representatives always act as trustees—making policy only on their own personal judgment in the best interest of their constituents—as sometimes the people have a clear preference that may be at odds with the representative's judgment. Ratliff's constituents, for example, did not have a clear preference for a specific policy regarding public school finance (Robin Hood), but they certainly did have a clear policy preference regarding the issue of a state income tax. A representative then must take a more pragmatic approach to policy decisions. In practice, the representative must combine these two approaches. Senator Ratliff would seek the input from a variety of sources and interests—including special interest groups, party leaders, other representatives, constituent opinion— and include his own personal judgment. Ratliff would not weigh all input equally. He understood that some groups had a specific stake in the decision that was not necessarily in the best interest of all. Further, Ratliff gave greater weight to public opinion than to professional lobbyists. Political scientists have labeled this the "politico" approach to representation, meaning that on issues that have a low degree of public opinion, elected officials are able to use their own personal judgment and act more in line with the trustee model. Conversely, issues that carry a high degree of consistent public opinion, elected officials must act more in line with the delegate model. As is clear in earlier chapters, Senator Ratliff's character, his personal life decisions, and his political circumstances allowed him to be "free of the lobby." His constituents roundly supported him — he was "bulletproof" — and he did not need nor want the money or support of lobbyist or big donors.

PILGRIM'S PRIDE

The large oversized double doors to the Texas Senate were open wide for Bo Pilgrim as he approached the Senate Chamber. The room was crowded with staffers, notebooks, senators chatting with one another, and even a few members of the press. The Senate was in recess for the morning. Although not open to the public, access to the Senate floor is sometimes granted to more than the usual senators and staffers. Bo Pilgrim was not the typical visitor to the Texas Capitol. As he walked onto the plush deep green carpet[29] on the Senate floor he approached a long table that had been placed in the middle of the room to allow the space to be used as a committee meeting room. Pilgrim had a problem and he wanted it addressed by the powerful men and women of the Texas Senate.[30] In fact, he had been lobbying to have his problem addressed for over a year. The Texas House had voted to help Mr. Pilgrim. The Senate was not sure it was willing to make the changes in the law he wanted — seven senators had yet to decide if they would or not. Pilgrim came to the Senate Chambers to see if he could convince those seven senators to support his solution. In fact, while some senators favored the bill that would help Pilgrim, the Senate had rejected it just days earlier in a vote that was not recorded.[31] Pilgrim knew just which seven of the thirty-one senators he needed to convince.

Chickens

Lonnie "Bo" Pilgrim was born on May 8, 1928, in a small house in Pine, Texas, where his father was the postmaster and ran a general merchandise store.[32] Pine is a very tiny village (about 100 people)[33] about eighteen miles south of Mt. Pleasant, deep in East Texas. In 1939, when Bo was ten years old his father died, leaving Bo's mother and his six siblings with little support. Three years later Bo's mother decided to remarry. At thirteen, the teenager did not approve of the remarriage, and he went to live with his grandmother.[34] Pilgrim has often said, "I haven't asked a person for a penny since I left home at age thirteen."[35]

Pilgrim enjoyed the unearned advantage of his grandmother's property. His grandmother owned land and had several "sharecroppers" (a sharecropper is a tenant farmer who gives a part of each crop to the owner as rent).[36] Using his grandmother's property and the sharecropper income allowed Bo to "butcher hogs, raise chickens, and sell them."[37] In 1946, Bo's brother, Aubrey, borrowed money[38] from a local bank and a local dentist to purchase a feed and seed store for $3,500 from W. W. Weems in Pittsburg, Texas.[39] Almost a year later, Aubrey asked Bo to join him in the growing business. Over the next twenty years, Aubrey and Bo expanded that chicken business to include a feed store, a feed mill, and warehouse.[40] Aubrey died of a heart attack in 1966 leaving the company to Bo. The Pilgrim brother's small chicken enterprise grew into a chicken slaughterhouse business and then over the next twenty years grew into one of the largest chicken processing corporations in North America — slaughtering about 2.25 million chickens each week.[41] In January 1986, Bo opened a processing plant in Mt Pleasant.[42] The new plant would employ about four thousand people who worked long and dangerous days slaughtering and processing chickens.[43]

There are many serious safety and health hazards in chicken processing plants. Workers are frequently exposed to high noise levels, dangerous equipment, slippery floors, musculoskeletal disorders, and hazardous chemicals.[44] Employees are often exposed to the biological hazards of handling live birds or poultry feces which can increase risk for many diseases.[45] In short, workers in chicken plants are often injured on the job and need substantial healthcare.[46] Healthcare for injured employees is expensive, so in the early 1900s "workers' compensation" insurance was created to cover the injured worker and to keep costs down for the business owner. Under a worker's compensation program, the business owner (like Mr. Pilgrim) would agree to pay for the healthcare of a worker injured on the job — if the worker would agree not to sue the owner for negligence.[47] By the late 1980s, one of Bo Pilgrim's biggest problems was the cost of workers' compensation insurance.[48] According to Senator Ratliff, "Pilgrim was paying 50 cents per man hour in his Texas plants for workers compensation insurance and 2 1/2 cents per man-hour in Arkansas."[49]

Pilgrim's primary concern was that the House and Senate were deadlocked on a Worker's Compensation reform bill that would deny injured workers a trial by jury if they rejected the award determined by an administrative procedure. The House bill would have eliminated a trial and only allowed further appeals to a judge. The Senate bill would have preserved the trial by jury option. Businessmen like Bo Pilgrim did not like the trial option as it was costing them to defend themselves in court. Before the summer ended this issue was in large headlines with Senator Ratliff's name on front pages of Texas newspapers.

Business leaders and insurance providers wanted the jury trial eliminated from the system, while the Texas Trial Lawyers Association led the fight to preserve the option for a trial by a jury. As a freshman senator,

Ratliff said he was perhaps too new to catch all of the political undercurrents—but he well understood that big chips were at stake in the workers' compensation fight.[50] Ratliff said, "This could be a critical turning point between the business community and the trial lawyers association."[51]

"Basically, you had two elements involved here," Ratliff explained, "You had the business community, which needs and wants major workers' compensation reform, and the trial lawyers who want no reform."[52]

Mr. Pilgrim Goes to Austin

The morning after the July 4th celebrations in 1989, Bo Pilgrim drove a few miles down U.S. Highway 271 from his home (nicknamed by locals as "Cluckingham Palace")[53] for his usual oatmeal breakfast at Herschel's Family Restaurant.[54] While waiting for his breakfast, Pilgrim handed out $20 bills tucked inside "Jesus Saves" pamphlets.[55] After breakfast, Mr. Pilgrim drove to the airport and was flown in his King Air 300 private airplane to Austin to visit with the Texas Senate about his workers' compensation problem.[56]

By the time Pilgrim reached the Capitol early in the day on Thursday July 6, it was already 88°F in Austin.[57] Once in the Capitol, Mr. Pilgrim's first stop was to see the Senator from District 1. Pilgrim had supported Ratliff's run for the Senate and the two men had previously discussed the workers' compensation issue.[58] However, Senator Ratliff was not in his office. He was in San Angelo with his father, Thomas, who was in the hospital having suffered a series of "shower" strokes.[59] Senator Ratliff's assistant, Vatra Solomon, helped Mr. Pilgrim with appointments and the locations of the senators who had not yet decided how they would vote on the pending workers' compensation bill.[60] Several of the senators were working in a committee meeting on the floor of the Senate. So Pilgrim made his way to the Senate Chambers.

IMPROPER, UNETHICAL, AND PROBABLY ILLEGAL

Mr. Pilgrim's actions that day would (within hours) shock the nation.[61] As Pilgrim eased his way around the conference table he handed out $10,000 checks to several senators in the Senate Chambers—two days before the crucial vote on the worker's compensation bill.[62] Over the next few hours, Bo Pilgrim gave $10,000 checks to Senators Hugh Parmer (D-Fort Worth), O. H. "Ike" Harris (R-Dallas), Gene Green (D-Houston), Chet Edwards (D-Duncanville), Bob Glasgow (D-Stephenville), Tate Sanstiesteban (D-El Paso), and John Whitmire (D-Houston).[63]

Senator Hugh Parmer, one of the recipients of the Pilgrim checks, commented, "I was in the Senate Chamber and got up to stretch, as I walked toward the member's lounge at the back of the Chamber, Senator Harris stopped me to introduce me to Mr. Pilgrim."[64] Pilgrim told Senator Parmer that he was in the poultry business, showed him a few papers to demonstrate expenses for worker's compensation insurance, and talked with him for a few minutes about his problem. Parmer told Pilgrim that one of the big issues they were working on involved jury trials for disputed worker compensation claims. Pilgrim replied, "that's what we want to get rid of because that costs us money."[65] Senator Parmer and the East Texas businessman concluded their conversation and Parmer got up to go on to the member's lounge but was stopped by Pilgrim who said he wanted to give Parmer some papers.[66] Pilgrim then gave the Senator some papers that included a small folded piece of yellow paper and said, "We don't want to bribe anybody," and then he added "but we need some help."[67] The small piece of yellow paper was a check for $10,000 with nothing filled in for the payee.[68] Senator John Montford (D-Lubbock) was nothing short of irate at the offer, he refused to accept the check and said he directed Mr. Pilgrim out of his office commenting, "It was improper, unethical, and probably illegal."[69]

Once the news of the checks hit the newspapers an investigation was launched. Pilgrim blamed the investigation on Senator Parmer. "Hugh Parmer, the senator who I hear is hooked in with the trial lawyers that want a trial where they can rip off all businesses large and small, broke the story for the name recognition," said Pilgrim.[70] He went on to say Parmer did so because "the name Bo Pilgrim draws attention."[71]

Not Very Sophisticated

Governor Clements, who had in the past received campaign contributions from Pilgrim, defended Bo. "I have to agree that he's a little unsophisticated in this approach he had," said the governor. Bo Pilgrim agreed, "I'm not very sophisticated, I've got a high school education and I've been in business 44 years. I mow my own yard. The last couple of years I gave over $1 million to different people—politicians, preachers, education institutions, and so forth. So $10,000 may excite you, but it don't me," said Pilgrim.[72] "I've known Bo a long time. I consider him a friend, but I wouldn't say he's a close friend," Ratliff said. "Knowing Bo as I do, he moves in some strong circles. He probably didn't think $10,000 was a lot of money."[73] Ratliff and Pilgrim would not always remain friends.

I Thought They Were Joking

After an investigation, Travis County District Attorney Ronnie Earle—who was charged with investigating the incident—said that state law prohibits political contributions thirty days prior to and after a regular session of the Texas Legislature. But it did not prohibit such gifts during a special session. "The bribery statute has a loophole big enough to drive a truck through," said District Attorney Ronnie Earle.[74]

Legal or unsophisticated or not, Bo Pilgrims $10,000 checks prompted calls for ethics reform and campaign finance reform.[75] District Attorney Earle said the incident showed it was time to change the state's campaign finance laws. "It would be very difficult to make it into a bribery case," he said. "In Texas, it's almost impossible to bribe a public official as long as you report it."[76] "I think it's outrageous," said Mr. Earle. "It offends the integrity of the whole process." Senator Kent Caperton said that when he first heard about the checks, "I thought they were joking."[77]

Ratliff explained that in the early 1990s, there were many reasons why the legislature needed ethics reform.[78] Lobbyists were routinely paying for not only meals but luxury vacations and expensive entertainment for legislators.[79] Lobbyists and legislators were often engaged in partnerships in land purchases and business ventures.[80] Legislators were even collecting consulting fees from lobbying firms.[81] "There were members of the legislature who actually carried a credit card which was paid by one or more lobby groups. We heard testimony of members who went into one of the high end men's stores in downtown Austin and bought two or three suits of clothes and charged them to such a credit card."[82] One might think that this type of arrangement would constitute bribery if the member then took an official action (voted) favorable to that lobby. However, according Texas law, the prosecutor had to prove a specifically agreed to quid-pro-quo between the lobbyist and the member, or it would not constitute bribery. Therefore, there was very little to no chance of prosecution.[83] "It's just so outrageous," Senator Caperton (D-Bryan) said, "The law needs to be changed. We need more limits about when we can take money and how much."[84]

SB 1—THE BO PILGRIM BILL

A bill filed before the session began contained a provision barring campaign donations in public buildings. "I guess that's the Bo Pilgrim memorial provision," said Ratliff. "It's a little ridiculous when you think about it. You could walk out on the lawn and do it and it would be perfectly legal."[85] Bo Pilgrim's $10,000 checks—which he called "campaign contributions"—along with Speaker Gib Lewis's indictment for receiving an illegal gift pushed the state's leaders to call for change and new legislation.[86] Indeed, Governor Ann Richards made ethics reform a central and urgent priority. On January 18, 1990, Richards wrote: "Dear Honorable Speaker, Honorable Lieutenant Governor, and Honorable Members of the Legislature: Today I am submitting as emergency matters the accompanying measures under the provisions of Article III, Section 5, of the

Constitution of the state of Texas. I urge your prompt consideration and enactment of these measures. I herewith submit as emergency matters the following: (1) Ethics legislation and Election reform; and, (2) A constitutional amendment and legislation establishing a state lottery. Respectfully submitted, Ann W. Richards, Governor of Texas, Austin, Texas."[87]

A New Wind Blowing

Speaking to a group of lobbyist at the time, District Attorney Ronnie Earle warned, "There is in the new Texas a new wind blowing, and the stage is set for a change in your business."[88] Ratliff and many others had different ideas of what should or should not be allowed. Bob Bullock's original proposal was to limit all honoraria—fees accepted by legislators for making speeches—and that "suits me fine," said Ratliff. Senator Ratliff felt that the Senate's bill was stronger, "I probably would get some push back from the people in the House of Representatives at the time but I do believe that the Senate bill was the more stringent of the two, and was calling for more accountability than the House version."[89] The House and the Senate passed similar provisions that prohibited legislators from taking "pleasure trips" paid by lobbyists. But both bills allowed lobbyists to pay members travel expenses to conferences or fact-finding trips in connection with their duties. Ratliff questioned why special interests should pay for trips related to state business. "We read about 100 members of Congress going to Barbados on a fact-finding trip," said Ratliff, "It sounds like a loophole you can drive a truck through."[90] None of the other nine committee members agreed. Representative Rick Crawford (R-Amarillo) argued that it would save taxpayer money if the lobby paid for such trips.[91] The committee also failed to solve differences on limiting gifts to legislators, banning lawmakers from representing clients in front of state agencies or requiring income disclosure by members and lobbyists. Ratliff wanted to ban lobby gifts over $50.[92] The House favored disclosing the gifts but not banning any of them—including even cars to legislators. The Senate rejected Ratliff's proposal that stopped lawmakers from using their campaign contributions to pay themselves or their businesses for work done for their campaigns.[93] "If for instance, a legislator owns a company, he can take money out of his officeholder or campaign account and pay his company for services. I could contract with myself for my services as a consultant, and by virtue of that I could launder campaign contributions into my personal account."[94]

As they neared the end of the legislative session Ratliff became increasingly frustrated with his colleagues, "All the provisions are far from unanimous. Some want to water it down and some, like me, want to stiffen it up. So it's not a done deal."[95] Finally, the two houses passed bills (SB 1 and HB 1 on May 17 and 18)—but they were very different and those differences had to be reconciled in a conference committee. A conference committee is a temporary committee appointed to resolve differences in similar legislation, a committee consisting of five members from each House. A conference committee solution is not subject to amendment by the House or Senate but must be accepted or rejected in its entirety.[96]

SHOUTING AT THE TOP OF THEIR LUNGS

The ethics conference committee, chaired by Pete Laney for the House and Bob Glasgow for the Senate, was appointed to reconcile the differences—but made very little progress as the session came to an end. For seven straight days, from May 20 to the 27, the conference committee argued and fought over the details of the two ethics bills. Ratliff was a member of the conference committee (which was a little unusual in that this was a major battle and he was in only his second legislative session), but because of his junior tenure Ratliff mostly observed as the conference committee battle heated up.[97] The conference committee met in the last days of the session which ended on May 27 at midnight. The Legislature was under serious pressure to pass a bill because of the intense amount of publicity the $10,000 checks and other ethics abuses received.

On the evening of the last day of the session, the ten conference committee members met in the Lt. Governor's conference room and the volume of the shouted discourse increased by the minute. Speaker of the House, Gib Lewis, who was himself a central reason for the legislation, was also in attendance but was mostly quiet.[98] Pete Laney led most of the battle for the House. The Conference Committee Chair, Bob Glasgow, "had been living on cigarettes and coffee for about three days, and was bouncing off the walls," recalls Ratliff, "he was so hyper."[99] At one point, Lt. Governor Bullock and Rep. Bruce Gibson[100] (D-Cleburne)[101] literally were almost nose-to-nose with each other both shouting at the top of their lungs.[102] Ratliff said, "This is the only time in my Senate service that I was ever afraid that blows would be struck."[103] The committee argued for hours about the details.

Sine Die

Ratliff recalled, "With about an hour to go before the midnight deadline, someone suggested that the only two rational people in the room were me and Representative Curt Seidlits (Curt was also in his second session and had also been mostly an observer to the battle), and the only chance we had of actually reporting a bill was to let the two of us put together a bill."[104] The committee agreed that Seidlits and Ratliff should go off into another room and finish the editing of the bill.[105] As the clock moved on toward midnight the two feverishly worked to finish the bill.

The Latin term used for adjournment of the Texas legislative session is "sine die." Sine die means "without assigning a day for a further meeting or hearing."[106] To adjourn the legislature "sine die" is to adjourn it for an indefinite period. The Texas legislative body adjourns this way so that it may be called back into special session. In June 2015, Harold Cook tweeted this humorous explanation, "#txlege newbies: 'sine die' is the last day of session. 'Sine' is Latin meaning 'OMG if they stay any longer I'm just gonna.' Die means die."[107] At about fifteen minutes before sine die, Ratliff and Seidlits still worked on the bill. Scattered across the the table were actual pages of the bill. The two men worked to create a document that reflected the wishes of the committee. Working from handwritten notes scribbled in the margins and actual cut out paragraphs including many words and sentences lined-out, the two literally patched, pasted, and stapled the final bill together with only minutes to spare before sine die. The ethics bill passed at five minutes to midnight and "for years afterward, many of the members who voted for the bill, and who were unhappy with some of the campaign finance accountability and the lobby restrictions, would complain that they had no idea what was in the bill, but they had to vote for it or be seen as being against lobby reform."[108] Ratliff said of the ethics bill, "That bill is a good example of the old saying that there are two things you don't want to see being made—sausages and laws. Both will turn your stomach."[109]

Seidlits and Ratliff's patchwork bill was the first major ethics legislation to pass the Texas Legislature since the ethics reforms enacted in the early 1970s after the Sharpstown stock fraud scandal.[110] Bob Bullock signaled the passage of the legislation by banging a golf club instead of a gavel, a joking referral to the practice of some lawmakers of playing golf at local clubs on the tabs of lobbyists.[111] The next month, Ratliff spoke about the ethics bill to the Henderson County Kiwanis Club. He told the Kiwanis members that it was "a bloody battle to get the ethics bill passed before the end of the last the legislative session."[112] He said that the bill has been widely criticized as a watered down reform or "another rug to sweep the dirt under."[113] "The reason I would like to discuss this reform is I was on the conference committee for that bill and it was a bloody battle. There were at least half of us on the committee trying to make it tougher and half that felt it was too hard."[114] The legislation required all lobbyists to register. It also prohibited lobbyists from taking legislators on trips (except if the legislator was to make a speech). Spending limits by lobbyists were set at $500 for entertainment and $500 per gift (other than travel). "That is a lot of money, I would have preferred it to be lower, but it is the first time there has been any kind of limit," said Ratliff.

REGULATION OF THE LOBBY

Those who seek to lobby the government in Texas are required to register their activities and to file reports about their lobbying actions.[115] The law that Ratliff and Seidlits completed, just minutes before the end of the session, included a substantial reform. The bill then created the Texas Ethics Commission.[116] The Commission was granted the power to oversee the lobby and campaign finance reporting laws. Ratliff and the majority of the Senate and House voted in favor of requiring lobbying efforts and campaign contributions to be reported and made public.[117] The rationale for the law was to allow the public to know who supported certain legislators, policies, and who stood to gain from them.[118] They wanted the public to know who wrote the $10,000 checks and who received those checks. Some legislators opposed the reporting requirements arguing that the law violated the basic right to freedom of expression of the donors and lobbyists.[119] Today, all registered lobbyists and their clients are made public and that information is available from the Texas Ethics Commission website. Public records of lobbying and campaign contributions promote transparency and helps keep Texans informed about the influence of lobbyists.

Some critics have argued that the Texas Ethics Commission does not vigorously enforce reporting requirements nearly enough.[120] The conference committee, in Bob Bullock's office that late night, hotly debated the enforcement and prosecutorial authority of the new Texas Ethics Commission. Ratliff explained, "one of the things which was heatedly debated when we passed the ethics bill was how much criminal prosecutorial authority would be given to the Commission."[121] In that legislative session, the majority of both houses was still in the hands of the Democrats and the District Attorney of Travis County was a Democrat. "Since the ethics commission was to be a bipartisan group," said Ratliff, "the Democrats felt they would be better served if the Commission did not have prosecutorial power, but was required to forward any violations to the District Attorney for prosecution. While this solution prevailed, I think it was a mistake. The Commission has proven to be a fair and responsible group, and should be empowered to prosecute offenses on its own authority."[122]

MAKING A LIVING

"Most members of the legislature are paid the same salary," said Ratliff, "some were making a living off being in the legislature. There are two ways that they did this. First, they would accept honorariums for speaking engagements. An honorarium was an odd ball in the previous law, as it was not a campaign contribution, therefore it did not have to be reported as such, and it went into the legislator's pocket. Members of an interest group that wanted a piece of legislation in the next session would invite the legislator to speak, pay him, and then during the next legislative session, approach the legislator and want him to carry their bill through."[123] The new law prohibited conversion of campaign contributions to personal use. "A legislator would start a small business, such as a public relations firm, and would hire and pay this firm to do his public relations. This way, campaign money would go directly to him—but not for what it was intended. Now the law prohibits any business using campaign funds wherein the legislator owns more than 10 percent of the business," said Ratliff.[124] "This reform is not perfect, but we have come a long way from anything we have had in the past and we hope for improvement in the future" said Ratliff.[125] "We had some members of the legislature who had credit cards billed to a lobby, and private club members. Now a lobby has to record everything they do. For $50 and up, they have to say what they spent the money on," said Ratliff, "I pressed for $25. I think there ought to be a low enough limit, where the people of Texas can go to the records and see who's doing me favors."[126]

A Kiwanis Club member commented saying, "We're going to lose a lot of politicians." To which Ratliff replied, "In my opinion, that's the purpose of this bill. It makes it bribery to take a campaign contribution from a group, then vote in their favor. It used to be only if you pocketed it. I think we did something. I think we cleared up a lot of Austin. I hope it retires a few folks who don't have any other way to make a living." Ratliff added that "the legislative salary of $600 a month should be raised to something a person can live on."[127]

Texas legislators are among the lowest paid legislators in the country, receiving an annual salary of only $7,200 (plus $150 per diem when in session). Texas legislators' salaries must be approved by Texas voters and there has not been an increase since 1975. After the ethics bill battle, Ratliff argued that legislator's pay should be increased to a professional-level salary. Ratliff saw a real conflict between the larger public interest, the personal making of a living, and private business of lawmakers. The salary increase, "doesn't make a big difference to me. As people say, I knew what it paid when I ran," said Ratliff.[128] "But my concern is, I had pretty much finished a 30-year career so I could do this. But what you do is restrict the number of people who can run for office to either people in my circumstance or to people who have a vested interest in what's going on down there. People wonder why the legislature is full of lawyers. Well, it's because there is an advantage to them being there," he said.[129] "They can afford to do that as an investment. If the pay were reasonable, I think we might have a broader cross section of types of people."[130]

OBI-WAN KENOBI

The University of Texas at Tyler campus sits among tall pine trees in a beautiful park-like setting on two small lakes in East Texas. The Bill Ratliff Science & Engineering Building is a magnificent modern six-story structure set at an angle on the north lake. On the top floor of the south building (the structure has both a north and a south building connected with skywalks) is a beautiful suite of rooms called the Ratliff Suite. In one room is a highly polished mahogany conference table (seating about twenty). Seated at this table one can see both lakes and students making their way to classes (or perhaps reading this book next to the lake). On the walls of this conference room are framed photos of the famous East Texas senator smiling with many other famous political leaders. Two beautiful double doors open from the conference room to a very large room with a high ceiling, several tables, comfortable chairs, and display cases. The room has the look and feel of a museum office and it is. Shelves with built-in lights line the walls. On those shelves are awards, years of mementos, books, photos, and two Star Wars replica light sabers.

The toy sabers were a gift to Senator Ratliff in the 1997 session to go with his affectionate nickname, "Obi-Wan Kenobi," after the legendary Jedi sage of the Star Wars movie. The nickname was given by fellow senators to Ratliff because of his intelligence, calm, and moral leadership. The Obi-Wan nickname fit and stuck. By the end of his second term, Ratliff's role in the senate had changed—the senator had grown from student to master. Ratliff—like Obi-Wan—was viewed by many as a wise mentor. His example, words, and actions inspired those around him. Bill was the "conscience" of the Texas Senate.[131] Like Obi-Wan, Ratliff led by example. He put policy ahead of politics and expected others to do the same. "Ratliff's calm demeanor, unshakable integrity, and analytical skill prevented many a disagreement from disintegrating into the legislative equivalent of a food fight."[132]

In the senate, in his district, and across the state more generally, the senator served a role that Toni Morrison calls the "ancestor."[133] For Professor Morrison, "ancestors" may be parents, grandparents, teachers, or elders in a community.[134] Morrison defines the ancestor as "benevolent, instructive, and protective."[135] Senator Ratliff filled this leadership and mentor role in the Senate. He was (and is) a wise, benevolent, instructive elder, and mentor. During his years in the public service, Ratliff provided honest, sensible, and reliable information, a connection with the past, protection of the vulnerable (he was always focused on the people of Texas), and he educated not only his colleagues but also everyone he worked with and served. In the ancestor or Obi-Wan role, Ratliff was an interested, benevolent, and guiding leader who was concerned about the good of all.[136]

In the coming years Senator Ratliff rose to the pinnacle of power. He chaired not only the Education and State Affairs committees—but chaired the most powerful and probably most difficult committee of all in the Texas Legislature—the Senate Finance Committee. For three years he was one of the four principal leaders of the state of Texas. His policy choices and leadership principles led to many decisions that made him enemies. Those enemies would ask if he was indeed "Republican enough?"[137]

NOTES

1. Lincoln Douglas Debates, First Debate: Ottawa, Illinois August 21, 1858 Full text of the Ottawa Debate online at (http://www.nps.gov/liho/learn/historyculture/debate1.htm).

2. The Gettysburg Address: "Four score and seven years ago our fathers brought forth on this continent, a new nation, conceived in Liberty, and dedicated to the proposition that all men are created equal. Now we are engaged in a great civil war, testing whether that nation, or any nation so conceived and so dedicated, can long endure. We are met on a great battle-field of that war. We have come to dedicate a portion of that field, as a final resting place for those who here gave their lives that that nation might live. It is altogether fitting and proper that we should do this. But, in a larger sense, we cannot dedicate—we cannot consecrate—we cannot hallow—this ground. The brave men, living and dead, who struggled here, have consecrated it, far above our poor power to add or detract. The world will little note, nor long remember what we say here, but it can never forget what they did here. It is for us the living, rather, to be dedicated here to the unfinished work which they who fought here have thus far so nobly advanced. It is rather for us to be here dedicated to the great task remaining before us—that from these honored dead we take increased devotion to that cause for which they gave the last full measure of devotion—that we here highly resolve that these dead shall not have died in vain—that this nation, under God, shall have a new birth of freedom—and that government of the people, by the people, for the people, shall not perish from the earth." Abraham Lincoln November 19, 1863

3. Mount Pleasant Daily Tribune September 17, 1989.

4. Ibid.

5. A Lobbyist by Any Other Name? National Public Radio January 22, 2006 (http://www.npr.org/templates/story/story.php?storyId=5167187).

6. Ibid.

7. Ibid.

8. See The Union as a Safeguard Against Domestic Faction and Insurrection by James Madison Friday, November 23, 1787. (http://thomas.loc.gov/home/histdox/fed_10.html).

9. Texas Monthly October 1991 page 151.

10. Henderson Daily News 24 June 1992. p. 1.

11. Marshall News Messenger March 7 1990

12. Ibid.

13. Ibid.

14. Ibid.

15. Ibid.

16. Ibid.

17. Longview News Journal Dec 29 1990.

18. Ibid.

19. SB 84 72nd Regular session (http://www.lrl.state.tx.us/LASDOCS/72R/SB84/SB84_72R.pdf#page=3).

20. Ibid.

21. Ibid.

22. Marshall News Messenger March 7 1990

23. See Because I Care History (http://bictexas.org/history.htm) and see also Marrow Donor Meets Recipient In Longview (http://www.kltv.com/story/2524020/marrow-donor-meets-recipient-in-longview).

24. Texas Monthly Best Legislators 1991.

25. Interview with Ratliff 2013.

26. . See Political Representation in the Stanford Encyclopedia of Philosophy (http://plato.stanford.edu/entries/political-representation/)

27. Ibid.

28. Ibid.

29. The plush historically accurate carpet for the Texas Senate comes from England. State historical records show the Senate's first carpet probably arrived in 1889. It wore out and was replaced a dozen years later, then again in 1917 with a heavy cut-pile woven carpet that carries the same pattern as today's version. See Not your average carpet replacement under the pink dome by Mike Ward, The Houston Chronicle December 1, 2014

30. Texas Businessman Hands Out $10,000 Checks in State Senate, The New York Times Published: July 9, 1989 (http://www.nytimes.com/1989/07/09/us/texas-businessman-hands-out-10000-checks-in-state-senate.html).

31. Ibid.

32. See Interview by Marv Knox in the Baptist Standard, Pilgrim's Progress: East Texas businessman Bo Pilgrim accessed online December 2015. (http://assets.baptiststandard.com/archived/2002/1_14/pages/pilgrim.html).

33. Ibid.

34. Ibid.

35. Not Clucking Around: Texas Poultry King Bo Pilgrim Takes on Senate Finance Committee Chairman Bill Ratliff, Austin Chronicle by Robert Bryce, Fri., Nov. 3, 2000. (http://www.austinchronicle.com/news/2000-11-03/79226/).

36. Ibid.

37. Ibid.

38. The Pilgrim's Pride Corporation History (http://www.encyclopedia.com/topic/Pilgrims_Pride_Corp.aspx).

39. See the About Us page at Pilgrim's Pride (http://www.pilgrims.com/our-company/about-us.aspx).

40. Ibid. Not Clucking Around: Texas Poultry King Bo Pilgrim Takes on Senate Finance Committee Chairman Bill Ratliff, Austin Chronicle by Robert Bryce, Fri., Nov. 3, 2000. (http://www.austinchronicle.com/news/2000-11-03/79226/).

41. Ibid.

42. But by 2008, the chicken market had changed dramatically. Record-high corn prices, an oversupply of chicken and financial constraints combined to force Pilgrim's Pride to file for Chapter 11 bankruptcy protection in December 2008. In December 2009, Pilgrim's emerged from its reorganization as a stronger, more competitive company. JBS USA, a unit of JBS S.A. in Brazil, acquired 64% of Pilgrim's stock in December 2009.

43. Ibid.

44. See The United States Department of Labor Safety and Health Topics Poultry Processing (https://www.osha.gov/SLTC/poultryprocessing/).

45. Ibid.

46. See Lives On the Line: The high human cost of chicken Oxfam Report 2015 (https://www.oxfamamerica.org/livesontheline).

47. See Hurting for Work: How disdain for government regulation sparked a "Texas miracle" economy—while tearing down protections for the workers who built it. Texas Tribune by Jay Root, June 29, 2014

48. See Dallas Morning News, 8 July 1989.

49. Mount Pleasant Daily Tribune July 7 1989

50. The Paris News July 9, 1989.

51. Ibid.

52. The Paris News July 23, 1989.

53. Not Clucking Around: Texas Poultry King Bo Pilgrim Takes on Senate Finance Committee Chairman Bill Ratliff by Robert Bryce, November 3, 2000.

54. Pilgrim's Pride town stays calm despite bankruptcy Saturday, December 06, 2008 by Paul J. Weber, Associated Press Writer (http://www.foxnews.com/printer_friendly_wires/2008Dec06/0,4675,PilgrimapossPridePittsburg,00.html).

55. Ibid.

56. Ibid.

57. See Historical weather Austin, Texas (https://www.wunderground.com/history/airport/KATT/1989/7/6/DailyHistory.html?req_city=&req_state=&req_statename=&reqdb.zip=&reqdb.magic=&reqdb.wmo=).

58. Mount Pleasant Daily Tribune July 7 1989.

59. Interview with Ratliff 2013.

60. Interview with Vatra Solomon 2014.

61. Texas Businessman Hands Out $10,000 Checks in State Senate The New York Times Published: July 9, 1989 (http://www.nytimes.com/1989/07/09/us/texas-businessman-hands-out-10000-checks-in-state-senate.html).

62. Ibid.

63. Fort Worth Star-Telegram July 8, 1989.

64. Ibid.

65. Ibid.

66. Dallas Morning News, 8 July 1989.

67. Ibid.

68. Ibid.

69. Dallas Morning News, Checks Prompt calls for campaign finance reform - What the senators did with the checks - July 8, 1989.

70. Ibid.

71. Ibid.

72. The Tyler Courier-Times July 7, 1989 p 1.

73. Austin American Statesman July 7, 1989.

74. Ibid.

75. Dallas Morning News, 8 July 1989.

76. Ibid.

77. Texas Businessman Hands Out $10,000 Checks in State Senate, The New York Times (http://www.nytimes.com/1989/07/09/us/texas-businessman-hands-out-10000-checks-in-state-senate.html) published: July 9, 1989

78. . Interview (email) with Bill Ratliff February 3, 2016.

79. See "Is the Legislature for Sale" by Paul Burka in Texas Monthly p. 118, February 1991. P 122.

80. Ibid.

81. Ibid.

82. Interview (email) with Bill Ratliff February 3, 2016.

83. Ibid.

84. Texas Businessman Hands Out $10,000 Checks in State SenateThe New York Times (http://www.nytimes.com/1989/07/09/us/texas-businessman-hands-out-10000-checks-in-state-senate.html) published: July 9, 1989.

85. Ethics Panel Refuses to tighten loophole Austin American Statesman May 23, 1991.

86. See "Is the Legislature for Sale" by Paul Burka in Texas Monthly p. 118, February 1991.

87. See Texas Legislation Online Governor Ann Richards January 18, 1991.

88. Quoted in "Is the Legislature for Sale" by Paul Burka in Texas Monthly, February 1991. p. 118

89. Email interview with Bill Ratliff February 22, 2016.

90. Mount Pleasant Daily Tribune July 14, 1991.

91. Austin American Statesman May 23, 1991.

92. Mount Pleasant Daily Tribune July 14, 1991.

93. Ibid.

94. Ethics Panel Refuses to tighten loophole Austin American Statesman May 23, 1991.

95. Longview News Journal Jan 20, 1991.

96. See Guide to Texas Legislative Information (Revised) Prepared by the Research Division of the Texas Legislative Council March 2015.

97. Interview with Bill Ratliff February 3, 2016.

98. Ibid.

99. Ibid.

100. Gibson would retire from the House in 1992 to become executive assistant to Texas Lieutenant Governor Bob Bullock. Bullock hires state Rep. Gibson as aide Date: January 16, 1992 Publication: Austin American-Statesman Page Number: B2 Lt. Gov. Bob Bullock announced Wednesday that he has hired state Rep. Bruce Gibson, D-Godley, a member of the House since 1981, to be his executive assistant. The hire gives Bullock, the presiding officer of the Texas Senate, a top aide who is a highly respected veteran of legislative wars and knows the House inside out.

101. Ibid. Gibson was a member of House Speaker Gib Lewis' leadership team.

102. Interview with Bill Ratliff February 3, 2016.

103. Ibid.

104. Ibid.

105. Ibid.

106. See Frequently Asked Questions Legislative Reference Library of Texas online (http://www.lrl.state.tx.us/genInfo/FAQ.cfm#sineDie).

107. The best #sinedie Tweets from the #txlege by Hannah Thornby Austin American Statesman June 1, 2015.

108. Interview with Bill Ratliff February 3, 2016.

109. Mount Pleasant Daily Tribune July 14, 1991.

110. "Is the Legislature for Sale" by Paul Burka in Texas Monthly p. 118, February 1991.

111. Need source.

112. Henderson Daily News 24 June 1992.

113. Ibid.

114. Henderson Daily News 24 June 1992.

115. Texas Ethics Commission Rules Chapter 34. Regulation of Lobbyists (https://www.ethics.state.tx.us/legal/ch34.html#subB).

116. For a full history see House Research Organization Legislative Report Major Issues 72nd Session.

117. Ibid.

118. On November 5, 1991, Texas voters approved an amendment that added a new provision, Article III, Section 24a, to the Texas Constitution. The constitutional amendment created the Texas Ethics Commission.

119. Ibid.

120. Texas gets D+ grade in 2012 State Integrity Investigation Why Texas ranked 27th of 50 states by Kelley Shannon November 2, 2015.

121. Interview with Bill Ratliff February 3, 2016.

122. Ibid.

123. Ibid.

124. Ibid.

125. Ibid.

126. Henderson Daily News 24 June 1992.

127. Ibid.

128. The Paris News October ,29 1989.

129. Ibid.

130. Ibid.

131. See Best Legislators Texas Monthly 1997.

132. Ibid.

133. See Writing African American Women: An Encyclopedia of Literature by Elizabeth Ann Beaulieu page 9.

134. Ibid.

135. Ibid.

136. There is a great deal of support for this- see for example Paul Burka in Texas Monthly "Saint Bill" 2003.

137. Republican Enough for the GOP? By Ross Ramsey, The Texas Tribune March 5, 2001.

SIX

Lt. Governor: The Right Republican

HIS MARGINS HAVE BECOME LARGER

Senator John F. Kennedy described three types of pressures faced by senators: pressure to be liked, pressure to be reelected, and the pressure of interest groups.[1] Even though Senator Ratliff was greatly liked and respected in Austin and much loved in his home district, he would face significant, often ugly, and vitriolic pressure from interest groups. One of Senator Ratliff's constituents, Lloyd Bolding, who owned an oil field services company in Kilgore, said, "Every year he's run his margins have become larger. I think people look at Bill Ratliff as a guy who's working for their interests harder than you'd expect him to. He digs out the facts, he looks at the pros and cons."[2] Mr. Bolding liked his senator, but tensions and divisions were brewing within the Republican Party across the state. Some in the extreme-right of the GOP were quite critical the Senator's bipartisan evenhanded approach. As Ratliff's power over politics and policy increased many of his decisions and floor votes were unpopular in some Republican circles. However, it would be incorrect to say that the senator was not conservative. Ratliff described himself as "a moderate Republican, and I have more of a problem with the extreme right Republicans that I do with Democrats. The extreme right does not understand my ideology and I do not understand theirs."[3] Still, it is clear that Ratliff stood for conservative values and principles even in facing a very popular newly elected Democratic governor. But, some critics began asking if Ratliff was indeed "Republican enough for the GOP?"[4] To which Ratliff famously said, "I am a Republican for the same reason I am a Methodist—I agree with them *at least* 51 percent of the time." He emphasized the words "at least."[5] The Senator from Mount Pleasant—who did not follow his brothers on to the debate and drama stages in high school—was about to take center stage in the high stakes game of politics.

WHAT WE USED TO CALL THE "NUMBERS GAME"

The citizens of Texas elect a governor every four years and in 1990 elected a fiery, silver-haired activist, named Dorothy Ann Richards. As the second woman to be elected governor in Texas, Ann Richards planned to use her position to bring about a "New Texas."[6] In her campaign, Richards beat Attorney General Jim Mattox for the Democratic nomination. Richards promised Texans that she would be a champion for civil rights specifically for minorities, women, gay men, and lesbians.[7] In attack ads against Richards, Jim Maddox claimed he could cure all the state revenue problems with a lottery.[8] In order to blunt this attack, Richards also endorsed a lottery, the proceeds from which she declared would go to help fund public schools.[9] After she won, Governor Richards needed to fulfill this campaign promise and pushed hard for passage of the lottery legislation.[10] The conservative Republican, Ratliff, opposed the lottery.

Since the 1876 Texas Constitution prohibited lotteries,[11] Governor Richards and the legislature proposed a Constitutional amendment to permit the legislature to authorize the state to operate a lottery. That amendment, like all amendments, required voter approval. The bill (HB 54) to create the amendment came to the Senate Finance Committee, chaired by Senator John Montford (D-Lubbock).[12] Quite out of the ordinary, Governor Richards decided to testify in favor of the lottery bill before the Senate Finance Committee.[13] Richards made an impassioned plea for allowing the amendment to be voted on by the people of Texas.[14] Sitting before Senators Montford, Ratliff, and nine others, the governor said, "Frankly, it is just plain nervy of us to suggest that those of us who are fortunate enough to be more affluent have any business telling people with modest incomes whether or not they can spend their money on one activity or another."[15]

After the governor had completed her testimony, Ratliff said, "Governor, I once heard David Brinkley[16] say that the only difference between the lottery and what we used to call the 'numbers game' was the fact that the state runs the lottery and the mob ran the numbers game. They took 20 percent of the proceeds and and we take 50 percent—and they use to do it on credit and break your knees if you didn't pay your bills, but maybe there is one more difference—they didn't have to advertise—theirs was all word of mouth and it seemed to be a real big success."[17] Richard's replied, "Well, it is very likely, Senator Ratliff, that it would not be necessary to do a great deal of advertising in Texas."[18] Ratliff would later say that Governor Richards "was not too happy with me."[19] The Democratic governor and Republican senator were not allies.[20]

I'm Not in Favor of a Lottery

The next morning, Senator Ratliff introduced an amendment to the lottery bill that would not allow state funds to promote or advertise the lottery.[21] On the Senate floor Ratliff said, "Now members, I'm not in favor of a lottery in any case, but let me tell you the one thing I find the most abhorrent about a lottery, we know from experience in other states that in the early going a lottery generates a lot of money because people are excited and it's something new. After a few years they begin to find out that this is an elusive dream, that they're not going to win any big money, and the interest drops off. And so the state of Texas will be in the position of having to entice people to throw their money away."[22] The Senate voted down his amendment 21 to 10.[23] Ratliff argued that the revenue to be gained from a lottery would be relatively small, would not prevent future tax increases, and that a lottery is a highly regressive tax[24]—as most participants are people with low incomes.[25] Now decades beyond this discussion, studies show that the lottery is indeed a tax on the poor.[26] In the 2014–2015 Biennium the state lottery accounted for just 1.5 percent of the total Texas budget.[27] Ratliff made it well known that he was not a supporter of the lottery or of gambling.[28] Senator Ratliff took his lead from Lieutenant Governor Bullock on Governor Richards. Ratliff would say, "I actually had little direct contact with her while she was governor."[29] He wrote, "In the quiet of his office, Bob Bullock was fond of saying that Ann Richards was a 'show pony.' That is, she did not have much influence on the legislative process, and he was quick to say that he (along with the Speaker possibly) made the decisions regarding state government. He had very little regard for Richards as a state leader, and as a result the members took their lead from him, not from the governor's office."[30] It is also important to note that Ratliff did not disagree with Ann Richard's policy of including people from the LGBT community in her campaign and in government posts.[31]

OH GOD, SHE KNOWS

Governor Richards was well known in Austin for giving lesbians and gays leadership positions in her campaign and administration.[32] For example, candidate Richards granted an opportunity and a nod of acceptance to two of her young campaign volunteers—Celia Israel and her girlfriend. Israel explains, "Anybody who knew Ann knew those blue eyes could look right through you."[33] "She gave us that look one day, and she said, 'Why, don't you guys look like a couple of bookends?' And you knew exactly what she was saying.[34] We were like, 'Oh god, she knows.' Back then, it was kind of a big deal that your boss knew you were gay. It was kind of a relief that she said it."[35] To date, Governor Richards is the only governor in Texas history to take an openly pro-gay stand. Unlike Walter Jenkins and his boss, Celia Israel's boss gave her acceptance. Twenty-four years later, Celia Israel (D-Austin) joined Representative Mary González (D-Clint) as the only two Texas state legislators who publically identify as lesbians.[36]

This Is Horse Manure

In 1994, Ann Richards underestimated her challenger for the Texas Governor's position—a man named George W. Bush. Bush challenged the incumbent governor promising Texans that he would improve public education and reform the state's tort laws. Several reporters and books about Bush and his campaign strategist, Karl Rove, have pointed to Governor Richards's support for lesbians and gays as a significant reason for Bush's successful challenge in 1994.[37] *Dallas Morning News* reporter, Wayne Slater, and his coauthor James Moore, in their books[38] about Bush and Rove, wrote that Rove attacked Richards as an advocate for the "homosexual agenda."[39] Rove was accused of using Senator Ratliff, who was then serving as Bush's honorary East Texas campaign chairman, to start a whisper campaign and personal attack on Richards. They claimed Rove and Bush used Ratliff so they would not be directly linked to the dirty campaign tactics. Slater says, "in every case, what I found was a duplication of the exact pattern of every Rove race, that Rove's opponent is attacked in a way that Rove can't be directly, clearly seen with his fingerprints, but that Rove's candidate benefits from."[40] *PBS Frontline* and others claim that Senator Ratliff "accused Richards of hiring avowed and activist homosexuals to high state offices."[41] Joshua Green from *The Atlantic* wrote, "Bush's 1994 race against Ann Richards featured a rumor that she was a lesbian, along with a rare instance of such a tactic's making it into the public record—when a regional chairman of the Bush campaign allowed himself, perhaps inadvertently, to be quoted criticizing Richards for "appointing avowed homosexual activists to state jobs."[42] The regional chairman was Bill Ratliff. None of these authors or reporters spoke with Senator Ratliff about these accusations. Neither Bush nor his political consultant used Senator Ratliff to start a whisper criticism about Richards for "appointing avowed homosexual activists" to state jobs.[43] "This is horse manure," said Richards's spokesman Chuck McDonald of Bush's denial, "George W. Bush is showing us what his idea of a positive campaign is. The election is seventy-six days away and he has stepped up his negative campaign."[44]

I DIDN'T NECESSARILY AGREE WITH THIS SENTIMENT

Ratliff explained, "I was asked by a reporter[45] who would carry East Texas, George W. or Ann Richards? I answered that George W. would. He asked me why I thought so. I gave him a list of three or four reasons, as I recall the last one of which was that the people of East Texas did not favor the appointment of avowed activist homosexuals to high public office." The reporter wrote that Ratliff said, "I simply don't agree to appointing avowed homosexual activists to positions of leadership, I think it elevates the lifestyle. It tends to elevate the lifestyle to the equivalent of the traditional family."[46] Ratliff stated that the reporter misquoted him as he was referring to the people of East Texas and which candidate would most likely carry that region.

"I now regret," wrote Ratliff, "that I did not preface this comment with the fact that I didn't necessarily agree with this sentiment, but I was asked about the people of East Texas and I answered in that context."[47] Ratliff was to underscore this statement in a very public and dramatic way just a few years later. Ratliff noted that it was an unfortunate coincidence that he had agreed to be the honorary chairman of the Bush campaign for East Texas (even though he had done nothing in that capacity before or after that news article). Bush and Rove both insisted that Ratliff was speaking independently of the Bush campaign.[48] Ratliff wrote, "There were those who accused George W. (and Rove on his behalf) of instigating this statement of mine, but that was not the case. I made the comment in response to the press' question without the knowledge or encouragement of the campaign."[49] When asked about the remarks at that time Bush said that he has never asked about anybody's sexual preferences and would not hesitate to appoint a gay or lesbian himself.[50] "That's not an issue to me," Bush said.[51] But, unlike Ratliff, Bush would come to contradict that sentiment with his words and legislative inaction in 1999.

HE IS AN INCURABLE TRASH TALKER

On November 8, 1994, Texas voters elected George W. Bush the forty-sixth governor of the state Texas. In 1998, Bush was reelected. In those years, Senator Ratliff and Governor Bush enjoyed a number of rounds of golf together in Austin and Dallas.[52] "Some of the most enjoyable times I had with him," said Ratliff, "were the times when he and Clay Johnson took on Senator David Sibley and me in golf matches."[53] Clay Johnson is perhaps President's Bush's closest longtime friend.[54] Johnson attended Andover and Yale with Bush and was one of his DKE fraternity brothers.[55] David Sibley is a lobbyist and attorney in Waco, Texas, who served in the Texas Senate from 1991 to 2002. Sibley and Ratliff gave Bush and

Johnson quite a challenge. "George is a VERY competitive person, and in a grudge match such as this, he is an incurable 'trash talker' (not profanity)," wrote Ratliff, "We played a number of times with these partners, and Sibley and I are convinced that we never lost, however, GW would never admit that."[56] The four men did not know it during those long rounds of golf, but Governor Bush came to play an important part in the upcoming chapter of Bill Ratliff's political life.

I've Learned You Cannot Lead by Dividing People

On June 12, 1999, Bush announced his candidacy for president. He joined a large field of candidates seeking the Republican party nomination saying, "I've learned you cannot lead by dividing people. This country is hungry for a new style of campaign. Positive. Hopeful. Inclusive. A campaign that attracts new faces and new voices. A campaign that unites all Americans toward a better tomorrow."[57] In addition, Bush promised to take Senator Ratliff's public school accountability[58] reforms with him to Washington and said that he would be a "compassionate conservative."[59] Bush said, "Everyone must have a first rate education, because there are no second rate children, no second rate dreams. It is conservative to cut taxes. It is compassionate to help people save and give and build."[60]

I Offer My Concession

On Tuesday, November 7, 2000, Americans voted for a new president (President Bill Clinton had served two terms). George W. Bush, the Republican candidate, was running against Al Gore, the Democrat. The election will long be remembered for the events that followed. The vote totals across the nation were so close that the race came down to the votes cast in Florida. On election night the Florida count was awarded to Bush by just 1,784 votes over Gore.[61] Florida law required an automatic recount because of the small margin and it was again determined that Bush had won the state by a very slim 537 votes.[62] On November 26, 2000, the state of Florida certified the Bush victory.[63] The Gore campaign protested that thousands of ballots had not been counted or had been improperly rejected by the vote-counting machines. The Gore campaign sued, and the Florida Supreme Court, by a vote of 4–3, ordered a manual recount.[64] The Bush campaign then appealed to the United States Supreme Court, which heard oral arguments on December 11 and December 12 and ordered the recount stopped by a vote of five to four.[65] On December 13, 2000, Al Gore reluctantly conceded defeat to the Texas governor. In a televised speech, Gore said, "I accept the finality of the outcome, which will be ratified next Monday in the Electoral College and tonight, for the sake of our unity as a people and the strength of our democracy, I offer my concession."[66] Gore's concession speech set off a chain of events that would just days later directly affect Senator Ratliff.

AUTHORIZING THE SENATE TO FILL THE VACANCY

The afternoon of June 12, 1999, when Governor Bush announced he was a candidate for president, the thirty-one members of the Texas Senate immediately began to wonder what it would mean for the Senate if he won. They would have almost two years to plan and ponder the prospect. If Bush won, Lieutenant Governor Rick Perry would become governor, and the lieutenant governor post would have to be filled, but how and by whom? The Texas Constitution provides guidance for the succession of the governor. If the governor is impeached and convicted, dies, resigns, the lieutenant governor becomes governor.[67] In 1999, the Senate Parliamentarian, Walter Fisher, had to dig all the way back to the 68th Regular Session in 1983 to find the method for selecting a lieutenant governor if that post was left vacant.[68] In 1983, Senator Grant Jones (D-Abilene) authored a resolution (SJR 22) proposing an amendment to the Texas Constitution to change the method of choosing a new lieutenant governor.[69] Senator Jones's proposed amendment required the Senate president pro tem to convene the Senate as a committee of the whole within thirty days after a vacancy occurs in the office of lieutenant governor. Then the Senate would elect a senator to perform the duties of lieutenant governor—in addition to his or her duties as senator until the next general election.[70] If that senator's term expired before the general election, another senator would be elected in the same manner.[71] The ballot language read: "The constitutional amendment authorizing the state senate to fill a vacancy in the office of lieutenant governor." Since the lieutenant governor is perhaps the most powerful political leader in Texas, the election of this person was a matter of great importance not only to the members of the Senate but to all Texans. On November 6, 1984, the voters of Texas approved Senator Jones's amendment.[72] However, the amendment failed to determine how the Senate should actually carry out the election—in public or by secret ballot?

God Put You Here For a Reason

Long before Al Gore's concession speech, six senators publicly acknowledged a desire to secure the position.[73] The Senate at that time was evenly split—sixteen Republicans and fifteen Democrats. With a major redistricting battle looming on the horizon, the stakes were high. In a letter, Ratliff quietly let his colleagues know he was interested in serving as lieutenant governor, but he added that he would not campaign for the position.[74] His golf partner, David Sibley, took the opposite approach.

Senator Sibley not only personally campaigned for the position—he also created a formal agenda and hired a campaign consultant.[75] Senators Teel Bivins (R-Amarillo), Buster Brown (R-Lake Jackson), Jeff Wentworth (R-San Antonio), and one Democrat, Ken Armbrister (Victoria) also let their colleagues know they too wanted the position.[76] Well before the 2000 election, in August 1999, David Sibley met with nearly every member of the Senate seeking to win support. He said, "I don't know why you want this spot if you don't have an agenda. God put you here for a reason."[77] While Sibley and others were campaigning, between the election date (November 7) and Gore's concession (December 13) the Senate devised a plan for voting.

SOMETHING THAT MUST BE DONE IN AN OPEN MEETING

With the Republicans' holding a slight edge over Democrats in the Senate, most of the senators feared political retribution if they lost or if the candidate they supported lost. So they decided that the election should be done by secret ballot. Many *Texas News* organizations did not like the secret ballot decision and filed a lawsuit in State District Judge Lora Livingston's court seeking a public vote.[78] Judge Livingston agreed with the news organizations. "In this case they aren't choosing a president of the Senate but they are choosing a lieutenant governor," Judge Livingston said, "It seems to me that is something that must be done in an open meeting."[79] Texas Attorney General John Cornyn, who represented the senators, immediately appealed Judge Livingston's decision in the Texas 3rd District Court of Appeals. The 3rd District Court agreed with Judge Livingston—the votes must be cast in public. Undeterred, Cornyn appealed to the Texas Supreme Court.

Let the Senate Work Its Will

Senator Sibley's approach of campaigning for the post and detailing an agenda was not well received by several in the Senate. He would later say, "There was a virulent strain of 'Anybody but Sibley' in the Democratic caucus." Ratliff, however, impressed his colleagues with his quiet and unassuming demeanor and message. If selected, he intended to follow Bill Hobby's management style and "let the Senate work it's will."[80] Ratliff said he would not have a mandate from the citizens of Texas and would therefore try to be a consensus builder in the Senate.[81] Ratliff indicated that he would work with both parties. In a bit of foreshadowing he also said that incumbents should be protected in redistricting.[82]

IF YOU SEE BLACK SMOKE, THEN YOU'LL KNOW THEY ELECTED ME

A thunderstorm was in progress and it was as dark as night at 12:00 noon in Austin on December 28, 2000. The Senate gallery was completely filled, with many standing. Many House members were in attendance, all of the Senate staffers present, and the press table was crowded. The Senate chamber's tall wooden shutters were closed, contributing to the level of excitement and electricity being felt by all in attendance. Not more than one-hundred yards away, the Texas Supreme Court was hearing the arguments about the secret ballot. As the time to convene neared, President Pro Tempore Rodney Ellis was advised by the Attorney General's office that the Senate should wait for the Court to make its decision which was expected within an hour. The appointed hour came and went. The crowd gathered in the Senate gallery became restless. One hour passed. Two hours passed.

As time passed, all thirty-one Senators mingled on the Senate floor, visited with one another, and exchanged stories about their Christmas holidays. Ratliff was proud of his colleagues, "I have never been so proud of the Senate as I was at about this time in the afternoon, there was no campaigning, no arm twisting, no arguments. The level of decorum was truly unbelievable considering the magnitude of the issue to be decided."[83]

Three hours passed, and finally, Senator Ellis received a message from the Attorney General that the Supreme Court had made a decision. The Texas Supreme Court settled the matter by ruling the courts had no jurisdiction in the matter. The Court ruled that the Senate could decide it's own rules in places where the Texas Constitution is silent.[84] In an 8-to-0 ruling, Justice Nathan Hecht wrote, "The parties have argued policy reasons for and against an election by secret ballot. These arguments are not for us to consider; the Constitution, by allowing but not requiring a secret ballot, commits that choice to the Senate."[85]

The Senate turned to Parliamentarian Walter Fisher, Secretary of the Senate Betty King, and Senator Ellis, the president pro tempore, to manage the election of the lieutenant governor. The leading contenders seemed to be Senators Brown, Ratliff, and Sibley. Senator Ellis, who is an African American, "joked that the Senate would select its next leader the way the cardinals in Rome select a pope, signaling a decision with white smoke—but, added Ellis, 'If you see black smoke, then you'll know they elected me.'"[86]

Betty King prepared thirty-one slips of colored paper and distributed one to each Senator. Each Senator wrote his/her first ballot choice on the slip and returned it to Mrs. King who went to her office and tallied the vote. After King returned Senator Ellis announced which members received the fewest votes and were thus eliminated from the voting. Mrs.

King then distributed another slip of a different color to the thirty-one members, and the voting proceeded.

Sixteen votes were required to win. Candidates polling the fewest votes were dropped from each succeeding secret ballot until only four contenders remained. After about two hours of voting, Senator Ellis announced the four finalists: Senators Brown, Ratliff, Sibley, and to the surprise many in the Senate gallery, Senator Judith Zaffirini (D-Laredo).[87] In the next round of ballots Ratliff picked up Zaffirini's votes.

In the eighth round of voting, the only two remaining candidates were Senators Sibley and Ratliff. Mrs. King returned with the result, she handed it up to Senator Ellis on the Senate dais. Senator Ellis motioned for Senators Sibley and Ratliff to join him on the dais. Senator Ellis quietly reported the result. Senator Sibley turned to Ratliff and asked, "would you allow me to make a motion for acclamation?" Ratliff replied, "I would be honored."[88] Senator Sibley honorably made a motion to name Ratliff by acclamation.[89] The motion unanimously passed and the Texas Senate chose the Republican from Mount Pleasant as new lieutenant governor—arguably the most powerful political post in the state of Texas. Senator Sibley was gracious in defeat saying, "He will have no more loyal soldier than I."[90]

I THANK YOU FROM THE BOTTOM OF MY HEART

After the Senate agreed to Senator Sibley's motion, Bill immediately "walked over to the rail and kissed my bride."[91] Just moments later, at 5:20 p.m., Texas Supreme Court Chief Justice Tom Phillips stepped to the dais in the Senate Chambers and waited for Bill and Sally. Taking Sally's hand, the inseparable couple walked to the dais. Justice Phillips carefully handed Sam Houston's old tattered Bible to Sally. The worn and torn brown two-hundred-plus-year-old Holy Book serves a symbolic link to the great Texas leaders all the way back to Sam Houston.[92] When Bill Ratliff laid his left hand upon it and raised his right, swearing allegiance to the state and its laws, he joined with those leaders, and yet, this would be only the first of the links between Bill Ratliff and the courageous Sam Houston. With Sally holding Houston's Bible, Ratliff was sworn in by the chief justice.[93] "I thank you from the bottom of my heart," a tearful Ratliff said after the applause in the chamber died down. "There truly is no greater honor than to be selected by your peers for an office as responsible as this one because, after all, you know all of my faults as well as I do having worked together all these years," said Ratliff, "I am truly honored. I hope and pray that you will believe that your confidence was not misplaced. Thank you from the bottom of my heart for giving me the opportunity to show you that I can live up to your confidence."[94] In 2016, Ratliff commented, "there is no doubt that that day stands out as one of my top two favorite memories of my service in the Senate."[95] The other memory is surprising and occurred two years into the future. When asked by a reporter about running for the statewide office in two years, Ratliff would not commit. Ratliff said, "Sometime when the session's over, why, my wife and I will sit on a log somewhere and decide whether we want to make that first statewide race at the age of 65. Right now, I feel pretty good about it."[96]

Bill Needs Me

After being elected, Ratliff became immediately aware that he and the Senate had less than two weeks to prepare for the coming regular session of the legislature. The newly elected lieutenant governor had very little time to make committee assignments, chair appointments, and to assemble a lieutenant governor's staff (Governor Perry had taken most of his lieutenant governor's staff with him to the governor's office). Ratliff needed to hire a staff of about twenty people to perform the duties assigned to the lieutenant governor's office.

Bill's old friend, Don Edmonds, came to help once again. "When Don heard on the news that Bill had indeed been selected as Lieutenant Governor, he immediately went to his bedroom and started packing," said Bonny, "I asked him what he was doing. Don responded, 'Bill needs me.'"[97] The next day, December 29, Don arrived in the Texas Capitol prepared to help his old friend. It was a hectic time for all, Don interviewed hundreds of applicants for the lieutenant governor's staff and "put together one of the best staffs ever assembled in the Capitol building. Many of these staff members have gone on to very successful careers in and out of government," said Ratliff.[98]

Ratliff asked Don if he would consider serving as his chief of staff, but he politely declined. Don explained, "I was comfortable with assembling a staff and with those personnel matters, but didn't believe I would operate well in the Capitol political environment."[99] A few weeks later, with all the staff in place and the office running smoothly, Don said, "My work is done here. I am headed back to Tyler."[100] "I cannot overemphasize," said Ratliff, "what his help meant to me. It is hard to describe how comforting it is to have someone whom you trust so totally to throw into a situation such as this and have total confidence that it will be handled as well or better than you ever could have done."[101]

MUCH TO HIS CREDIT

The lieutenant governor sent word to the Senate members that they should each contact Ms. Vatra Solomon to arrange to visit with the lieutenant governor about their committee assignments and chair preferences. "It was important," said Ratliff, "that I have adequate time to visit individually with each member to hear their desires and try to accommodate them where possible."[102] Employing the principles of fairness and bipartisanship, he appointed members of both parties to powerful committee chairs. In appointing members to committees, Lieutenant Governor Ratliff made a mistake. Ratliff surprised the GOP and Democrats by naming his friend Senator Ellis to head the state's most influential legislative committee.[103] With this appointment, Senator Ellis was the first African American to preside over one of the state's most powerful and influential legislative committees.[104] Ratliff also appointed Ellis, who represented an inner-city Houston district, two other very important Senate committees—jurisprudence and redistricting.[105]

As the grumbling and cheers for Ellis's appointment echoed around the state, Ratliff was hit with a substantial oversight. He made a mistake in not appointing any Hispanics to the very important redistricting committee. The coming redistricting battle would redraw electoral boundaries and redefine power for the first decade of the twenty-first century and beyond. The lieutenant governor swiftly admitted his mistake and took steps to remedy the oversight. Ratliff quickly appointed Hispanic Senator Judith Zaffirini (D-Laredo) to the redistricting committee.[106] "I think Bill Ratliff showed real leadership by recognizing that he didn't have a Hispanic and he didn't have someone from South Texas on the committee," said Ellis.[107] Senator Zaffirini said the steps taken by the lieutenant governor were "impressive and much to his credit."[108]

SENATOR SHAPLIEH, YOU ARE NOT RECOGNIZED FOR THAT PURPOSE

As lieutenant governor, "Obi Wan" judiciously presided over the Senate, creating committees, controlling the flow of legislation, promoting some bills, and allowing others to die. One of the more significant powers of the lieutenant governor is the ability to control the flow of legislation. On January 9, 2001, Representative Juan "Chuy" Hinojosa (D-McAllen) introduced HB 514 in the Texas House. Hinojosa's bill drew the attention of a soon to be infamous lobbyist and an evangelical church leader who were working as lobbyists for native American gambling interests. Jack Abramoff and Ralph Reed worked together as a lobbying team to represent the interests of several native American tribes—including the Alabama and Louisiana Coushatta.[109] While the Jack Abramoff lobbying scandal has been widely written about elsewhere, there is one piece of the story that is directly about Lieutenant Governor Ratliff and should be addressed.[110]

Author John Anderson in *Follow the Money: How George W. Bush and the Texas Republicans Hog-Tied America*, makes two claims which Ratliff states are false. Ratliff wrote, "The story by Reed and Abramoff taking credit for stopping casino gambling in Texas is total fiction."[111] First, Anderson infers that Ralph Reed convinced Ratliff to stop Hinojosa's gambling bill. Second, Anderson writes, "Former lieutenant governor says he talked to Reed only once—and over the telephone at that. 'My recollection is he called me about redistricting,' Ratliff told the *Atlanta Journal-Constitution*,' 'but I can't say that for sure. I don't remember it being about gambling."[112] Anderson goes on to write, "'Jack Abramoff would seem to have remembered things differently." In a 2003 email Abramoff warned that the Indian casino bill had ben resuscitated yet again in the Texas House and that "'the current speaker, Tom Craddock [sic], is a strong supporter.' Worse still there will be no Bill Ratliff to fall back on in 2003: 'Last year we stopped this bill after it passed the House using the Lt. Gov. Bill Ratcliff [sic], to prevent it from being scheduled in the State Senate.'"[113] Ratliff had a long history of opposing gambling. In fact, he had "told many people that, if there were ever an issue over which I would mount a personal filibuster, casino gambling would be that issue."[114]

Ratliff wrote, "Sometime during this period, I did receive a telephone call from Reed (whom I had never before met or talked to) which I took. He asked me what my stance was on casino gambling and I told him that I was solidly opposed. He thanked me for the information and, as I recall, he then asked me some questions about redistricting which was hot on the agenda at that time."[115] Senator Eliot Shapleigh (D-El Paso) was pushing hard to get his casino gambling bill (SB 253, the companion bill to HB 514) to the Senate floor. At one point in the session, there was another bill on the floor, the subject of which made a casino gambling amendment germane. During the debate on that bill, Senator Shaplieh asked to be recognized for an amendment. "I asked him to state the purpose of the amendment," said Ratliff, "and he said it was to authorize casino gambling. I stated, 'Senator Shaplieh, you are not recognized for that purpose.'" Senator Shaplieh was not happy with Ratliff's ruling, but the subject of casino gambling did not again arise during Ratliff's tenure as lieutenant governor. "Nowhere, in all this time, did I communicate with Mr. Abramoff nor with Reed other than the time I stated above."[116]

DO RIGHT AND RISK THE CONSEQUENCES

A courageous person is not oblivious to fear and loss. A person of courage stands upon principle even in the face of fear and loss. "Do right and risk the consequences," Sam Houston famously said. In 1854, Houston sacrificed for principle all he had ever won. Standing in opposition to Southern pro-slavery extremists and the powerful Senator John C. Calhoun of South Carolina, Houston was the only Southern Democrat to

refuse to support the Kansas-Nebraska Act—a bill that would have re-
pealed the Missouri Compromise of 1820.[117] The citizens of Texas did not
forget Houston's "anti-Southern" vote and he was defeated and dismissed from the Senate by the Texas Legislature in 1857.[118] Like Sam
Houston, Lieutenant Governor Ratliff would stand on principle even
when it would have been easier and simply expedient to be quiet, not act,
and to not say anything. Lieutenant Governor Ratliff would soon take a
stand against those who hate. Fortunately, they are small in number, but
there are those who have been taught to hate others and to be intolerant
of people of different races, skin colors, religions, national origin, ancestry, disabilities, and sexual orientations. Late on a hot June night in the
small deep East Texas community of Jasper, James Byrd Jr. sadly met
three of those people who had been taught to hate.

I PRAY THAT HE WASN'T

On June 7, 1998, as he walked home on Saturday night, Mr. Byrd was
picked up by three men (Shawn Berry, twenty-three, Lawrence Brewer,
thirty-one, and John King, twenty-three) he did not know. The men (who
were covered with racist tattoos[119] and were known Ku Klux Klan supporters) immediately started a fight with Byrd.[120] They then took Byrd
into the woods, beat him, then chained him to their pickup truck and
dragged him behind their truck for more that three miles down deserted
country roads outside the community of Jasper. The following morning,
Byrd's body parts were found scattered across eighty-one different places
on the seldom-used roads.[121] In the trials of the three men, the prosecu-
tors presented evidence that Byrd was alive and conscious when the
dragging began and that he was likely conscious until decapitated by a
culvert.[122] "I don't know if he was conscious when he hit the culvert,"
pathologist Thomas Brown testified, "I pray that he wasn't."[123] The three
men dumped what remained of Byrd's body in front of an African
American church and then went to a barbecue.[124] The horror, hate, ruthless apathy, and racially motivated killing of Mr. Byrd shocked the
world. The three men were charged and later convicted of the brutal
murder of James Byrd Jr. When Brewer was sentenced to death, Jasper
County District Attorney Guy James Gray said, "I don't like the death
penalty, but that's what he deserves, the just punishment for his case and
these facts and circumstances is death." King was also sentenced to death
and the third man, Berry, was sentenced to life in prison.[125]

Hate Crimes

According to the FBI's 2015 hate crime report, law enforcement agencies reported 5,479 hate crime incidents in 2014.[126] Of the 5,462 single-bias

incidents reported in 2014, 47 percent were racially motivated.[127] The FBI states that hate crimes are motivated by sexual orientation, religion, ethnicity, gender identity, disability, and gender.[128] Individuals, like Mr. Byrd, were overwhelmingly the most common victims of a single-bias hate crime, accounting for 82.4 percent of the reported 6,418 offenses.[129] According to the FBI, of the over 113,000 hate crimes since 1991, 55 percent were motivated by racial bias, 17 percent by religious bias, 14 percent sexual orientation bias, 14 percent ethnicity bias, and 1 percent disability bias.[130] While Americans have made significant progress toward acceptance and tolerance since the 1960s when Walter Jenkins was forced to resign his position in the White House, the LGBT, minority, and other communities continue to be all too frequently victimized by violent hate crime as seen in the tragedy of the June 2016 mass shooting in Orlando, Florida.

In the matter of hate crimes, Americans have a great deal of work to do, and in 1999, Senator Rodney Ellis (D-Houston) and Representative Senfronia Thompson (D-Houston) sought to engage in that work. Senator Ellis introduced Senate Bill 275 (SB 275) and Thompson introduced the same bill, House Bill 938, to strengthen the state's hate crimes law.[131] They named their legislation after James Byrd. The James Byrd bill sought to increase punishment for crimes prompted by hate and prejudice about "sexual orientation, race, color, religion, national origin, ancestry, sex or disability."[132] These bills bitterly divided both houses of the Texas Legislature and many people all across the United States. Many Republicans did not approve of increasing penalties for hate crimes against particular groups of people. While most Democrats supported the bill, most Republicans specifically objected to the bill's inclusion of sexual orientation. Governor Bush, who at that time was contemplating a run for president, refused to support the legislation. Governor Bush opposed the specific protection of homosexuals and his opposition was believed to have been instrumental in the bill's death in the Senate Criminal Justice Committee.[133] In 2001, with George Bush moved on to Washington, Rick Perry in the governor's office, and Ratliff lieutenant governor, Senator Ellis and Representative Thompson would have opportunity to pass the James Byrd hate crime legislation.

The James Byrd Jr. Act Is One of Our Top Priorities

Senator Grant Jones's 1984 amendment to the Texas Constitution put Lieutenant Governor Ratliff in an unusual leadership position. While serving as lieutenant governor, Ratliff continued (according to the amended Texas Constitution) to represent the first Senate District in the Senate.[134] This may, in fact, be the only time in Texas government that a person is allowed to hold two official offices at the same time.[135] Normally, when the senate takes a vote, the lieutenant governor (president of the

Senate) may only vote in case of a tie. However, Lieutenant Governor Ratliff's case, he was allowed to cast his vote as a member of the Senate during a regular roll call vote.[136] Ratliff made it known that he did not intend to cast a vote for his Senate seat except in exceptional circumstances, and he would make that determination on a case-by-case basis.[137] He used the casting of his vote to signal importance of a bill—to make known his stand on legislation. On May 7, 2001, the lieutenant governor would cast a vote. That vote on that day was significant in several important and dramatic ways. Ratliff may not have understood just how significant, but he did know that he was making a decision that while right—would likely have serious consequences. Indeed, that vote on May 7, would come to play an important part in the career of the senator from Mt. Pleasant.

Senator Ellis and Representative Thompson led the fight to punish hate crimes in Texas. They worked tirelessly for years trying to strengthen the state's hate crimes law. Their efforts were blocked in 1999 when, after a bill similar to the 2001 bill passed the House, Governor Bush refused to back it despite lobbying from Mr. Byrd's daughter, Renee Mullins. In May 2001, Ellis and Thompson were finally successful in getting the bill to the floor of the House and Senate for a full vote. In a press release on the morning of May 7 Senator Ellis reported, that the James Byrd, Jr. Act had cleared a major hurdle. The bill was approved by the Senate Criminal Justice Committee by a vote of 5–1.[138] "I am very pleased by the Senate Criminal Justice Committee's approval of the James Byrd Jr. Hate Crimes Act," said Senator Ellis. "Today's vote, sends a clear signal that passing the James Byrd Jr. Act is one of our top priorities."[139]

SHOW THE CHAIR VOTING "AYE"

The stage was set for an "important call of the roll" in the Senate.[140] Senator John Kennedy wrote, "He may want more time for his decision . . . but when that roll is called he cannot hide, he cannot equivocate, he cannot delay—and he senses that his constituency, like the Raven in Poe's poem, is perched there on his Senate desk, croaking "Nevermore" as he casts the vote that stakes his political future."[141] The Senate was scheduled to vote on one of the most contentious issues of the time. Most Republicans felt that the law was unnecessary and strongly objected to the special provision for "sexual orientation." The bill was voted out of committee *without* the provision which would have included "sexual orientation" to the list of hate crimes.[142] The Texas Senate was in a pitched battle over a proposed amendment to add the sexual orientation provision back into the bill.[143] The Republican right-wing mounted a strong campaign against this amendment, and the required two-to-three vote to suspend senate rules was very close.[144]

Politics is the authoritative allocation of values.[145] But before those values can become law they must be debated and accepted. Managing this battle of ideas, emotions, and values from the Senate dais, Lieutenant Governor Ratliff allowed the Senate to work its will. Ratliff drew upon a lifetime of experience and lessons—from Tom and Bess, from Jack and Shannon, from the endless days of sandlot baseball, from years of problem solving as a parent and engineer, from years of teaching Sunday school lessons, to thousands of hours of testimony, to over a decade of standing for his constituents and on principles in the Senate. "After much introspection, I had decided," said Ratliff, "that a crime committed because of one's hatred for the victim was equally as heinous notwithstanding the rationale for the act."[146] Ratliff had been quiet during the storm—only managing the debate and not involving himself by voicing his thoughts. "Bill is always" said Sally, "very calm even in the midst of great stress and trouble."[147] The vote to include "sexual orientation" in the bill was very close. When the vote to suspend was called, the secretary began the roll call. Starting with Senator Armbrister (D-Victoria) in alphabetical order, she worked her way down the roll. When she reached the Rs, Bill Ratliff stepped forward on the Senate dais and stated into the microphone, "Show the chair voting aye."[148]

As the presiding officer, Ratliff was not expected to cast a vote. The Republican from Mount Pleasant could have easily ducked the controversy. No one would have even noticed. Ratliff's vote was the very definition of integrity—"doing the right thing, even when no one is watching."[149] "I do not remember what the final vote was," Bill later said, "nor do I know whether my casting this vote from the chair made any difference to the other members. I only know that I decided that the right thing to do in this case was to vote my convictions."[150] Later that day, the Senate joined the House, and approved the James Byrd Jr. hate crime bill. It was two years after Senate allies of Governor George Bush had suppressed similar legislation opposed by conservatives—the law specifically includes protections for gay people. "This is truly a historic day for the state of Texas," said Senator Ellis, "The Texas Senate has sent a message that our state is not a safe haven for hate."[151] Governor Rick Perry signed the bill into law on May 11, 2001. Right-wing Republicans, like Dr. James Leininger, from San Antonio, were not happy with the legislation or the lieutenant governor's vote.

INTRINSICALLY SINFUL

James Leininger's parents, Hib and Berneta, practiced the religion of the very strict "Missouri Synod."[152] The Missouri Synod is a branch of the German Evangelical Lutheran Church that was organized in 1847—the Synod of Missouri name simply reflects the geographic location of the founding congregation.[153] The doctrine of the Missouri Synod is centered on the belief that the Bible is inerrant—the Bible is inspired by God and is without error.[154] For young Jim, growing up in the 1950s, this meant "Sticking exactly to the Bible and no funny business," Jim's mother once said.[155] The Missouri Synod followers rely on the Book of Concord—a series of confessions of faith written by Lutherans in 1580 to explain the Bible's scriptures. The Missouri Synod believe that, "the Lord teaches us through His Word that homosexuality is a sinful distortion of His desire that one man and one woman live together in marriage as husband and wife. God categorically prohibits homosexuality. Our church, the Lutheran Church—Missouri Synod, has declared that homosexual behavior is "intrinsically sinful."[156]

Jim Leininger took his parents and the Missouri Synod teachings to heart. After growing a successful business in the 1980s, Leininger became increasingly involved in Texas politics by supporting ultraconservative Republicans and creating and contributing to conservative political action committees (PACs).[157] Although supporting other values (like tort reform) Leininger sought to promote his specific religious values in Texas politics. Jim and his wife, Cecilia, became major donors in Republican circles and—from behind the stage—contributed significantly to the political discussion in Texas and nationally.[158] According to the Texas Freedom Network, "James Leininger has used his fortune to support the religious rights' rise to power. Texas has witnessed the increasing influence of extravagantly wealthy donors who use their vast fortunes to advance a hard-right social agenda. Dr. Leininger has been the most important of these ideological super-donors."[159]

THEY CAME AFTER ME WITH ALL THEIR VITRIOL

Dr. Leininger and the right-wing of the Republican party were ardently opposed to Senator Ellis's hate-crime bill—the legislation Lieutenant Governor Ratliff voted to support. The right-wing Republicans used that vote to try to discredit him and to try to remove him from office in multiple ways over the next few years.

In 2002, Bill Ratliff was running for reelection, and the right-wing Republicans recruited a former House member, Jerry Yost, to challenge him. Leininger's Free Enterprise Political Action Committee (FreePAC), contributed $11,345.03 to the Yost campaign.[160] However, Yost was not a real threat, Ratliff received over 70 percent of the vote, but the right-wing of the GOP "came after me with all their vitriol," said Ratliff. Leininger (who owned a direct mail business) and FreePAC, sent thousands of mailers to Ratliff constituents with pictures of a shirtless man in leather bondage gear, two men cutting a wedding cake, and two other men happily kissing. FreePAC's flyers said "Bill Ratliff Supports the Homosexual Agenda," and "State Senator Bill Ratliff voted to give homosexuals more protections than the rest of Texas citizens by adding 'sexual orientation' to the so-called 'hate crimes legislation.'"[161] FreePAC's mailer went on to say, "A bill similar to the one Bill Ratliff supported was used by Al Gore against President George Bush in the 2000 presidential campaign because Bush opposed it."[162] Ratliff held a news conference in Austin denouncing the mailers as "unconscionable attacks" by FreePAC. Ratliff said, "some of the contributors [to FreePAC] called me to say they regretted having contributed. I asked them if they would tell me who solicited the contribution, and they said Mr. Leininger had."[163] In the end Ratliff easily won reelection and comments on the FreePAC attack: "It wasn't any fun, but it didn't really bother me."[164] However, the right-wing of the GOP was not through using the issue and the vote against the lieutenant governor.

Not the Right Republican

On May 26, 2001, two days before the legislative session ended, lieutenant governor Ratliff, the people's champion from Mount Pleasant for more than a dozen years, announced his candidacy for lieutenant governor in the upcoming election. At the end of his first session as lieutenant governor, Ratliff generally followed Governor Hobby's example and let the Senate "work its will." He felt that the session had been a success: a statewide teacher health insurance plan had been created, Medicaid coverage had been extended to hundreds of thousands of additional poor children, and the Byrd hate crimes legislation had been added to the criminal justice system. Staying true to his promise, Ratliff only voted a handful of times in that session, including the one vote for the Byrd hate crimes law, he voted for a bill ending racial profiling by police, a bill to provide school employees with health insurance, and twice he voted for the state budget bill.[165] So, Ratliff decided to run for a full term for the position most considered the most powerful in Texas government.[166] One afternoon just days after he had announced his intention to run, two GOP donors from Dallas arrived at the lieutenant governors office and requested a meeting.[167] According to Ratliff, the meeting was "stiff and confrontational."[168] The two donors had come to express their distaste for Ratliff's bipartisan approach saying he was "not the right Republican for the job."[169] It became apparent that to some Republican contributors, as Ratliff explained, "the term 'moderate' doesn't go down well."[170]

I DON'T LIKE MYSELF VERY MUCH RIGHT NOW

On Monday afternoon, June 4, 2001, Bill and Sally drove the 265 miles from Mt. Pleasant to Houston. The first storm of the season, Allison, was brewing from a tropical heat wave out in the Gulf. Houston was hot and humid. The couple checked into the Hilton Hotel on Post Oak Road and rested before two evening political events. A few days after making his announcement for the statewide office, his consulting team told Bill that it would require a campaign war chest of a minimum of $10 million to make a competitive run for the office.[171]

Ratliff's advisors explained that, unlike his previous campaigns for the Senate, he could not run a statewide campaign on $50, $100, or even $500 contributions. A statewide race required major contributions from Republican "heavy hitters."[172] In keeping with that philosophy, Bill's team hosted a reception in Houston to which several of the major contributors were invited. Bill and Sally attended two events in Houston, the reception held at a prominent Republican's home, and dinner afterward at a local restaurant.[173]

Bill and Sally arrived early at the home of the "heavy-hitter" Republican. They were greeted kindly and warmly and handed drinks (diet coke) as they waited for the visitors to arrive. At six o'clock the visitors began to arrive at the reception. The first heavy-hitter through the door walked up to Bill with a very combative and belligerent attitude and, before Bill even had an opportunity to engage the donor in cordial conversation the man said, "I don't care what you are using it for, a state budget of $200 billion is just too god-damn much."[174]

In the quiet friendly confines of such polite company, wealth, and luxury, Bill was so taken aback that he was at a loss for words. The heavy-hitter right-wing Republican launched into a tirade about the appointment of Senator Ellis as the Chair of the Senate Finance Committee and berated the Texas Legislature and the lieutenant governor for such reckless decisions and spending. Not wishing to be rude, Bill politely attempted to redirect and to lighten the atmosphere with an innocuous comment, but he was totally unsuccessful as the tirade loudly and rudely continued. It was very apparent to all in the room that the rude guest had no idea what was in the state budget or the various needs of the people of the state, but was only venting in hyperbolic generalities. In the twelve previous legislative sessions Senator Ratliff had worked hard and with great care to create fair and conservative state budgets.[175]

Later that evening, the guests, Bill, and Sally made their way to a restaurant for dinner. The dinner included some of the same donors who had been at the earlier event as well as some who had not been invited to the earlier reception. Bill and Sally were seated adjacent to another couple identified as potential major contributors. During dinner, the conversation turned to the subject of the African American struggle for civil rights and then to the Byrd hate crime legislation. Bill's vote supporting the hate crime bill and his support for including "sexual orientation" in the law was heatedly discussed. During the discussion about the African American struggle, the wife of one of the potential big donors said, "I don't know what those people are complaining about. If we hadn't brought them over from Africa, they would all be dying of AIDS."[176] For the second time that evening, Bill was stunned. Sally was embarrassed.[177] Out of politeness, the gentleman from Mount Pleasant did not respond to the horrible comment.

The next day, Sally and Bill drove to Mt. Pleasant for a much needed respite—a long weekend at home. A couple of hours into the trip, Sally commented, "you are very quiet, what is on your mind?" Bill replied, "I don't like myself very much right now."[178]

As the long-married partners drove north along U.S. Highway 59, Sally gently inquired further and Bill explained, "If I had not been trying to impress those 'heavy-hitters,' and win their major contributions, I would have taken them to task for both of their comments."[179] Bill later recalled, "there had never been a time in my life when I would have remained silent in the face of such bigotry, arrogance, and insensitivity, but I had remained silent because of my desire to raise campaign contributions. Perhaps these two incidents happening in my very first fund-raising jaunt was an anomaly, but I feared I would find myself routinely excusing such behavior in the name of campaign expediency, and I didn't think I could face myself in the mirror each morning if I should do so."[180] The very next afternoon with Sally at his side, Bill announced that he was withdrawing his candidacy for the office of lieutenant governor. When asked what prompted his reversal, Bill simply responded that he was not prepared to do the things necessary to raise $10 million dollars; he was not willing to be "repackaged" for $10 million dollars.[181]

THE FATAL DISEASE IS INDEPENDENCE AND MODERATION

In conversations about politics, Americans too often tend to focus on the strategies of men like Karl Rove, or on the hateful self-serving statements and decisions made by candidates or elected leaders, or on the outrageous scandals of men like Jack Abramoff or on the influence of men like Dr. Leininger. Those tactics or elements should be uncovered, pointed out, and redressed. But we must also celebrate and learn from the men and women who stand for right, good, and who serve with great distinction. We must celebrate the courageous decisions that are made when the senate clerk calls the roll. In stepping out of the lieutenant governor's race, Ratliff said he was saddened by his decision not to run but, more than that, he was relieved.[182] Ratliff said, "I do not love politics, especially the kind involved in running a $10 million campaign. I don't think you can be as independent, as fiercely independent, as I have been in these last 12 years and be successful."[183] Ratliff discussed his exit from the race with his longtime friend and advisor, Don Edmonds. Don jokingly suggested, "Why don't you say you are dropping out because you have a fatal disease?" Bill replied, chuckling, "The fatal disease of independence and moderation."[184] In the next dramatic and final chapter of Ratliff's political career, that fierce independence and bipartisan moderation would shake the very foundations of his party. His "audacious disdain for narrow partisanship" would earn him both further vitriol and high honor.[185]

NOTES

1. . In the preface to Profiles in Courage, John F. Kennedy discusses his interest in the "problems of political courage in the face of constituent pressures, and the light shed on those problems by the lives of past statesmen." Published in 1954.

2. Ratliff ending 15-year political career in GOP with resignation, AP Austin Lubbock Avalanche Journal Friday, November 21, 2003

3. Interview with Bill Ratliff 2013.

4. Republican Enough for the GOP? by Ross Ramsey Texas Tribune March 5, 2001.

5. Ibid.

6. Ann Richards, Plain-Spoken Texas Governor Who Aided Minorities, Dies at 73, By Rick Lyman, The New York Times September 14, 2006.

7. Ibid.

8. Bill Ratliff email February 26, 2016.

9. Let the People In: The Life and Times of Ann Richards by Jan Reid October 3 2012.

10. See Texas Legislation Online Governor Ann Richards, January 18, 1991.

11. See the Texas Constitution, Article III, Section 47.

12. Bill: HB 54 Legislative Session: 72(1) (http://www.legis.state.tx.us/BillLookup/ History.aspx?LegSess=721&Bill=HB54).

13. Email from Bill Ratliff 2016 and Texas State Library and Archives Commission Recording: 720915a Session: 72nd 1st C.S. Committee: Finance Committee Date: 8/8/ 1991 Description: 72nd Finance Committee (1) 8/8/91 Tape 1 of 2 Sides 1 & 2, 2:30pm HB 54 all Senate Finance Committee Senate Chamber 8/8/91 Tape 1 Side 1 2pm Subjects: HB 54

14. Ibid.

15. Ibid.

16. David McClure Brinkley was an American newscaster for NBC and ABC from 1943 to 1997.

17. Ibid. Senator Ratliff and Governor Ratliff exchange is at 28:15.

18. Ibid.

19. Bill Ratliff email February 26, 2016.

20. Interviews with Bill Ratliff 2013, 2014, 2015, and March 2016.

21. See Texas State Library and Archives Commission Recording: 720275b Session: 72nd 1st C.S. Committee: Floor Date: 8/9/1991 Description:72nd Leg. 1st Session 8/9/91 Tape.

22. Ibid.

23. Ibid.

24. See Analyses of Proposed Constitutional Amendments November 5, 1991 (http://www.lrl.state.tx.us/scanned/Constitutional_Amendments/Amendments72_tlc_1991-11-05.pdf).

25. Ibid.

26. See for example: University study proves Maine's lottery amounts to a multi-million-dollar tax on the poor By: Dave Sherwood, Contributing Writer © Maine Center For Public Interest Reporting October 21, 2015.

27. Comptroller of Public Accounts 2014–2015 Certification Revenue Estimate December 2013. (www.texastransparency.org/State_Finance/Budget_Finance/Reports/Certification_Revenue_Estimate/cre1415).

28. In an email on March 6, 2016 Bill Ratliff wrote, "I had made it known very early in my career that I opposed anything resembling casino gambling in Texas (As I said earlier, I was an adamant foe of the lottery too)."

29. Bill Ratliff, email to the author, March 6, 2016.

30. Ibid. See also For Ann Richards, Spats With Bob Bullock Were Constant by Jan Reid Texas Tribune Oct. 2, 2012

31. Bill Ratliff, email to the author, March 6, 2016.

32. See Let the People In: The Life and Times of Ann Richards, by Jan Reid, The University of Texas Press 2012.

33. Celia Israel recalls coming out to Ann Richards, looks ahead to Jan. 28 special election runoff for Texas House by John Wright 4 Jan, 2014 (http://www.lonestarq.com/celia-israel-recalls-coming-ann-richards-looks-ahead-jan-28-run-off/).

34. Ibid.

35. Ibid.

36. Israel Defeats Van DeWalle in HD-50 Runoff by Edgar Walters Texas Tribune Jan. 28, 2014.

37. See: Bush's Brain: How Karl Rove Made George W. Bush Presidential Paperback by James Moore and Wayne Slater January 5, 2004; Rove Exposed: How Bush's Brain Fooled by James Moore and Wayne Slater October 20, 2005; Karl Rove in a Corner by Joshua Green in The Atlantic November 2004; Don't Mess With Texas: Gay governors, oil money, KKK fish camps and Karl Rove by Lou Dubose in LA Weekly. September 16, 2004; Karl Rove's Ashley Judd problem The big loser of the 2012 campaign cycle is incapable of helping his party close the gender gap by David Brock Tuesday, Feb 19, 2013.

38. Bush's Brain: How Karl Rove Made George W. Bush Presidential by Wayne Slater.

39. See PBS Frontline "Karl Rove: The Architect" transcript (http://www.pbs.org/wgbh/pages/frontline/shows/architect/etc/script.html).

40. Ibid.

41. Ibid.

42. Karl Rove in a Corner by Joshua Green in The Atlantic, November 2004.

43. Email to the author from Bill Ratliff March 6, 2016.

44. San Antonio Express News, An East Texas senator's criticism of Gov. Ann Richards Associated Press Publish Date: August 27, 1994.

45. Ibid.

46. Ibid.

47. Email to the author from Bill Ratliff March 6, 2016.

48. San Antonio Express News, An East Texas senator's criticism of Gov. Ann Richards Associated Press Publish Date: August 27, 1994.

49. Email to the author from Bill Ratliff March 6, 2016.

50. San Antonio Express News, An East Texas senator's criticism of Gov. Ann Richards Associated Press Publish Date: August 27, 1994.

51. Ibid.

52. The score cards for some of these golf rounds are in the University of Texas at Tyler Archive. The story was relayed to me in an email from Bill Ratliff February 26, 2016. President George W. Bush sent his best wishes to Ratliff when asked to comment on this in February 2016, but did not comment further.

53. Ibid.

54. Ibid.

55. PBS Frontline Choice 2000 Interview with Clay Johnson (http://www.pbs.org/wgbh/pages/frontline/shows/choice2000/bush/johnson.html).

56. Email to the author from Bill Ratliff February 26, 2016. President Bush sent his best wishes to Governor Ratliff when asked to comment on this in February 2016, but did not comment further.

57. Bush Remarks Announcing Candidacy for the Republican Presidential Nomination June 12, 1999 at The American Presidency Project (http://www.presidency.ucsb.edu/ws/?pid=77819).

58. In an email to the author (February 24, 2016) Bill Ratliff wrote, "One of the things many people do not recall about this bill [SB 7] was that it not only established the recapture concept, it also contained the first comprehensive accountability system for the state (which was later carried to Washington DC by George W and became the early concept for "no child left behind", but later was bastardized so badly at the national level)."

59. Ibid.

60. Ibid.

61. See the American Presidency Project (http://www.presidency.ucsb.edu/florida2000.php)

62. Ibid.

63. Ibid.

64. Ibid.

65. Bush v. Gore, 531 U.S. 98. See also The New York Times, The Vote: The Overview; Study of Disputed Florida Ballots Finds Justices Did Not Cast the Deciding Vote by Ford Fessenden and John M. Broder: November 12, 2001, "Contrary to what many partisans of former Vice President Al Gore have charged, the United States Supreme Court did not award an election to Mr. Bush that otherwise would have been won by Mr. Gore. A close examination of the ballots found that Mr. Bush would have retained a slender margin over Mr. Gore if the Florida court's order to recount more than 43,000 ballots had not been reversed by the United States Supreme Court."

66. See the American Presidency Project (http://www.presidency.ucsb.edu/florida2000.php)

67. Article 4, section 16 of the Texas Constitution, gives the lieutenant governor the authority to take over gubernatorial responsibilities if the governor vacates the position.

68. "A representative of the parliamentarian's office is always present in the chamber when the House or Senate is in session. The Senate and House parliamentarians sit next to the presiding member. The advice a parliamentarian provides is not binding, and the presiding member of the House or Senate can reject that advice at any time." Texplainer: What Does the Parliamentarian Do? by Elizabeth Koh, The Texas Tribune June 27, 2013.

69. See Texas Archive SJR 22, 68th Regular Session Proposing a constitutional amendment relating to the manner in which a vacancy in the office of lieutenant governor is to be filled. Proposition Prop. 5 - The constitutional amendment authorizing the state senate to fill a vacancy in the office of lieutenant governor. Outcome: Adopted Election date: 11/06/1984 Votes for: 2,377,602 Votes against: 1,426,217 Enabling legislation No enabling legislation required. Articles affected Article 3 : Amends §9

70. Ibid.

71. Ibid.

72. Outcome: Adopted Election date: 11/06/1984 Votes for: 2,377,602, Votes against: 1,426,217 Enabling legislation No enabling legislation required. Articles affected Article 3 : Amends §9

73. After Dispute Over Ballots, Texas Senate Picks a Leader by Ross E. Milloy, The New York Times Published: December 29, 2000.

74. Bill Passes: How Bill Ratliff Became Lieutenant Governor and What It Means For Texas by Patricia Hart Texas Monthly February 2001.

75. Ibid.

76. Texas Uses Secret Vote to Elect Official from Associated Press December 29, 2000 (http://articles.latimes.com/2000/dec/29/news/mn-5939).

77. Bill Passes: How Bill Ratliff Became Lieutenant Governor and What It Means For Texas by Patricia Hart Texas Monthly February 2001.

78. See Judge: Texas Senate Must Vote in Public Austin AP Thursday December 28, 2000.

79. Ibid.

80. Email from Bill Ratliff January 28, 2016.

81. Ibid.

82. Bill Passes: How Bill Ratliff Became Lieutenant Governor and What It Means For Texas by Patricia Hart Texas Monthly February 2001.

83. Email from Bill Ratliff April 2, 2016.

84. After Dispute Over Ballots, Texas Senate Picks a Leader by Ross E. Milloy, The New York Times Published: December 29, 2000.

85. Ibid.

86. Ibid.

87. Ibid.

88. Email from Bill Ratliff March 2, 2016.

89. Ibid.

90. Ibid.

91. Ibid.

92. See The Texas Supreme Court: The Mystery of The "Sam Houston" Bible (http://www.txcourts.gov/supreme/about-the-court/court-history/the-mystery-of-the-sam-houston-bible.aspx).

93. Ibid.

94. Quoted in the Texas Senate media release Senator Bill Ratliff is the New President of the Texas Senate December 28, 2000.

95. Email from Bill Ratliff February 10, 2016.

96. Ratliff's about-face draws a mixed reaction Polly Ross Hughes, Houston Chronicle Austin Bureau, January 7, 2001

97. Interview with the author Bonny Edmonds September 2014.

98. Email from Bill Ratliff March 2, 2016.

99. Interview with Don Edmonds 2014.

100. Email from Bill Ratliff March 2, 2016.

101. Ibid.

102. Ibid.

103. See Ratliff's about-face draws a mixed reaction by Polly Ross Hughes, Houston Chronicle Austin Bureau, January 7, 2001.

104. Rodney Ellis chairs influential Texas Senate Finance Committee, LBJ School Record Online (http://www.utexas.edu/lbj/archive/pubs/record/spring01/ellis.html).May 14, 2001

105. Texas Legislative Online

106. Ibid.

107. Ratliff's about-face draws a mixed reaction, by Polly Ross Hughes, Houston Chronicle Austin Bureau, January 7, 2001.

108. Ibid.

109. Follow the Money: How George W. Bush and the Texas Republicans Hog-Tied America by John Anderson p. 102.

110. In several places online (including Wikipedia) one can find this statement "Abramoff claims that he had influenced the Lieutenant Governor of Texas, Bill Ratcliff, to prevent a bill, which would allow the Tigua to open their casino, from being scheduled for a vote in the State Senate. The efforts succeeded, and the Tigua officially closed their casino on February 12, 2002."

111. Email from Bill Ratliff to the author March 6, 2016. I ask Ratliff directly about the claims made in John Anderson's book Follow the Money p. 102.

112. Follow the Money: How George W. Bush and the Texas Republicans Hog-Tied America by John Anderson page 102.

113. Ibid footnote on 102.

114. Email to the author from Bill Ratliff March 6, 2016.

115. Ibid.

116. Bill Ratliff also wrote, "As a matter of fact, I did not know who Abramoff was until his scandal came to light, and I learned that he was taking credit for my stopping the bill. By the way, I never heard from Mr. Anderson regarding this matter. I find it strange that he would include such a statement in his book without even the courtesy of a telephone call."

117. Profiles in Courage by John F. Kennedy 1955.

118. Ibid.

119. Brewer had a tattoo of a cross burning and an intertwined KKK (see James Byrd's killer: 'I'd do it all over again' KHOU Houston. KHOU.com 12:14 p.m. CDT September 20, 2011.

120. See Man executed for dragging death of James Byrd, by the CNN Staff, September 22, 2011.

121. Ibid.

122. Ibid.

123. Second Man Convicted in Texas Dragging Death by Paul Duggan Washington Post Staff Writer, Tuesday, September 21, 1999; p. A2

124. Ibid.

125. Man executed for dragging death of James Byrd by the CNN Wire Staff September 22, 2011.

126. See Latest Hate Crime Statistics Available Report Contains Info on Offenses, Victims, and Offenders 2015 (https://www.fbi.gov/news/stories/2015/november/latest-hate-crime-statistics-available/latest-hate-crime-statistics-available).

127. Ibid.

128. Ibid.

129. Ibid.

130. Ibid.

131. See Legislative Reference Library of Texas, SB 275, 76th Regular Session, Relating to the investigation and prosecution of an offense motivated by bias or prejudice and to other remedies for and protections against certain hateful acts. Author: Rodney Ellis Coauthor: Carlos Truan | Mario Gallegos, Jr. | Royce West | Gonzalo Barrientos | Mike Moncrief | Eddie Lucio, Jr. | Gregory Luna | David Cain | John Whitmire | David Bernsen | Eliot Shapleigh; Companion: HB 938 (Identical)

132. Ibid.

133. Hate crime bill given approval by Senate Measure would toughen law by Clay Robison, Houston Chronicle Austin Bureau Published 6:30 am, Thursday, February 8, 2001

134. See Texas Archive SJR 22, 68th Regular Session Proposing a constitutional amendment relating to the manner in which a vacancy in the office of lieutenant governor is to be filled. Proposition Prop. 5 - The constitutional amendment authorizing the state senate to fill a vacancy in the office of lieutenant governor.

135. You need to check on this.

136. Ibid.

137. Email to the author from Bill Ratliff March 6, 2016.

138. James Byrd Jr. Hate Crimes Act Clears Major Hurdle, Senate Press Release From the Office of State Senator Rodney Ellis February 7, 2001.

139. Ibid.

140. Senator John F. Kennedy wrote about the important call of the roll in Profiles in Courage, p. 39.

141. Ibid p. 40.

142. Email from Bill Ratliff March 6, 2016.

143. The digital recording of this debate is found on The Texas Digital Archive.

144. Ibid.

145. David Easton wrote this widely used definition of politics.

146. Bill Ratliff, email to the author, March 6, 2016.

147. Interview with the author Sally Ratliff September 2013.

148. The digital recording of this debate is found on The Texas Digital Archive.

149. Quote from C.S. Lewis.

150. Bill Ratliff, email to the author, March 6, 2016.

151. Texas Senate Passes Hate Crimes Bill That Bush's Allies Killed by Ross E. Milloy, The New York Times Published: May 8, 2001.

152. Mr. Right: Can you name the most influential Republican in Texas? It's not Rick Perry or any other elected official. It's James Leininger, a little-known San Antonio physician whose ideology and millions are pushing the GOP to be more conservative than ever. by Karen Olsson Texas Monthly published November 2002.

153. From the Missouri Synod website "Belief and Practice, The Lutheran Church—Missouri Synod (http://www.lcms.org/belief-and-practice).

154. Ibid.

155. Mr. Right by Karen Olsson Texas Monthly 2002.

156. From the Missouri Synod website "Belief and Practice, The Lutheran Church—Missouri Synod (http://www.lcms.org/belief-and-practice).

157. Mr. Right by Karen Olsson Texas Monthly 2002.

158. Ibid.

159. Quoted in Who is James Leininger? by The Texas Tribune Aug. 26, 2011. See also, The State of the Religious Right: 2006 The Anatomy of Power (http://tfn.org/cms/assets/uploads/2015/11/SORR_06_ReportWEB.pdf).

160. Source: Texas Ethics Commission (the Commission Ratliff helped establish).

161. These quotes are directly from the flyer. A photo of the flyer can be found on Capitol Chronicle The Politics of Hatred: FreePAC's Gay-Bashing Reveals the Dark Side of Texas Politics by Michael King, Fri., March 15, 2002 (http://www.austinchronicle.com/news/2002-03-15/85232/).

162. Ibid.

163. Dallas Observer: Thursday, February 17, 2005 (http://www.dallasobserver.com/news/right-hand-of-god-6382731)

164. Ibid.

165. Ratliff withdraws from lieutenant governor race, by Clay Robison, 2001 Houston Chronicle Published Tuesday, June 5, 2001

166. A Power in Texas Governing Finds Fault in Texas Politics, by Jim Yardley, The New York Times, June 9, 2001.

167. Interview with Ratliff in Mt. Pleasant 2013.

168. Ibid.

169. Ibid. Ratliff did not recall the names of the men or did not want to say.

170. A Power in Texas Governing Finds Fault in Texas Politics, by Jim Yardley, The New York Times, June 9, 2001.

171. Ibid.

172. Ibid.

173. Bill and Sally Ratliff told the author this story in an interview in Mt Pleasant in 2013. Each time we talked about this story it was obvious that it was an emotional moment in their lives. They had only shared it with a few close friends and family. Bill Ratliff would later email answers to details about the series of events. I have done my best to retell it as they told it to me.

174. Ibid.

175. Ibid.

176. Neither Bill nor Sally would reveal the names of these donors. It would be possible find the names, however, I decided not to seek that information as the names are not really relevant to the point of this book. The people involved know who said these offensive remarks, but the point of retelling this story is to share Ratliff's decision, the factors that went into that decision, and his character.

177. Sally Ratliff interview 2013.

178. Ibid.

179. Ibid.

180. Bill Ratliff, email to the author, October 2014.

181. A Power in Texas Governing Finds Fault in Texas Politics, by Jim Yardley, The New York Times, Published: June 9, 2001.

182. Ibid.

183. Ibid.

184. Don Edmonds told me this story and it was also retold in A Power in Texas Governing Finds Fault in Texas Politics, by Jim Yardley, The New York Times, June 9, 2001.

185. Quote from Profiles in Courage, by John F. Kennedy, page 78.

SEVEN

The Stand: Free of Partisanship

FREE OF EGOTISM

It was never about ego. From his earliest days in office, Ratliff had ruled out a bid for a US Congressional seat. "Yes, I would rule it out," he said, "I'm really not interested in being a member of Congress. I've had people ask me, but I think I can have more of an impact for Northeast Texas in Texas than in Washington."[1] This promise, however, would not prevent Washington—both Congress and the White House—from calling on the Senator in the long hot summer of 2003. After refusing to change his stripes or forgo his principles for $10 million dollars, Lieutenant Governor Ratliff considered new plans, not based on ego but rather on the principle of service.

On Friday, August 1, 2001, Bill and Sally drove the sixty miles from Mt. Pleasant to Kilgore, Texas to make an announcement. After considering his options in June and July, Bill had decided to seek reelection to return to Austin as a Senator for one more legislative session. On that hot August afternoon in East Texas, Ratliff warned the hundreds of gathered supporters that lawmakers would have some tough decisions to make in the upcoming session. He did not know how true warning would actually end up being. Ratliff also noted that the Senate would be losing some significant senior leadership. "I figured they might need a little gray hair in there one more time," said Ratliff.[2] Indeed, the Senate would need "Obi Wan." Democrats and Republicans in Austin and Washington came to depend upon him as the 78th Texas Legislature in 2003 was pulled into a feverish national partisan battle that turned out to be "one of the most extraordinary political events of the past fifty years."[3] Before that event unfolded the Senator from Mt. Pleasant set out to reshape Texas civil torts.

149

TORTS AND TRIAL LAWYERS

Since winning his Senate seat in 1988, Ratliff had written and led major landscape-changing legislation leading to stronger ethics laws for lawmakers, a more equitable and improved education system for Texas children, balanced State budgets, and served as the State's forty-first Lieutenant Governor. However, he still had work to do. The 78th Legislative session required the engineer to find a solution to the State's "tort" law issue.

Tort law reform was neither a new issue for Texas or for Senator Ratliff. In 1988, in his first run for office, Ratliff had called for change in the State's tort laws and challenged the "trial lawyers." As far back as 1975, Lieutenant Governor Bill Hobby called for reform in a "tort reform" speech to the Galveston Chamber of Commerce. In that speech, Hobby detailed his "plan for dealing with the rising medical malpractice insurance rates in Texas."[4] Hobby stated his intention to establish an "interim committee to look into the entire problem and determine the feasibility of establishing an alternative system for Texas."[5]

In 1975, Lieutenant Governor Hobby asked Senator A. R. "Babe" Schwartz[6] (D-Galveston) to create an interim committee to look into the tort reform issue.[7] Hobby asked the famous dean from the University of Texas School of Law, Page Keeton,[8] to chair a special malpractice study committee.[9] One of the nation's foremost authorities on tort law, Keeton (along with professor William Lloyd Prosser) authored *the* primary textbook on tort law.[10] Generations of first-year law students all across the nation were required to read *Prosser and Keeton on Torts* in order to learn the elements of tort law—duty, breach, and proximate cause. According to Keeton, a "tort" is a "civil wrong" that has been recognized by law as grounds for a lawsuit.[11] Professors Prosser and Keeton wrote that the primary aim of tort law is to provide relief for the damages incurred and deter others from committing the same harms.[12] Among the types of damages, the injured party may recover are for loss of earning capacity, pain and suffering, and reasonable medical expenses.

Doctors Are Abandoning the Medical Profession

Insurance companies, corporations, and especially medical practitioners, argue that court costs and excessive damage awards have unnecessarily driven up insurance premiums and medical costs. In 2003, Governor Rick Perry declared medical malpractice reform legislation to be an emergency issue. On January 23, 2003, Governor Perry sent an emergency message to the Senate and House.[13] In that message, Perry wrote, "All across Texas, doctors are abandoning the medical profession because of soaring malpractice rates and the plague of frivolous lawsuits. If this issue is not addressed soon, the medical malpractice crisis will do lasting damage to the practice of medicine in Texas and undermine the access Texans have to the quality, affordable health care they need."[14] Governor Perry requested that the Texas Legislature cap "noneconomic losses to plaintiffs at $250,000."[15] Senator Ratliff and Representative Joe Nixon (R-Houston) took on the task of addressing Perry's emergency legislation.

On February 17, 2003, Representative Nixon introduced a tort reform bill (HB 4) in the House. On February 26, 2003, the Texas House Civil Practices Committee held a full day of public hearings. Among others, Shannon Ratliff, and Richard Trabulsi Jr. testified in favor of HB 4.[16] Trabulsi, along with Leo Linbeck, Hugh Kelly, and Richard Weekley, founded the Texans for Lawsuit Reform (TLR) lobbying group. TLR is a highly influential and very conservative lobbying group that primarily advocates for tort reform and limiting lawsuits.[17] TLR is one of the largest and best-funded tort reform groups in the United States.[18] TLR has become a dominant financial engine for legislative races and has helped "to create a Legislature that's not only more conservative about legal issues, but more conservative, period."[19]

I Was Being Lobbied Hard

Representative Nixon and his committee worked on the lengthy and detailed bill until March 31, 2003, when it was finally sent to the Senate. Governor Perry and Lieutenant Governor David Dewhurst turned to Senator Ratliff to carry the bill in the Senate. Ratliff and his State Affairs Committee colleagues made many significant additions and changes to HB 4. The Conference Committee report "Section-by-Section Analysis" shows that Ratliff and his committee made more than two hundred additions and changes to the House version of the legislation.[20]

As he had done with every other difficult issue of public policy, Ratliff turned his efforts to understanding the problems, issues, and stakeholders before seeking solutions. There was no shortage of input about what was to be done or not done with Texas tort law. "I was being lobbied hard," said Ratliff, "by both the Texas Association of Business and their allies as well as the Texas Trial Lawyers Association and their members."[21] Ratliff was lobbied by groups representing the defendants in civil actions, the Texas Civil Justice League, Texans for Lawsuit Reform, insurance companies, and a wide range of business and medical groups who sought to limit liability in civil tort cases. "I spent many hours with those groups in my office," said Ratliff.[22] Chairing the State Affairs Committee, Ratliff and his colleagues listened to more than sixty-five hours of public testimony on tort reform from April 7 to May 13.

Receiving thousands of pages of information about existing tort law, tort reform ideas, and hours and hours of lobbyists input during the final days of testimony, Ratliff decided that he needed a full day to engage in informal learning—away from the office. Bill called on his brother's legal

Senate Committee on State Affairs—78th Regular Session (2003)
Committee Members

Bill Ratliff, Chair

Todd Staples (R-Palestine), Vice Chair	Tommy Williams (R-The Woodlands), Vice Chair
Ken Armbrister (D-Victoria)	Robert Duncan (R-Lubbock)
Rodney Ellis (D-Houston)	Troy Fraser (R-Horseshoe Bay)
Chris Harris (R-Arlington)	Frank Madla (D-San Antonio)
Jane Nelson (R-Flower Mound)	Florence Shapiro (R-Plano)

expertise. Bill's brother, University of Texas School of Law Professor, Jack Ratliff, offered his ranch home as a private and quiet meeting place.

LET'S NOT BULLSHIT EACH OTHER

Jack Ratliff described Saturday, May 10, 2003, as "one of those glorious hill country days."[23] Senator Ratliff fondly recalled that "there is no doubt that it stands out as perhaps my favorite memory of my service in the Senate, second only to the day I was chosen Lieutenant Governor."[24] Early that morning, Bill and Sally drove West out of Austin on Highway 290 toward Dripping Springs. Just past Dripping Springs, deep in the Texas hill country, they turned off the main highway onto Creek Road and drove another eight miles to Jack's ranch house. Jack and his wife, Clare, lived in a beautiful limestone house designed by an architect with a tin roof built in the Texas hill country Fredericksburg esthetic.[25] The home, on a hill in sight of Onion Creek, is not far from President Lyndon Johnson's ranch.[26] Jack and Clare are gracious hosts and had prepared for a day-long meeting. Shannon arrived just after Bill and Sally. Bill also asked Robert Duncan (R-Lubbock)[27] to take part in the informal tort-discussion in the hill country. Senator Duncan is a lawyer with many years of legal experience and was a key member of Bill's State Affairs Committee (Senator Duncan would later become Chancellor of Texas Tech University). Jack had invited his UT Law School Dean, Bill Powers, to the meeting. Powers (like Dean Keeton before him) is a leading national authority on tort law.[28] Powers (who later served as President of the University of Texas at Austin) and Jack Ratliff had published an article on tort law together.[29] Jack was also teaching tort law at the University of Texas School of Law at that time. These five men, three brothers, Bill, Jack, and Shannon Ratliff, along with Bill Powers, and Robert Duncan spent the day trying to make sense of mountains of testimony and Governor Perry's urgent call for tort reform.[30] "It was a very constructive day," recalled Powers, "we said, let's not bullshit each other, let's figure out what we really ought to do."[31] They spent most of the day on a large high-ceiling porch sitting in rustic leather easy chairs made from large bentwood branches. Not quite fifty yards away from the porch where they sat was the fence of an exotic game ranch. The owner of that ranch had collected exotic game from all over the world. That day, while debating tort law, the men saw a herd of bison and later a herd of zebra grazing along on the other side of the fence.

He Was Clearly the Decider and Judge

Politics is, according the Professor Harold Lasswell, the process that determines who gets what, when, and how, in a society. Seated on that porch next to an exotic game ranch, five Texas leaders debated the issue of torts or who would get what, when, when, and how under tort law in Texas. "Tort reform" is a heated and contentious political issue precisely because the stakes are high for medical consumers (all of us), injured patients, physicians, insurance companies, and lawyers. Individuals on the various sides of the issue claim their solutions simply must be put into law if people are to have access to quality healthcare, or to avoid disaster for patients, or to protect doctors.

As a light breeze blew in, reminding them of the nearby zebras, the senators, Ratliff and Duncan, asked questions. The lawyers, Jack, Shannon, and Bill Powers provided answers and the debate. "Bill would ask a question," recalled Jack, "hear the different arguments for different positions and then sometimes 'rule' about which he thought he might use in the bill, other times not committing and just moving on to the next issue. In other words, he sat as a judge and everybody addressed their arguments to him. The odd part was that everybody on the porch was a lawyer except Bill, however, he was clearly the decider and judge in that situation."[32]

Shannon, sitting deep in a rustic leather rocker facing the exotic game, argued for the defendants and Governor Perry's reforms. Shannon had extensive personal experience in tort cases. He had been the main negotiator in many cases, representing the business side. Shannon had already testified in favor of the House version of the bill and easily made the argument for the corporations, the medical community, and the insurance companies.[33] Shannon argued that too many doctors in Texas were being confronted with expensive malpractice claims, that even the medical malpractice claims that the plaintiffs failed to win were very expensive to defend, and that these costs were hurting not only doctors but also the quality of healthcare in Texas.[34]

Just Trying to Get a Better Deal

With his back to the grazing exotic game, Bill Powers took the role and tone of the torts professor. "Jack and I were the academics," said Powers.[35] Taking the plaintiff side, Powers stated that doctors, hospitals, and malpractice insurers would likely grow millions of dollars richer by devaluing the claims of injured patients. To Powers the tort reform cap requested by Governor Perry, doctors, and insurers, was simply an "arbitrary" redistribution of wealth from malpractice victims to the proponents of the tort reform.[36] Powers said, "I put on my plaintiff's cap whenever caps on damages come up as it's just arbitrary to place a cap on the damages."[37] Jack argued that HB 4 could put contingent fee lawyers out of business. Jack said, "I don't mind telling you that I favored leaving the tort setup alone, especially when it came to caps on damages. I was okay with some limit but my idea was much higher limits than the others."[38] "Placing caps on damages," said Powers, "is just trying to get a better deal."[39]

As the day wore on there were disagreements and spirited discussions. Powers recalled, "the discussion was at an extremely high level, academic, extremely friendly."[40] "The 'heated' discussions I recall," said Jack, "were mainly between Shannon and me, in an odd way, they replayed the kind of discussion and debate that was a staple of our parents' home in earlier days. We both got red in the face during the back and forth, but, after the debate was over, there was never any residual bad feeling, at least none that I could see."[41] Bill recalled, "one of my reactions to the session was that, even though Jack and Bill Powers tended to state the plaintiff arguments, and Shannon and Robert tended to state the defendant position, I was always struck by the fact that everyone seemed to try to give me the countervailing arguments from a balanced perspective as best they could from their experiences, and without hyperbole."[42] Senator Duncan later said, "The group was not constrained by lobbyists sitting outside the door or the media spinning every word being stated. Rather, the group was able to speak freely in agreement and disagreement as to the recommendations that were being formulated in those discussions. It was truly a discussion of the highest level and one that was focused on policy and not necessarily politics."[43] Senators Duncan and Ratliff took that day of informal debate and discussion back to the Senate.

Ten Gallon Tort Reform

The House floor debate continued for eight record setting days; the Senate floor debate running from early morning until very late into the night, lasted six days. The people's representatives in the Texas Legislature debated the values of Texas's society. "Politics," Professor David

Easton famously argued, is the "authoritative allocation of values for a society."[44] On June 11, 2003, Governor Rick Perry signed into law a bill (HB 4) that the *Wall Street Journal* called a "Ten Gallon Tort Reform."[45] The values were debated and then given the authority of law for all Texas citizens. The central and most important reform to tort law in 2003 was a cap placed on "pain and suffering" awards. Representative Nixon and Senator Ratliff's 2003 tort law limited noneconomic damages. A Texas jury cannot award more than $250,000 in noneconomic damages.[46]

REPUBLICAN IN NAME ONLY

Senator Ratliff was at his best when working with the heavy lifting of complex policymaking. He was a workhorse who relished the detailed work of a ninety-six-page bill that included hundreds of floor amendments. Bill Powers later said, "Ratliff would tackle the big issue, even if it was a hot and controversial topic, he was a very responsible legislator, who was for a successful session and for resolving the issues and getting the legislative job done."[47] Tort reform "was a hard fought political battle over an issue that called for compromise, and that was Bill Ratliff," said Powers, "so it was an issue that was teed up for him."[48] Compromise was necessary in the reform of tort law, just as in education law and in budgeting, as there are many and competing interests. Lawmakers like Ratliff who seek common ground, who compromise, and work across party lines are often criticized by those in their own parties for doing so. To some far-right, ultraconservatives, Ratliff's willingness to compromise made him what they call a RINO, a "Republican In Name Only."[49] The RINO insult is for those who are not *real* Republicans.[50] While some far-right Republicans used the derogatory term RINO for Ratliff, he was, in fact, one of the principle architects of the conservative 2003 tort reform that has been roundly cheered by ultraconservative groups across Texas and the United States.[51] Senator Duncan said, "The term RINO became popular as the Republican Party began placing its own membership into categories. What was becoming lost was the importance of the "ability to govern" and find solutions for the State's problems and issues. Bill Ratliff was the ultimate problem solver. Texas is a large and diverse state. In order to solve problems impacting all Texans, compromise is absolutely necessary. Bill tried different methods during his time as Lt. Governor, including appointing Rodney Ellis, a leading Democrat, as Chairman of the Senate Finance Committee. By doing this, he enlarged the tent of problem solvers which allowed solutions to issues utilizing the various and wide talent available in the Senate, whether or not the talent fit into some specific political label. I think this is what made Bill successful as a legislative leader and later as an influential person in Texas public policy."[52]

PEOPLE WANT EFFECTIVE REPRESENTATION

In an era of hyperpartisanship many people tend to think that they should support only those who score the closest to their own values on narrow ideological or even single issue tests or on voting record rankings. Political scientists have long used roll call votes to measure a legislator's ideology. Professor Mark Jones, of Rice University's political science department, regularly ranks representatives based on their voting records.[53] Other groups use these rankings (or groups like "Empower Texans" create similar rankings) to make decisions about who to support—financially. Like Senator Kennedy's Raven these rankings are perched on each representative's desk croaking "nevermore" as they cast votes.[54] The rankings matter—not so much because the citizens actually care about each specific roll call vote—but because political action groups use the rankings or "scores" to support candidates that support their specific agenda. Few voters know or even care about many of the thousands of issues their representatives handle each legislative session. The scorecard has the potential to change the way a representative does his or her work as the ranking often means significant flows of cash.

Empower Texans (and Texans for Lawsuit Reform) gave the most money to specific Texas candidates in the 2016 election cycle.[55] Empower Texans is an ultra-right wing conservative political action group that supports Tea Party candidates such as Bryan Hughes (R-Mineola) in his bid for Senator Ratliff's old seat and Matt Rinaldi (R-Irving) who defeated Bill Ratliff's son, Bennett Ratliff (R-Irving) for a seat in the Texas House of Representatives. Empower Texans creates a "Texas Scorecard" that ranks a legislator's votes. The group awarded Rinaldi with a perfect 100 percent score and an A+ rating—meaning that the Rinaldi voted exactly as Empower Texans wished 100 percent of the time.[56] Professor Mark Jones summed up the Rinaldi and Bennett Ratliff race saying, "While Rinaldi ranked as *the* most conservative of the 154 Republican representatives (over the last three sessions), Ratliff ranked as the 126th most conservative. The vast ideological gap separating these candidates provides GOP primary voters in northwest Dallas County with two very disparate ideological options on March 1."[57] Professor Jones and Empower Texans argue that their scorecards are important to voters. However, the scorecard rankings do not appear to have made much difference in the total dollar amount of individual contributions made to each of these two candidates in the 2016 race.

Bennett Ratliff and Matt Rinaldi raised nearly equal amounts from individual contributors during both 2015 and 2016. Rinaldi raised $111,000 compared to Ratliff's $110,870.[58] But Rinaldi had a clear advantage in support from groups like Empower Texans, with $205,600 to Ratliff's $66,500.[59] Empower Texans contributed $125,000 to Rinaldi's campaign.[60] The founder of Empower Texans, Midland oilman Tim Dunn, also personally gave Rinaldi another $5,000.[61] Between January 1, 2015 and February 22, 2016, Empower Texans contributed $1,497,458 to candidates vying for the Texas Senate, House, and the State Board of Education.[62]

In the 2014 Rinaldi versus Ratliff race, more than 8,200 votes were cast and a mere 92 votes determined the winner.[63] "People want effective representation," said Bennett Ratliff during the campaign, "somebody who will go to Austin and actually get something done. They realize there is a stark contrast between my record of accomplishing conservative results, and my opponent's record of just voting no."[64]

Like father like son, Bill Ratliff stood "just fifteen degrees to the right of center and was motivated by two things," said Bill Powers, "representing his constituents, and a resolve to find solutions to the issues to get the legislative job done."[65] About Bennett's father, Powers said, "He would not last a single session today with the Koch brothers and Empower Texas."[66] It seems likely that Senator Sam Houston would also have had low ranking with Empower Texans after his famous vote against his party in 1857. Perhaps it is not the perfect ideological scorecard that voters need and or want—but rather men and women who are authentic in their pursuit of common ground and in effective governing. In a letter to a Democrat constituent, dated October 8, 1992, Lieutenant Governor Bob Bullock, also a Democrat, explained why he supported the Republican candidate, Senator Ratliff.

Dear David,
Tony Proffitt[67] told me about your call regarding the event I plan to attend October 19 in New Boston on behalf of Senator Bill Ratliff.
I want you to know that your feelings and your opinion on this mean a great deal to me. You have been my friend for a long time and I would

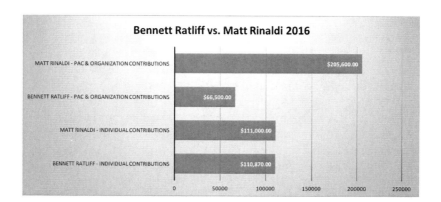

Figure 7.1.   Created by the author (Data source: The *Texas Tribune*, February 23, 2016 (https://www.texastribune.org/2016/02/23/after-bowing-out-or-getting-beat-several-former-la/).

not do anything to imperil our friendship or detract from my appreciation of the support you have given me in the past.

But in this instance, I must do what I feel is right about a man who is a good Texas Senator and who has put public responsibility ahead of politics. My first session as Lieutenant Governor was a tough one and the Republicans in the Texas Senate did nothing to make it any easier—with one exception, Bill Ratliff.

By way of example, I can cite two of the toughest—and most critical—votes cast in the Senate last year, the school finance bill and the tax bill to keep the school doors open. Bill Ratliff voted for both bills. He was the only Republican to do so and he has taken a lot of heat from his own party over it. Right now he is taking heat from Democrats and Republicans alike over the corporate franchise tax revision which he voted for and without which the state budget could not have been balanced.

But more than just voting for bills, Senator Ratliff has been a worker, a contributor in putting those bills together in a businesslike form, when other Republicans—and unfortunately, a few Democrats from time to time—said no.

Partisan politics in Washington has brought Congress to a standstill. I simply won't permit that in the Texas Senate.

So as Bill Ratliff has put partisan politics aside when he works with me in the Texas Senate, I have put partisan politics aside in going to New Boston and telling any who cares to listen that Bill Ratliff is like my friend David Glass—a good man who has given me his hand in friendship, confidence, and help.

Sincerely,

Bob Bullock

Lieutenant Governor

BB: cgw[68]

THIS MEASURE WILL COST YOU AND ME OUR SEATS

In the 2003 legislative session, Bill Ratliff stood firmly on principle and for his constituents in one of the most dramatic political events of the last fifty years. The event moved Senator Ratliff from the work he enjoyed—finding solutions and policymaking—to the part of politics he hated—center stage in a national partisan battle for power and control. Ratliff's example, once again, stands as a testament to courage and of a representative seeking to serve the people rather than a political party or narrow individual interests. The Senator from Mt. Pleasant is not alone in his staunch independence and standing against narrow partisanship. Senator John Quincy Adams, during his single term in the US Senate, demonstrated an "audacious disdain for narrow partisanship."[69] Adams was also an independent thinker with a willingness to break from his party. In 1803, seeking to be fair, Senator Adams proposed giving the Jeffersonian (or Democratic) party proportional representation on an important council.[70] His nonpartisan independence, Adams later said, "marked the principle by which my whole public life has been governed from that day to this."[71] In 1807 Adams, like Senator Ratliff in 2003, irreparably split with his party. Senator Adam's break concerned foreign policy, Senator Ratliff's concerned redistricting politics—both Senators later found themselves to be men without a party. "This measure will cost you and me our seats," Adams remarked, "but private interest must not be put in opposition to public good."[72] Like Adams, Ratliff took a stand for public good.

In January 1990, the *Texarkana Gazette* headline declared, "Redistricting Promises to Be Battle of Decade!"[73] In 2003 that headline became true as Democrats and Republicans waged a highly partisan battle over where voter district lines would be drawn on the Texas map. While redistricting may seem like an "inside baseball" aspect of politics, it is not complicated. It is, however, critically important to all Americans.

IT IS *ESSENTIAL* TO SUCH A GOVERNMENT

The creation of voter districts is a critical and a foundational component of American democracy. Early in American history, political leaders realized the remarkable power found in the shape, reshaping, and the size of voter districts. Attempts to manipulate district lines for political advantage and gain date back to the country's origin. It is important to remember that the drawing of voter districts is—at its most basic and fundamental level—about political power. It is about getting and or keeping power.

In a democracy the people are sovereign—meaning that citizen voters should ultimately hold the power and have the final authority over their own lives. The American political system, as James Madison wrote, "derives all its powers directly or indirectly from the great body of the people. It is *essential* [emphasis in original] to such a government that it be derived from the great body of the society, not from an inconsiderable proportion, or a favored class of it."[74] The government's power and authority must come from the people—all of the people. The people must vote for their representatives. Representatives must be elected by a specific geographic group of people. Lines must be drawn on a map.

The actual and practical drawing of geographic districts is done with census data. The Texas Constitution requires that the State Legislature reapportion Texas voter districts during the first regular session after every federal census—which occurs every ten years.[75] Using census data the legislature divides the population into equal districts for every elected position—both state and national. Political power is derived from the actual drawing of the district lines.

Perrymandering

Drawing legislative districts to give a political advantage is commonly called "gerrymandering."[76] The term "gerrymander" comes from the name of a Massachusetts governor, Elbridge Gerry, who, in 1812, signed into law an unpopular redistricting plan that included one state Senate district shaped like a salamander.[77] In 2003, many renamed it "Perrymandering," after Texas Governor Rick Perry.[78] Until the 1960s, many politicians even deliberately created districts that were malapportioned—meaning that the districts did not contain the same number of voters. In a series of cases in the early 1960s, the United States Supreme Court ruled that the unequal distribution of population (drawing districts with one area substantially larger or smaller than another) is unconstitutional.[79] In a 1964 decision, *Reynolds v. Sims*, and again in 2016, *Evenwel v. Abbott*,[80] the Supreme Court ruled that voting districts must contain very close to the same number of people—one-person-one vote.[81]

The mere fact that the issue of redistricting is so very often litigated further supports the proposition that it is an important and powerful factor in American politics. In 2016, the Court resolved, in *Evenwel v. Abbott*, yet another challenge to the one-person-one vote rule.[82] The Court was asked whether voting districts should contain roughly the same number of people or the same number of eligible voters. This challenge was again about power, as counting all the people amplifies the voting power of places that have large numbers of residents who cannot register to vote—including children and people who are legal residents but not citizens. In 2016, those areas tended to be urban and tended to vote Democratic. Republicans would have benefited from changing the one-person-one vote rule to meaning only eligible voters at that point in history. For the Court, Justice Ruth Ginsburg wrote, "Nonvoters have an important stake in many policy debates—children, their parents, even their grandparents, for example, have a stake in a strong public-education system—and in receiving constituent services, such as help navigating public-benefits bureaucracies. By ensuring that each representative is subject to requests and suggestions from the same number of constituents, total population apportionment promotes equitable and effective representation."[83] By the ruling of the United States Supreme Court, one-person-one vote rule is the law of the land.

Even with significant Supreme Court restrictions on voter districts, politicians still draw district maps to gain power and to shape policy. Politicians use redistricting as a political tool in a number of different ways. One of the most obvious is that they use it to select their voters. They draw district lines around those voters they know will support them and dilute and divide those communities they know will not. Redistricting is also used to defeat competitors and to support the incumbent. Some politicians use the redrawing of district lines to eliminate challengers (by excluding them from the district) or to defeat incumbents (by placing them in a new unwinnable district). Most importantly, politicians use redistricting to shape and reshape a state's representation in the United States House of Representatives. In 2001 and 2003, Republicans in Washington set about using redistricting to increase their power and control of politics and policy. They intended to take long-term control of Congress.

THE TWO-THIRDS RULE

As required by the Texas Constitution, in 2001, the Texas Legislature and Lieutenant Governor Ratliff took up the redistricting challenge. Ratliff appointed a Republican senator, Jeff Wentworth (San Antonio), to chair the Redistricting Committee. Senator Wentworth and his committee created a plan that would have moderately increased the number of Republicans in Washington and kept most—but not all—incumbents in place.[84] But Wentworth and the Republicans had a problem. They could not bring the plan to the floor of the Senate for a vote because of a nearly seventy-year-old Senate rule requiring two-thirds of the thirty-one senators to approve before bringing a bill to the floor. This Senate rule was called the two-thirds rule.

Senate Rule 5.13 stated, "No bill, joint resolution, or resolution affecting state policy may be considered out of its regular calendar order unless the regular order is suspended by a vote of two-thirds of the members present."[85] It was the Senate tradition until 2015,[86] that an insignificant bill, referred to as a "blocker bill" was placed at the top of the Senate's calendar. That bill was left there all session. In order for a bill to be considered before the blocker bill was considered, two-thirds of the senators must vote their approval—thus, in effect, requiring two-thirds approval for every bill that would reach the Senate floor. The two-thirds rule require the majority of senators to include the minority in the decision to bring a bill to the floor. The rule forced the senators to be more collegial, to work together, and to be less partisan. Bill Ratliff, as a senator and as Lieutenant Governor greatly supported and respected the two-thirds rule. The rule fit Ratliff's principles—namely the principles of bipartisanship and inclusiveness. Ratliff's bipartisan approach to politics and policymaking dovetailed perfectly with the two-thirds rule—as the rule clearly made the Senate a less partisan institution.

In 2001, Senator Wentworth could not rally the support of twenty-one senators needed to bring his redistricting bill to the floor for a vote. Wentworth asked Lieutenant Governor Ratliff to suspend the two-thirds rule.[87] Ratliff refused. Wentworth's bill died. U.S. Congressman Tom Delay (R-Sugarland) phoned Lieutenant Governor Ratliff to see if he would insist on the two-thirds requirement in a special session.[88] True to form,

Ratliff told Delay that he would always follow Senates rules. Ratliff's strict adherence to the Senate rules and his refusal to "engage in 'breaking some arms' to pass an aggressively partisan congressional redistricting plan" left the Washington Republicans with few options.[89] With Ratliff as the presiding officer they failed. Governor Perry did not call a special session and the 2001 redistricting of Texas fell to the courts. When Texas lawmakers are not able to agree on district maps, the State constitution places the duty on the Legislative Redistricting Board (LRB). In 1990, the LRB staff wrote a handwritten poem to the freshman from Mount Pleasant. In that session, Ratliff spent many long hours drafting maps. This LRB poem highlights two important lessons. First, redistricting is and always will be an issue. Second, by 2003, Ratliff very well knew and understood the implications of redistricting.

Ode to a Sweet Cookie[90]

"He eats those sweet cookies
To bolster his knowledge.
But in his office where no one lookies,
There are notebooks enough to start his own college!

Those notebooks he has,
With lots of yellow marks
Denote his intensity—
He's almost never in the dark.

In redistricting particularly, he designs lots of maps.
And the staff makes a promise to Sen. Ratliff, the frosh!
Keep furnishing those sweet cookies at least once a month,
And we won't put on your district the official kibosh!"

Thanks L.R.B Staff

Washington Republicans were not yet done with their attempt to redraw the Texas voter districts. The would try again in the next session. In 2003, Congressman Delay and the Bush administration had big plans for the Texas Legislature. Washington Republicans were focused on achieving a favorable and highly partisan redistricting of the Lone Star state. The Republicans decided to attempt an unprecedented second congressional redistricting in Texas—since they had failed in 2001. Their goal was to "maximize the number of Democratic seats that could be eliminated" and correspondingly increase the number of Republican seats in Washington.[91] Even though Ratliff was no longer the presiding officer, Republicans in Austin and in Washington knew that without Senator Ratliff's support their redistricting plan would likely die.[92] To apply some pressure, President George Bush's Chief of Staff, Karl Rove, decided to call his old client.

WOULD IT MAKE A DIFFERENCE IF THE PRESIDENT CALLS?

Senator Ratliff's assistant, Vatra Solomon, took the call from the White House.[93] Ratliff knew Rove well. Rove had worked for Ratliff's reelection campaign years before. Rove wanted the senator to know just how important his support was to President Bush.[94] Rove intended to persuade the senator to support Congressman Delay's efforts to redraw the lines of power in Texas. Washington Republicans wanted the Senator to fall into line with his party and vote to support larger party interests. After explaining how much his party needed him, Rove asked, "Senator, can we count on your support?" To which Ratliff replied, "Karl, you know me. I'll look at the details of the plan and see how it effects the people of my district."[95] And then in a strong and even tone he added, "the people whose interests I represent."[96] Hearing the note and the tone of independence and the possibility that the senator may not fall into line, Rove asked, "Would it make a difference if the president calls?" "I'd be happy to speak with the president," replied Ratliff, "but you may relay to him that I remain open and will carefully consider any and all fair plans."[97] The Republican senator did, in fact, carefully consider his party's plans and then took a valiant stand that would shake the foundation of his party.[98]

The Republican Strategy

The 2003 Republican strategy included redrawing some districts that had been heavily Republican and dividing those voters into districts which had favored Democrats.[99] They also sought to include more Republican voters in the swing districts in order to improve the overall Republican congressional majority. Congressional District One[100] (CD1) had historically been a compact set of rural Northeast Texas counties with an almost homogeneous commonality of issues. As an illustration of the commonality of this district, the boundaries of CD1 and SD1 (State Senate District One) were almost coterminous, and yet CD1 had been represented by Congressmen James Louis "Jim" Chapman (D) and then Max Allen Sandlin Jr. (D), at the same time that SD1 had been represented by Bill Ratliff.

The Washington redistricting plan proposed to cut Congressional District 1 in half. Tom Delay proposed including several Republican precincts from the Dallas area (Rockwall, Sherman, etc.) in Congressional District 1 to insure that a Republican would be able to dominate that district. In fact, Delay's plan added so many of the Dallas Republican precincts to Congressional District 1 that, not only would it guarantee a Republican would represent the northeast corner of Texas but, Senator Ratliff contended, that the Republican most often elected would be a resident of the Dallas metropolitan area—not from an East Texas community. Thus, not only was Northeast Texas to be cut in two districts—dividing their commonality of interests—it was to be diluted by being included in a nonrural district. Ratliff argued that the congressman that served that district would very likely be a resident of the Dallas metropolitan area. Thus, the Northeast corner of Texas (Ratliff's constituents) would in effect lose its representation in the United States Congress.

NEVERMORE

The summer of 2003 will long be remembered in political lore. That summer many of the people's representatives found themselves facing career-defining moments over the aggressive redrawing of voter districts. Each representative faced Senator Kennedy's Raven—Nevermore—risking personal financial loss, facing career-ending votes, and making personal and public decisions. Books have been written about the 2003 historic redistricting war.[101] Chapters have been written about the individual battles.[102] Careers ended. Friendships died. Five Democratic members of the United States House of Representatives soon lost their jobs.[103] The nation watched as Democrats bolted from the House and Senate to Oklahoma and New Mexico. Airplanes were tracked. Buses were chartered. House and Senate Chamber doors were locked. Fines imposed. Emotions were extremely high. Tempers were short. In all of this partisan ranker and emotion was the calm, fair, and consistent leadership of Senator Ratliff. He earned great respect for doing what he felt was right.

After months of fighting, House Democrats were unable to stop the highly partisan redistricting bill. It soon became clear to all involved that the critical battle would have to be fought among the thirty-one members of the Texas Senate. Republicans held nineteen seats and Democrats held twelve seats in the Senate that summer. Basic math and the Senate two-thirds rule stood in the way of the Republican redistricting bill. Republicans needed twenty-one votes to move Delay's bill past the "blocker bill" onto the floor of the Senate. Senator Ellis had sponsored a bill (HB 53) that sat in the blocker bill spot at the top of the Senate calendar blocking the redistricting bill.

In June, Lieutenant Governor David Dewhurst, a Republican with Washington ambitions, said he would follow Lieutenant Governor Ratliff's precedent and adhere to the Senate two-thirds tradition. Needing twenty-one votes meant that it was imperative that all Republican senators support the Delay plan, so Ratliff's support became critical. It was not important that Ratliff support the bill itself, but it was critical that he vote to allow the bill to come to the floor for a vote. As the Senate boiled in the Austin heat, it became clear that twenty-one votes was out of reach for Delay and the Republicans.

I Will Be Your Eleventh

The Democrats were in a pitched battle. The Republicans faced intense party pressure. But Ratliff was not the only Republican to disagree with Congressman Delay's new map. On the evening of July 10, Senator Ratliff met three of his Republican colleagues at a restaurant on Lavaca Street in Austin.[104] All three of the Republicans told the senior Senator that they did not favor Delay's plan. Over dinner they asked the senior senator from Mount Pleasant to go public with his opposition. That night Bill Ratliff decided to take a stand. He later recalled, "when faced with a decision which pitted my loyalty to my constituents against my loyalty to the Republican party, my loyalty had to be with my constituents. I felt that the Delay redistricting plan was not in the best interest of my constituents, and that I had to oppose its adoption."[105]

The next morning, Senator Ratliff met with the Democratic Dean of the Senate, John Whitmire (D-Houston). Whitmire told Ratliff that he had ten Democrats[106] who were willing to stand in the way of Delay's plan. Ratliff said, "If you can give me those written in blood that they will not vote to suspend the rules, I will be your eleventh."[107]

UNALTERABLE OPPOSITION

By Monday morning, July 14, ten Democrats had signed the letter flatly declaring their "unalterable opposition" to considering any redistricting map on the Senate floor. The letter addressed to Lieutenant Governor David Dewhurst, stated their intention to "oppose any motion to bring such a redistricting bill to the Senate floor for debate." The letter was boldly signed by Senators Gonzalo Barrientos (D-Austin), Rodney Ellis (D-Houston), Mario Gallegos (D-Houston), "Chuy" Hinojosa (D-McAllen), Eddie Lucio (D-San Benito), Eliot Shapleigh (D-El Paso), Leticia Van de Putte (D-San Antonio), Royce West (D-Duncanville), John Whitmire (D-Houston), and Judith Zaffirini (D-Laredo).

Tensions were high on Monday afternoon when Senator Ratliff held a press conference. Ratliff told a throng of reporters, "I have advised Lieutenant Governor David Dewhurst, that I am in possession of a statement signed by ten senators stating their unalterable opposition to any motion to bring redistricting to the Senate floor. I have advised the lieutenant governor that I am adding my name to the statement." In the Senate under the two-thirds rule, Ratliff's signature, the eleventh, meant that the redistricting bill would not be considered. Ratliff's announcement sent shock waves from Austin to Washington.

I Felt That This Mantle Fell to Me

Ratliff felt that the Republican party had asked him and his colleagues to "fall on their swords" for a national gain in power.[108] A vote to support Delay's plans was not in the best interest of his constituents. Ratliff signed his name to that letter not only for his constituents but also his Republican colleagues who were unable to stand against the party. "As a senior Republican in the Texas Senate, I felt that this mantle fell to me," said Ratliff.[109] Ratliff bravely and independently stood for the people, his colleagues, and against narrow partisanship. Like Senators John Quincy Adams and Sam Houston before him, Senator Ratliff was now a man without a party.

As the months wore on, Lieutenant Governor David Dewhurst succumbed to the right-wing pressures in the Republican party and suspended the Senate's two-thirds rule. Ratliff observed, "each step that's taken destroys the Senate that I knew."[110] Democrats fought to keep the rule but failed and then bolted for Albuquerque, New Mexico, in an attempt to keep the Senate from voting. Frustrated and angry, Ratliff walked out of a Republican caucus meeting when his colleagues decided to impose fines upon the boycotting Senate Democrats saying, "I will not be a party to any of this."[111]

RUTHLESS QUEST FOR POWER

"Senator Van de Putte said that walking out of the Senate and staying away to break quorum was 'the bravest thing that I have ever done.'"[112] Democrats stayed away from the Senate and out of the state for four long weeks. In the end their boycott did not stop Delay and the Republicans "ruthless quest for power."[113] In October, senate Democrats had, as Senator Shapleigh said, "run out of options."[114] By a vote of seventeen to fourteen the Senate voted to approve the plan. Two Republicans voted against the plan—Senator Ratliff and Troy Fraser (R-Horseshoe Bay).

The effects of the of the 2003 Texas redistricting are many—but six stand out. First, the 2003 redistricting resulted in significant Republican gains in Congress (twelve seats).[115] Second, those seat gains in Congress had a significant effect on budget policy—President Bush's $726 billion tax cut plan for example.[116] Third, the strong Republican majority in Congress led to significant changes in environmental and civil rights legislation.[117] Fourth, the Republican majority has made significant steps to weaken the effects of the Voting Rights Act.[118] Fifth, Delay's plan created noncompetitive congressional districts.[119] Sixth, time has confirmed Senator Ratliff's fears about the plan. As a result of the 2003 redistricting, Northeast Texas lost much of its representation on matters that are common to its rural population. Since 2003, the person representing the previously homogeneous Northeast corner of Texas has been a Republican who is a resident of the Dallas metropolitan area. In 2016, Republican Congressman John Lee Ratcliffe (and before him Republican Ralph Hall) from the Dallas metropolis area represents the Tom Delay created district that stretches from the eastern suburbs of Dallas-Fort Worth all the way across rural East Texas to Texarkana.

Only 208 People in the World That Really Care

In 1990, Senator Ratliff told the *Texarkana Gazette*, "The one thing that will make this session so difficult is the fact that no matter what the issue is, no matter what's being debated on the floor, the question of redistricting will be the underlying issue."[120] The power and incentive in creating favorable voter districts is strong. Ratliff noted, "There are only 208 people in the world that really care about where those lines are, and all of them are either in Austin or Congress, and they care a lot."[121] Today, Americans are beginning to understand the implications of allowing lawmakers to choose their voters. Citizens in a number of states have taken the power away from their legislators and placed it in independent commissions. In 2015, the United States Supreme Court, in a 5–4 decision upheld Arizona citizen's right to take the redistricting power away from their state legislators.[122] According to a 2013 University of Texas poll, 43 percent of Texans support taking redistricting from lawmakers and giving it to an independent and appointed commission.[123]

"HOME TO MORE IMPORTANT THINGS"

Four months after the redistricting standoff ended, Senator Ratliff announced his resignation. Ratliff delivered a letter to Governor Perry's office that said he would retire effective January 10, 2004—exactly fifteen years from the day he was sworn into office. Ratliff's letter asked Governor Perry to call an election to fill his seat at the earliest possible date so the people of East Texas did not have to go without representation. In 1878, "hated by his party, Senator John Quincy Adams returned to private life."[124] In 2004, Bill and Sally returned to Mount Pleasant. "He's a man who has the inner peace that comes from the satisfaction of having done extremely well and gone back home to the more important things in life," said Bill Powers.[125]

In 2016, when asked about his accomplishments Lieutenant Governor Ratliff said, "my proudest accomplishment is raising three outstanding children who have each reared wonderful children of their own, and who have proven themselves successful adults in a difficult and competitive world."[126]

With the support of Sally, Fate, Tom, Bess, his brothers, and many teachers, many donors, and Texas taxpayers, Bill Ratliff had an extraordinary engineering career, reaching the pinnacle of the consulting engineering world at a very young age. With that success he decided to serve others. As we have seen, Ratliff was the key architect and driving force in the passage of six major pieces of legislation—SB7, SB1, Tort Reform, and three State budgets. Individually, each of those legislative efforts were extraordinary accomplishments.

SB7

Many policy makers had tried to solve the constitutional problem of the State's school finance system and had failed. Ratliff succeeded. This bill redistributed a percentage of property taxes from wealthy school districts to poorer ones. Today, many people are unhappy with the Robin Hood or recapture concept contained in SB7, but in the intervening twenty-three years no one has been able to come up with another solution which is constitutional and would pass in the legislature.

SB1

Ratliff was responsible for the total rewrite of the Texas education code. In the end, his efforts resulted in an extraordinary change in school governance in Texas. Those changes have made and will continue to make a positive difference in the public educations of generations of children.

Tort Reform

Ratliff's tort reform work resulted in a total rewrite of tort law in Texas. Because of his work Texas was no longer being viewed nationally as the preferred venue for the filing of tort lawsuits, particularly lawsuits aimed at medical providers.

Three State Budgets

No matter what other laws are passed, the State's priorities are almost universally controlled by how the State's resources are allocated. "The Texas Legislature can be a puzzling, frustrating, and at times exasperating mechanism for implementing democracy, but I am proud to have been one of those honored to do all I could to make it work for the people of this state," Ratliff said.   .

When asked what he would want a college student to know about his career Lieutenant Governor Ratliff said, "I would hope that students would understand that public service through political office can be a worthy and satisfying experience." Ratliff received many honors and a great deal of recognition for his service.

Texas Monthly

Many people are not aware that the *Texas Monthly* Annual Ten Best list is not simply compiled by the writers of the magazine. During each legislative session, *Texas Monthly* journalists, Paul Burka and his staff, visited with members of the legislature, veteran staffers, respected lobbyists, and compiled that information into their Ten Best/Ten Worst list. Ratliff's peers and Capitol insiders (who knew the members best) selected him for the prestigious Best list an unprecedented seven times (of his eight legislative sessions).

Forty-First Texas Lieutenant Governor

It is hard to imagine a bigger compliment than that of having been selected by one's peers to be the Lt. Governor and President of the Senate. Ratliff did not campaign for this position and would not list it as an accomplishment but he added, "I do consider this the ultimate high honor in the Texas Capitol."[127]

The University of Texas at Tyler Engineering and Science Building

Each year students from all across the United States and the world find themselves learning in the multimillion dollar state-of-the-art engineering building named for Senator Ratliff. "It came as a complete surprise," said Ratliff, "I was honored beyond belief when I learned of it.[128] It is especially meaningful in that I can imagine college students for generations walking into the facility. I doubt that they will ever know what prompted my name to be on these buildings, but that does not diminish my pride in the recognition."[129] Bill Ratliff helped make that magnificent facility of learning possible and for those efforts and his many accomplishments there is a suite of offices dedicated to him the top floor of the building. In that suite, among the many documents, memorabilia, and photos sits the Kennedy Foundation Profiles in Courage Award.

The President John F. Kennedy Profiles in Courage Award

In 2005, the man his colleagues nicknamed Obi-Wan Kenobi was awarded the John F. Kennedy Foundation Profile in Courage Award.[130] The Profile in Courage Award, "seeks to make Americans aware of the conscientious and courageous acts of their public servants, and to encourage elected officials to choose principles over partisanship—to do what is right, rather than what is expedient."[131] The award is presented each year to "elected officials who, acting in accord with their conscience, risk their careers by pursuing a larger vision of the national, state, or local interest in opposition to popular opinion or powerful pressures from their constituents."[132] A sterling silver lantern, modeled after the lantern on the USS *Constitution*, the oldest commissioned ship in the United States Navy was awarded to Senator Ratliff. The lantern was designed by Edwin Schlossberg and crafted by Tiffany & Company and is today in the Ratliff Suite in the Ratliff Science and Engineering Building at the University of Texas at Tyler. Bill Ratliff's name is included on a list of less than fifty extraordinary Americans—including President George H. W. Bush, President Gerald Ford, and Senator John McCain.

A TOTALLY FREE MAN

In 1991, Paul Burka, Patricia Hart, and Ellen Williams, writing for *Texas Monthly* magazine named Senator Ratliff one of the Ten Best Legislators of the Year. They wrote, "Ratliff's stature rests on a single trait that sets him apart from the great mass of the Senate. He's a totally free man—free of partisanship (he cast a rare Republican vote to raise taxes, but he protested to Bullock when no Republicans were named to a crucial conference committee), free of egotism (a Ratliff press release qualifies for the rare documents collection), free of ambition, free of the lobby, free to act as every senator should but few actually do: Look at every issue from both sides and decide what is right."[133] Wrapped in the penumbras of this statement are the keys to Bill Ratliff's courage and leadership.[134]

Senator Ratliff did not forget "wholly about himself in his dedication to higher principles."[135] Rather, it is the integrity of who he is—his character—that enabled him to consistently and courageously stand on principle. *Texas Monthly* said his "stature rests on a single trait—he's a totally free man." Ratliff was "free" because he was not dependent on others for his position. He would not sell himself—not even for $10 million dollars. Through hard work, he had obtained what he wanted and needed (and he was not interested in piling it higher). Senator Ratliff was able to be free—fiercely independent—in his actions and decision making because of his personal responsibility, dedication, and hard work.

Ratliff was "free of narrow partisanship" for several reasons. First, he was respectful and considerate of others—even his opponents. Senator Ratliff's actions in the Senate embody the "golden rule." Just as Tom and Bess had insisted that their sons be fair to and be respectful of their opponents on the playing fields in Sonora, Bill consistently treated others with the dignity and respect he expected from them. Second, Ratliff had earned the trust and support of his constituents. The strong support of the people of his district allowed him the freedom to vote his convictions in the Legislature and to ignore the pressures of partisanship. Finally,

Ratliff was also free of partisanship because he was an engineer looking for real-world solutions not ideological shortcuts. He was willing to do the hard work of understanding the issues confronting the Senate. Party ideology is almost always a poor guide to policymaking, as it fails to take into account the real-world complexities of problems. Bill Ratliff understood that neither citizens or policy makers could effectively cooperate and find solutions through purely partisan ideological approaches. When others were limited by their partisan filters about school finance, Ratliff loaded the entire problem on his laptop and wrote a solution.

Being "free of egotism" meant that Lieutenant Governor Ratliff did not draw his strength from the power of his position, from his seniority, or from his party. His sense of self-worth was not a product of his status. Rather his strength and courage were derived—not from the external—but from an internal and mature independence. Internal maturity and independence is the product of confidence and self-acceptance. Ratliff was free of the burden of self-importance.

Being "free of ambition" meant that his actions were not about his own personal gain but rather were about service to and for others. Ratliff made his life in the Senate about service and making a contribution to the people of his district, state, and country. He believed he had a responsibility to his community. Focusing on that responsibility allowed him to be free of personal ambitions. That freedom gave him the independence to do what he felt was right and to stand for his convictions.

Ratliff was "free of the lobby" for some of the same reasons he was free of his party—he was not dependent on the lobby for his well-being, in any sense. He did not need or want the support of the lobby. Ratliff understood the reasons many legislators were financially dependent on the lobby—they needed (or thought they needed) the income. Freedom and independence from the lobby allowed the self-reliant Senator to carefully listen, empathically understand, and even to courageously confront those who lobbied him. Bill Ratliff is a man-made free by principle.

The man President George W. Bush called "a calm, ramrod-straight, low-key Southern gentleman, and the gray eminence of the Texas Senate" served well in accordance with his conscience.[136] Ratliff stood firmly on the principles of honesty, hard work, justice, fairness, and respect for others and risked his career pursuing the greater good in opposition to powerful party pressures. The extraordinary story of Tom and Bess's son is our American story. It is a celebration of the values that we cherish. It is our story to read, to share, and to celebrate. It is important that we share it, be astonished by it, and allow it to enrich and inform our own lives and our collective American history. It is now your turn to serve.

NOTES

1. The Texarkana Gazette's Melanie Poppiewell July 4, 1989.
2. Ibid.
3. Lines in the Sand: Congressional Redistricting in Texas and the Downfall of Tom Delay, by Steve Bickerstaff, The University of Texas Press, p. 1.
4. See The Lieutenant Governor's by Bill Hobby March 7, 1975 on the Texas Legislative Archive.
5. Ibid.
6. See Reporter Returns to Texas Capitol, Where Father's Voice Still Rings by John Schwartz, The New York Times, September 3, 2013.
7. See The Texas Legislative Achieve, SR 234, 64th Regular Session Providing for creation of special interim committee to study professional liability insurance by A. R. "Babe" Schwartz
8. In an interview University of Texas at Austin President Bill Powers stated that he thought of "the Ratliff brothers like the famous Keeton brothers." Page Keeton and Robert Keeton both lawyers had long and very successful legal careers. Comparing Jack, Bill, and Shannon Ratliff to the Keeton brothers was a very high compliment.
9. See Oops! The Doctor Makes His Cut. The Lawyer and The Insurance Man Take Their Cut. You Just Get Cut. In Texas Monthly, March 1977 by Alan Waldman p. 82.
10. The University of Texas School of Law Early Deans, Page Keeton, 1949-1974 online at https://tarlton.law.utexas.edu/exhibits/early_deans/keeton.html.
11. See Prosser and Keeton, Hornbook on Torts, West Group 1984.
12. See Benjamin C. Zipursky, Legal Malpractice and the Structure of Negligence Law, 67 Fordham L. Rev. 649, 1998. p. 650.Available at: http://ir.lawnet.fordham.edu/flr/vol67/iss2/13
13. See: To The Senate and House of Representatives of the Seventy-Eighth Texas Legislature, Regular Session January 23, 2003. (http://www.lrl.state.tx.us/scanned/gov-docs/Rick%20Perry/2003/govmsg_health.pdf).
14. Ibid.
15. Ibid.
16. See Texas Legislative Archive HB 4, 78th Regular Session Senate Committee Report.   p.   632   (http://www.lrl.state.tx.us/LASDOCS/78R/HB4/HB4_78R.pdf#page=632).Relating to reform of certain procedures and remedies in civil actions.
17. See The Texas Tribune Tribpedia on Texan for Lawsuit Reform online (http://www.texastribune.org/tribpedia/texans-for-lawsuit-reform/).
18. What Comes with Tort Reform? by Ross Ramsey Texas Tribune August 29, 2011 online (http://www.texastribune.org/2011/08/29/collateral-politics-what-comes-tort-re-form/).
19. Ibid.
20. I counted the changes in the Conference Committee Report Section by Section Analysis. See Texas Legislative Archive HB 4, 78th Regular Session Senate Committee Report. (http://www.lrl.state.tx.us/LASDOCS/78R/HB4/HB4_78R.pdf#page=632).
21. Email from Bill Ratliff February 10, 2016.
22. Ibid.
23. Email from Jack Ratliff February 2, 2016.
24. Email from Bill Ratliff February 4, 2016.
25. Jimmie Vaughn of the Fabulous Thunderbirds, and the brother of Stevie Ray later bought the ranch from Jack and Clare Ratliff.
26. It is about thirty miles from the former Ratliff ranch to LBJ's ranch.
27. Longtime Lubbock resident, Alison Johnson Sterken proudly states that Senator Robert Duncan is the only Republican she has ever voted for.
28. See https://law.utexas.edu/faculty/wpowers/
29. Another Look at "No-Evidence" and "Insufficient Evidence" Points of Error, 69 Texas Law Review 515 (1991) (with Jack Ratliff).

30. This meeting as described here was described to me in individual interviews with Bill, Jack, Shannon, Clase and Sally Ratliff and President Bill Powers (March 22, 2016), and Chancellor Robert Duncan (April 5, 2016).

31. Interview with Bill Powers March 22, 2016.

32. Email from Jack Ratliff February 2, 2016.

33. Email from Jack Ratliff February 2, 2016 and Interview with Bill Powers March 22, 2016.

34. Ibid.

35. Interview with Bill Powers March 22, 2016.

36. Ibid.

37. Ibid.

38. Email from Jack Ratliff February 2, 2016.

39. Interview with Bill Powers March 22, 2016.

40. Ibid.

41. Ibid. Jack Ratliff wrote in an email dated February 2, 2016. "That was a process that was conducted in serious confidence. I'm not sure anybody but the participants ever knew such a meeting took place. Therefore, I don't feel free to quote what anybody said or what view he took. Except, of course, I feel free to tell what I thought. In fact, I'm not sure I'm at liberty to talk about it at all. I understand why it's important to your book as it's an illustration of the serious way Bill went about making his decisions. And I don't mean to say that all his views came out of this meeting. He was meeting with more people than he'd care to count and listening to opinions from all sides."

42. Email from Bill Ratliff February 4, 2016.

43. Email from Chancellor Robert Duncan June 24, 2016.

44. David Easton defined politics as the "authoritative allocation of value" in A Framework for Political Analysis and in A Systems Analysis of Political Life. 1965.

45. Quoted in Ten Years of Tort Reform: A Review by The Honorable Joe Nixon-Senior Fellow Texas Public Policy Foundation March 2013 p. 3.

46. See HB 4, 78th Regular Session Relating to reform of certain procedures and remedies in civil actions. Texas Legislative Archive.

47. Interview with Bill Powers March 22, 2016.

48. Ibid.

49. See 'RINO' label has two meanings, Ratliff says, by Gary Scharrer Houston Chronicle Blog, May 21, 2012 http://blog.chron.com/texaspolitics/2012/05/rino-label-has-two-meanings/

50. Ibid.

51. See for example Better Care, Thanks to Tort Reform by Howard Marcus Texas Tribune October 24, 2011 online (https://www.texastribune.org/2011/10/24/guest-column-better-care-thanks-tort-reform/).

52. Email from Chancellor Robert Duncan June 24, 2016.

53. See for example, The 2013 Texas House, From Right to Left by by Mark P. Jones Texas Tribune, October 15, 2013 (https://www.texastribune.org/2013/10/15/guest-column-2013-texas-house-right-left/).

54. Senator John F. Kennedy wrote about the important call of the roll in Profiles in Courage, p. 39.

55. Who Are the Biggest Spenders in Texas Races? by Becca Aaronson, The Texas Tribune March 1, 2016 (https://www.texastribune.org/2016/03/01/who-are-biggest-spenders-texas-state-races/).

56. See State Rep. Matt Rinaldi (R-Irving) on Empower Texans online (http://index.empowertexans.com/legislators/matt-rinaldi/2015-index).

57. Candidates' legislative records offer insights to primary voters by Mark P. Jones, The Texas Tribune January 25, 2016 online (https://www.tribtalk.org/2016/01/25/candidates-legislative-records-offer-insights-to-primary-voters/).

58. Former Lawmakers Make Bids to Return to Texas House by Julián Aguilar and Lauren Flannery The Texas Tribune February 23, 2016 online (https://

www.texastribune.org/2016/02/23/after-bowing-out-or-getting-beat-several-former-la/
).

59. Ibid.

60. Ibid.

61. Ibid.

62. Who Are the Biggest Spenders in Texas Races? by Becca Aaronson, Texas Tribune, March 1, 2016 online (https://www.texastribune.org/2016/03/01/who-are-biggest-spenders-texas-state-races/).

63. Old Rivals Meet Again in Dallas House Race by Morgan Smith The Texas Tribune February 12, 2016 online (https://www.texastribune.org/2016/02/12/two-old-rivals-fight-gop-votes-dallas-house-race/).

64. Ibid.

65. Ibid.

66. Interview with Bill Powers March 22, 2016.

67. Tony Proffitt was a longtime Austin political strategist who served as a trusted adviser to Bob Bullock. See more online (http://www.legacy.com/obituaries/statesman/obituary.aspx?pid=2725448#sthash.QxkOkL8F.dpuf).

68. A copy of this letter was found in the Ratliff papers in the The University of Texas at Tyler Archives.

69. Profiles in Courage by John F. Kennedy 1954, p 107.

70. Ibid.

71. Ibid p 108.

72. Ibid. p. 123.

73. The *Texarkana Gazette* by Melanie Wall, January 7, 1990 p. 1

74. The Federalist Papers: No. 39 The Conformity of the Plan to Republican Principles,For the Independent Journal by James Madison.

75. Evenwel v. Abbott, Oyez, https://www.oyez.org/cases/2015/14-940

76. For an excellent explanation of the history see All About Redistricting by Justin Levitt on Loyola Law School website online (http://redistricting.lls.edu/why.php).

77. Ibid.

78. Lines in the Sand: Congressional Redistricting in Texas and the Downfall of Tom DeLay by Steve Bickerstaff University of Texas Press 2007. p. 208.

79. See Baker v. Carr, 369 U.S. 186, 1962.

80. Plaintiffs Sue Evenwel and Edward Pfenniger were registered Texas voters who sued and claimed that the interim plan that was adopted and signed into law violated the Equal Protection Clause of the Fourteenth Amendment. They argued that the new districts do not adhere to the 'one person, one vote' principle, which the Supreme Court had previously held exists in the Equal Protection Clause of the Fourteenth Amendment, because they were apportioned based on total population rather than registered voter population, and while the new districts are relatively equal in terms of total population, they vary wildly in relation to total voter population.

81. Reynolds v. Sims, 377 U.S. 533 and Evenwel et al. v. Abbott, Governor of Texas,et al. No. 14–940. Argued December 8, 2015—Decided April 4, 2016.

82. Evenwel et al. v. Abbott, Governor of Texas 2016.

83. Ibid.

84. Lines in the Sand: Congressional Redistricting in Texas and the Downfall of Tom DeLay by Steve Bickerstaff University of Texas Press 2007. p. 30.

85. Suspension of the Regular Order of Business, Rule 5.13. No bill, joint resolution, or resolution affecting state policy may be considered out of its regular calendar order unless the regular order is suspended by a vote of two-thirds of the members present. Notes of Rulings: By suspending the regular order of business, the Senate may take up a bill before the day to which it previously was postponed (67 S.J. Reg. 1057 (1981)). A motion to suspend the regular order of business is not in order when the time set for consideration of a special order has arrived (67 S.J. Reg. 1558 (1981)) online (http://www.lrl.state.tx.us/scanned/rules/78-0/78R_SenateRules.pdf).

86. The two-thirds rule was suspended by a vote of 20 to 10 in 2015.

87. Lines in the Sand: Congressional Redistricting in Texas and the Downfall of Tom DeLay by Steve Bickerstaff University of Texas Press 2007. p. 31.

88. Ibid.

89. Ibid. p. 161.

90. The handwritten poem is in The University of Texas at Tyler Archives in the Ratliff paper.

91. Ibid. p. 85.

92. . Ibid. p. 162.

93. Interview with Vatra Soloman 2014.

94. Notes about Karl Rove come from interviews and from compiled from articles and excerpts from: Bush's Brain, by Wayne Slater; Frontline's "The Choice 2004;" and from PBS's "Karl Rove- The Architect."

95. Interview with Ratliff 2014.

96. Ibid.

97. Ibid.

98. The information in this section is derived from interviews with Bill Ratliff, Vatra Soloman, and adapted from Lines in the Sand: Congressional Redistricting in Texas and the Downfall of Tom Delay, by Steve Bickerstaff.

99. Email from Bill Ratliff March 2, 2016.

100. Reference here is to CD1 as the Northeast Texas Congressional District since that is what it was during Ratliff's tenure in the Senate. That district is now called CD4 and CD1 is currently represented by Congressman Louie Gohmert (R-Tyler).

101. . Lines in the Sand: Congressional Redistricting in Texas and the Downfall of Tom DeLay by Steve Bickerstaff, University of Texas Press, 2007.

102. Latina Legislator: Leticia Van de Putte and the Road to Leadership, Texas A&M University Press, October 2008.

103. The "Texas Five" were Martin Frost, Charles Stenholm, Max Sandlin, Nick Lampson, and Chet Edwards.

104. Interview with Ratliff. This story is also retold in Bickerstaff's Lines in the Sand, p. 177. In 2014 Ratliff told me that Senator Robert Duncan (R-Lubbock) was at this meeting—like he did with Professor Steve Bickerstaff he would not share the other names.

105. Ibid.

106. Two Democrats Frank Madla of San Antonio and Ken Armbrister of Victoria, remained undecided.

107. Quoted in Lines in the Sand: Congressional Redistricting in Texas and the Downfall of Tom DeLay by Steve Bickerstaff University of Texas Press, 2007. p. 178.

108. Ibid. p. 179.

109. Interview with Ratliff and also quoted in Lines in the Sand: Congressional Redistricting in Texas and the Downfall of Tom DeLay by Steve Bickerstaff University of Texas Press 2007. p. 179. Ratliff later (April 26, 2016) pointed out that Senator Buster Brown was the senior most Senator at that time.

110. Ibid. p. 203.

111. Ibid. p. 187.

112. Ibid. p 221.

113. Ibid. p. 221.

114. Ibid. p. 256.

115. Ibid. p. 2

116. Ibid.

117. Ibid. 3

118. Ibid.

119. Ibid.

120. The Texarkana Gazette December 5, 1990, p. 1

121. Ibid.

122. Arizona State Legislature V. Arizona Independent Redistricting Commission Et Al. No. 13–1314. Argued March 2, 2015—Decided June 29, 2015.

123.   University of Texas at Austin and Texas Tribune Poll: Partisan Splits on Guns in Texasby Ross Ramsey June 21, 2013 online (https://www.texastribune.org/2013/06/21/uttt-poll-partisan-splits-guns-texas/).

124.   Profiles in Courage by John F. Kennedy 1954, p. 132.

125.   Interview with The University of Texas at Austin President Bill Powers March 22, 2016.

126.   Bill Ratliff interview March 8, 2016.

127.   Ibid.

128.   Bill Ratliff, email to the author, March 8, 2016.

129.   Ibid.

130.   The John F. Kennedy Profile in Courage Award was created in 1989 by members of President Kennedy's family to honor President John F. Kennedy and to recognize and celebrate the quality of political courage that he admired most. Online (http://www.jfklibrary.org/Events-and-Awards/Profile-in-Courage-Award/About-the-Award.aspx).

131.   Ibid.

132.   Ibid.

133.   The Best and the Worst Legislators 1991, by Paul Burka, Patricia Hart, and Ellen Williams, *Texas Monthly* October 1991, online (http://www.texasmonthly.com/politics/the-best-and-the-worst-legislators-1991).

134.   I use the word penumbra to indicate the meaning or shadows cast. According to Legal Dictionary.com the term penumbra was created and introduced by astronomer Johannes Kepler in 1604 to describe the shadows that occur during eclipses. However, in legal terms penumbra is most often used as a metaphor describing a doctrine that refers to implied powers of the federal government. The doctrine is best known from the Supreme Court decision of Griswold v. Connecticut, 381 U.S. 479 (1965), where Justice William O. Douglas used it to describe the concept of an individual's constitutional right of privacy.

135.   Profiles in Courage by John F. Kennedy 1954, p. 488.

136.   See The University of Texas at Austin's Academy of Distinguished Alumni William R. Ratliff online (http://www.caee.utexas.edu/alumni/academy/49-alumni/academy/193-ratliff).

Epilogue

Today, Bill and Sally play a prominent role in community affairs in Mount Pleasant and East Texas. While Bill remains involved in the long struggle for good, spending his days fighting for quality education, he mostly does so in the Obi-Wan role—the wise mentor. Ratliff serves as advisor, guide, and teacher. He is frequently called upon to share his wisdom and decades of experience in the legislature and on college campuses. He serves as an advisor to both of his sons who are both very active and exemplary public servants.

Although his son, Bennett, lost his race to return to the Texas Legislature, in 2016, he also continues to fight the good fight for Texas and, like his father, in specific for Texas schoolchildren. Bennett continues to present solid leadership in a steady, measured, and pragmatic manner. The current Republican extremism has ushered in a wave of young political leaders who often, again and again, vote only to avoid the dreaded label RINO (Republican in Name Only). Representatives from Washington to Sacramento to Austin tend to vote, like Matt Rinaldi, to satisfy not their constituents needs or for good governance but out of fear of being "primaryed" unless they move ever more toward the extremes of the party. In late 2016 the extremes of the GOP are pulling at the very seams of the once big tent.

When Bill Ratliff retired from the Senate, his seat was won by the Honorable Kevin P. Eltife. Senator Eltife was sworn in on March 5, 2004, and until 2016 worked very hard to follow Ratliff's extraordinary example. "I was fine before I had this job," Eltife said, "If they kick me out of office, I'll be fine." Eltife was a solid and loud voice of reason in a legislature dominated by politicians who too often vote for the Empower Texans report card rather than reasoned public policy. Like Ratliff before him, Eltife brought reasoned political discourse to the Senate, but his fight was all too lonely. In direct opposition to extremist groups, Eltife fought to raise the gasoline tax to improve the state's highways. Standing on conservative principles, Eltife warned that the recent trend of borrowing money to pay for highways would saddle the state with unneeded debt. Voting against his Empower Texans report card, Eltife said that if acting responsibly got him defeated, so be it. Senator Eltife did not seek reelection in 2016.

On May 24, 2016, a University of Texas at Tyler graduate, Bryan Hughes (R-Mineola) defeated David Simpson (R-Tyler) to replace Senator Eltife and to serve in the seat once held by the father of modern education in Texas, Senator Aikin. Like Senator Aikin, Hughes is from deep East Texas and is the first member of his family to receive a college education. Hughes attended the public university that Senators Aikin, McKnight, Ratliff, and Eltife all voted to raise taxes to support. Will Hughes have Ratliff and Eltife's political courage? Running on an Empower Texans' platform of "cut spending, cut taxes" may be the expedient short-run way to win the seat. It may be the easy thing to do, but repeatedly voting "no" does nothing to solve the educational and major infrastructure problems facing citizens. Polls indicate that there is a substantial disconnect between these real-world problems and the public policy voting record of representatives like Matt Rinaldi.[1]

Political science research suggests that there are several reasons for the disconnect between constituent desires and the voting records of representatives.[2] First, older and more affluent Anglos-Americans are more likely to be registered and to vote. Those same voters tend to be more conservative than the less affluent, younger, and disproportionately non-Anglo citizens who are less likely to vote. Second, the gerrymandering of districts has created more competition within the party and less real competition across political parties. The primary winner of a gerrymandered district nearly always wins the general election. Bryan Hughes's defeat of David Simpson in the primary meant that he was elected in a district specifically drawn to elect a Republican. Voter turnout is low in primaries and reflects the more extremes of the political party. Third, many voters make their choice on the report card or single issue—rather than on reasoned and responsible governing. Because Bill Ratliff was willing to work with various interest and across party lines to represent all of the people in his district his vote choice on every single issue did not fit with every single voter. For example, single-issue voters who are intensely and passionately antigay or antitax are more likely to vote than the more moderate citizen. The fourth reason for the disconnect is structurally the most significant and the most difficult. The billionaire donors, like the Koch brothers, James Leininger, and Tim Dunn are able to define the parameters of the American political discussion. The influence of groups like Empower Texans and their support of public servants like Rinaldi and Hughes are disproportionally shaping politics and policy. The "heavy hitters," using billions in contributions are defining each legislator's vote and thus the policies that are considered politically acceptable, regardless of the views of the general public.

The fight for democracy and the struggle for a fair representation of the spirit of all citizens now falls on you. In the 2015 Star Wars movie, *The Force Awakens*, Rey inherits Luke's light saber. In the last scene of the movie, the light saber was passed from one generation to the next. Rey, like Luke before her, accepted the light saber from Obi-Wan Kenobi.

NOTES

1. See "The disconnect between Texans and their elected officials" by Stephen L. Klineberg, July 1, 2015 online (https://www.tribtalk.org/2015/07/01/the-disconnect-between-texans-and-their-elected-officials/).

2. Ibid.

Bibliography

Anderson, John. *Follow the Money: How George W. Bush and the Texas Republicans Hog-Tied America.* Scribner 2007.

Analyses of Proposed Constitutional Amendments November 5, 1991, accessed online October 2015. (http://www.lrl.state.tx.us/scanned/Constitutional_Amendments/Amendments72_tlc_1991-11-05.pdf).

Ball, Terence. *Lincoln: Political Writings and Speeches.* Cambridge University Press, 2012.

Belief and Practice, The Lutheran Church—Missouri Synod, website accessed November 2015. (http://www.lcms.org/belief-and-practice).

Bickerstaff, Steve. *Lines in the Sand: Congressional Redistricting in Texas and the Downfall of Tom Delay.* The University of Texas Press, 2007.

Bryce, Robert. "Not Clucking Around: Texas Poultry King Bo Pilgrim Takes on Senate Finance Committee Chairman Bill Ratliff," Austin Chronicle Nov. 3, 2000, accessed online December 2015. (http://www.austinchronicle.com/news/2000-11-03/79226/).

Burka, Paul. "Is the Legislature for Sale" Texas Monthly February 1991.

Burka, Paul. *The Best and The Worst Legislators The Best: Bill Ratliff.* Texas Monthly Press, October 1991.

Burka, Paul. Ambassador Teel Bivins dead at 62 by October 26, 2009, accessed online December 2015. (http://www.texasmonthly.com/burka-blog/ambassador-teel-bivins-dead-at-62/#sthash.lP9L7sAY.dpuf)

Burka, Paul and Patricia Hart, *A Perfect Team Bill Ratliff and Paul Sadler Texas Monthly The Best and the Worst Legislators 1995 July 1995,* accessed online December 2014. (http://www.texasmonthly.com/politics/the-best-and-the-worst-legislators-1995/#sthash.uZYyZTYk.dpuf)

Burns, Richard Allen, "Sweatt, Heman Marion," Handbook of Texas Online accessed February 04, 2016. (http://www.tshaonline.org/handbook/online/articles/fsw23).

Carlisle, Rodney P., J. and Geoffrey, Golson, *The Reagan Era from the Iran Crisis to Kosovo.* ABC-CLIO Press, September 2007.

Connally, John. *Charge to The Coordinating Board Texas College and University System,* September 20, 1965, accessed online December 2014. (http://www.thecb.state.tx.us/reports/PDF/0002.PDF?CFID=40927664&CFTOKEN=36115836).

Core Commitments: Educating Students for Personal and Social Responsibility created and established by the American Association of Colleges and Universities. Website accessed February 2013. (https://www.aacu.org/core_commitments).

Crisis of Confidence: Jimmy Carter delivered this televised speech on July 15, 1979 accessed online October 2015. (http://www.pbs.org/wgbh/americanexperience/features/primary-resources/carter-crisis/).

Duncan, Robert, (Chancellor of Texas Tech University, former Texas Senator) discussions with the author June 2016.

Edgewood Independent School District v. Kirby 777 S.W.2d 391 (Tex. 1989).

Edmonds, Bonny. Interview with the author 2014.

Edmonds, Don (Chief of Staff, Campaign Director for Bill Ratliff) in discussions with the author 2014.

Edmonds, Don. Unpublished Memoir and notes provided to the author October 2014.

Escott, Paul D. *Lincoln's Dilemma: Blair, Sumner and the Republican Struggle Over Racism and Inequality in the Civil War Era.* University of Virginia Press, 2014.

Haney López, Ian, *Dog Whistle Politics: How Coded Racial Appeals Have Reinvented Racism and Wrecked the Middle Class.* Oxford University Press, 2014.

Haney-Lopez, Ian. *Hernandez v. Texas and Ruben Munguia, A Cotton Picker Finds Justice: The Saga of the Hernandez Case* (http://www.law.uh.edu/Hernandez50/saga.pdf).

Hart, Patricia. "Bill Passes: How Bill Ratliff Became Lieutenant Governor and What It Means For Texas," Texas Monthly February 2001.

History of Columbia University website accessed 2014. http://www.columbia.edu/content/history.html.

History of Great Depression website accessed 2013. http://www.econlib.org/library/Enc/GreatDepression.html.

History of the U.S. Capitol Building website accessed 2013. (http://www.aoc.gov/history-us-capitol-building).

"Huey Long: The Man, Mission, and Legacy," website accessed July 19, 2013 http://www.hueylong.com/life-times/governor.php.

Jenkins, Walter W. Top Aide To Johnson In The White House by Marjorie Hunter, Special to the New York Times Published: November 26, 1985, accessed online November 2015. (http://www.nytimes.com/1985/11/26/us/walter-w-jenkins-top-aide-to-johnson-in-the-white-house.html).

Jillson, Cal. *Texas Politics: Governing the Lone Star State*. Routledge, 2015.

Johnson, Clay. Interview with PBS Frontline Choice 2000, accessed online December 2015. (http://www.pbs.org/wgbh/pages/frontline/shows/choice2000/bush/johnson.html).

Kennedy, John F. *Profiles in Courage*. Harper Perennial Modern Classics, 2006.

Klineberg, Stephen L. "The disconnect between Texans and their elected officials" July 2015, accessed online December 2015. (https://www.tribtalk.org/2015/07/01/the-disconnect-between-texans-and-their-elected-officials/).

Kosky, Philip, Robert T. Balmer, William D. Keat, George Wise. *Exploring Engineering: An Introduction to Engineering and Design*. Academic Press, 2012.

LBJ Aide Walter Jenkins Dies by By Bart Barnes November 26, 1985 The Washington Post, accessed online October 2015. (https://www.washingtonpost.com/archive/local/1985/11/26/lbj-aide-walter-jenkins-dies/f993fac7-d7a9-47bb-a5fc-6f9204dad30e/)

Legislative Reference Library Texas Legislators: Past & Present A.M. Aikin, Jr. website accessed November 2015. (http://www.lrl.state.tx.us/mobile/memberDisplay.cfm?memberID=350).

Lives On the Line: The high human cost of chicken Oxfam Report 2015 accessed online January 2016. (https://www.oxfamamerica.org/livesontheline).

Long, Huey P. *Every Man a King: The Autobiography of Huey P. Long*. Da Capo Press, 1996.

"History & Traditions pages of the University of Texas at Austin Cockrell Engineering College," website accessed 2015 (http://www.engr.utexas.edu/about/history/200-cockrell-school-history)

Milloy, Ross E. "Texas Senate Passes Hate Crimes Bill That Bush's Allies Killed," The New York Times Published: May 8, 2001.

McNeely, Dave. *Bob Bullock: God Bless Texas*. The University of Texas Press, 2008.

Olsson, Karen. "Mr. Right: Can you name the most influential Republican in Texas?" Texas Monthly, November 2002.

Powers, Bill (President of the University of Texas at Austin) recorded interview with Robert E. Sterken III March 2016.

Prosser William Lloyd, W. Page Keeton, *Hornbook on Torts*. West Group. 1984.

PBS "The Murder of Emmett Till," website accessed September 2013 (http://www.pbs.org/wgbh/amex/till/peopleevents/e_councils.html).

PBS "Karl Rove – The Architect PBS Frontline." website accessed March 2015. (http://www.pbs.org/wgbh/pages/frontline/shows/architect/interviews/whitman.html).

Pilgrim, Bo. Interview by Marv Knox in the Baptist Standard, Pilgrim's Progress: East Texas businessman Bo Pilgrim accessed online December 2015. (http://assets.baptiststandard.com/archived/2002/1_14/pages/pilgrim.html).

Plessy v. Ferguson (No. 210) 163 U.S. 537 May 18, 1896.

Public Attitudes toward Homosexuality by Tom W. Smith NORC/University of Chicago September, 2011, accessed online November 2015. (http://www.norc.org/PDFs/2011%20GSS%20Reports/GSS_Public%20Attitudes%20Toward%20Homosexuality_Sept2011.pdf).

Ramsey, Ross. "Republican Enough for the GOP?" The Texas Tribune March 2001.

Ratliff, Bill, in discussions with the author, 2012 to 2016.

Ratliff, Clara (sister-in-law of Bill Ratliff), in discussion with the author, October 2014.

Ratliff, Jack (brother of Bill Ratliff and University of Texas School of Law Professor), in discussions with the author, October 2014.

Ratliff, Sally (wife of Bill Ratliff), in discussions with the author, 2012 to 2016.

Ratliff, Sally (wife of Bill Ratliff), unpublished notes, cards, photos, 1988 to 2005.

Ratliff, Shannon (former University of Texas Board of Regent, lawyer), in discussions with the author, 2014.

Reid, Jan. *Let the People In: The Life and Times of Ann Richards*. The University of Texas Press, 2012.

Schwartz, John. "Reporter Returns to Texas Capitol, Where Father's Voice Still Rings," The New York Times, September 3, 2013.

Solomon, Vatra (administrative assistant to Lt. Governor Ratliff), in discussions with the author, 2014.

Slater, Wayne. *Bush's Brain: How Karl Rove Made George W. Bush Presidential*. Wiley, 2003.

"Texas Businessman Hands Out $10,000 Checks in State Senate," The New York Times July 9, 1989.accessed online December 2014. (http://www.nytimes.com/1989/07/09/us/texas-businessman-hands-out-10000-checks-in-state-senate.html)

Texas Ethics Commission Rules Chapter 34. Regulation of Lobbyists, accessed online March 2014. (https://www.ethics.state.tx.us/legal/ch34.html#subB).

Texas State Library and Archives Commission Recording: 720275b Session: 72nd 1st C.S. Committee: Floor Date: 8/9/1991 Description: 72nd Leg. 1st Session 8/9/91 Tape.

The American Presidency Project at UCSB website accessed December 2015. (http://www.presidency.ucsb.edu/showelection.php?year=1992).

The Devil's River News, Sonora, Texas January 1954.

The Gulf of Tonkin Incident, 40 Years Later Flawed Intelligence and the Decision for War in Vietnam accessed online 2013. (http://nsarchive.gwu.edu/NSAEBB/NSAEBB132/index.htm).

The Lyndon Baines Johnson Room, website accessed 2014. (http://www.lbjlibrary.org/assets/uploads/lbj/Lyndon_B._Johnson_Room.pdf).

The Man Who Said No to LBJ by Carlos Harrison published in: 2013 Texas Super Lawyers, accessed online October 2013 (http://www.superlawyers.com/texas/article/The-Man-Who-Said-No-to-LBJ/5187bd08-85a2-4f3f-af1f-81627136bfe9.html).

The Papers of US Supreme Court Justice Tom Clark at the University of Texas School of Law, Tarlton Law Library (https://tarlton.law.utexas.edu/clark/clerks.html).

The United States Department of Labor Safety and Health Topics Poultry Processing, accessed online December 2015. (https://www.osha.gov/SLTC/poultryprocessing/).

The University of Texas School of Law Early Deans, Page Keeton, 1949-1974, accessed online January 2016. https://tarlton.law.utexas.edu/exhibits/early_deans/keeton.html.

Waldman, Alan. "Oops! The Doctor Makes His Cut. The Lawyer and The Insurance Man Take Their Cut. You Just Get Cut," Texas Monthly, March 1977.

Wright, Eric (Chief of Staff for Lt. Governor Bill Ratliff), in discussions with the author, 2014.

Wright, John. "Celia Israel recalls coming out to Ann Richards, looks ahead to Jan. 28 special election runoff for Texas House," January 2014, accessed online November 2015. (http://www.lonestarq.com/celia-israel-recalls-coming-ann-richards-looks-ahead-jan-28-runoff/).

Yardley, Jim. "A Power in Texas Governing Finds Fault in Texas Politics," The New York Times, June 9, 2001.

Index

About the Author

Robert Sterken is associate professor of Political Science at the University of Texas at Tyler. Professor Sterken is a Senior Fulbright Scholar who has taught politics in many places around the world, most recently in Burma/ Myanmar, Thailand, and Cambodia. He has been teaching and writing about politics and power for twenty plus years. While serving as a Senior Advisor in Legislative Affairs for the University of Texas at Tyler Professor Sterken worked closely with legislators, lobbyist, and first met the Honorable William Roark Ratliff. He is an avid runner, yogi, reader and writer, traveler, and global soul who lives mostly in Tyler, Texas.